M-libraries

Libraries on the move
to provide virtual access

M-libraries

Libraries on the move
to provide virtual access

edited by
Gill Needham and **Mohamed Ally**

facet publishing

Published by Facet Publishing,
7 Ridgmount Street, London WC1E 7AE
www.facetpublishing.co.uk

Facet Publishing is wholly owned by CILIP:
the Chartered Institute of Library and
Information Professionals.

British Library Cataloguing in Publication Data
A catalogue record for this book is available
from the British Library.

ISBN 978-1-85604-648-0

First published 2008

Typeset from editors' disks by Facet
Publishing in 12/14 American Garamond
and Nimbus Sans.
Printed and made in Great Britain by MPG
Books Ltd, Bodmin, Cornwall.

Contents

Acknowledgements

Without the 1st International M-Libraries Conference there would be no book and so we would like to thank everyone who contributed to the success of the Conference: the Open University and Athabasca University who co-hosted the conference, the International Organizing Committee, Programme Committee and Local Organizing Committee, all our excellent conference speakers, session chairs, delegates, helpers and commercial sponsors.

Our thanks also go to all the authors who have contributed to the book and those who have helped to put it together. We would like to say a particularly big 'thank you' to Jeannette Stanley for her patience, hard work and good humour.

Gill Needham
Mohamed Ally

Contributors

Dr Anne Adams is an Institute of Educational Technology lecturer in theory and practice at the Open University, currently working with the OPEN CETL on research into e-learning and practice-based learning. Her previous research (at UCL and Nottingham) was conducted within many domains (building industry, telecommunication, health service and academia) but has always concentrated on technology and learning (e.g. digital libraries, multimedia communications and mobile technologies). The main focus of her research has been on social issues and identity. This research has in the past centred on usability, security, technology design/implementation processes and e-learning. Other interests include research methods, which are the focus of two current book chapters. She has presented at, and chaired sessions at, international conferences, and been both an invited and keynote speaker for academic, industrial and health organizations across the world. Over the past few years she was an invited speaker at the Royal Society of Medicine, Google, the Royal College of Surgeons, Microsoft and the HEA.

Dr Mohamed Ally is a professor at Athabasca University in Canada. He is currently conducting research in the areas of mobile technology in learning and training, the mobile library and skills required for the 21st-century graduate. He recently presented and published papers on the use of emerging technology to bridge the digital divide, mobile learning, and the mobile library. He has published papers in books, journals, and encyclopedias, and recently wrote a chapter on designing information for mobile government.

Geoff Butters is a Research Associate at CERLIM, the Centre for Research in Library and Information Management, at Manchester Metropolitan University. For more than a decade he has researched the delivery of library and information services via the internet and world wide web. Other research areas have included a hybrid library system, an electronic current awareness service, portal development, and a web-based citizens' local cultural heritage system.

Lynne Callaghan gained her PhD in psychology from the University of Plymouth in 2002. Since then she has worked on several pedagogic research projects employing a range of quantitative and qualitative methodologies in both the School of Psychology and the Faculty of Health and Social Work at the University. She is currently working as the postdoctoral research fellow supporting and leading a number of projects within the Centre for Excellence in Professional Placement Learning (Ceppl). Current projects include mobile learning, enhancing library access, student support on placement and the evaluation of practice assessment tools.

Yang Cao is the Digital Objects & Repository Network Developer in Library Services at Athabasca University in Canada. She received her Bachelor of Engineering from Northeastern University and her Master of Science in computer science from the University of Saskatchewan. Her research interests are in the areas of e-learning, mobile learning, and applying advanced technology in online distance education. She develops and maintains the Athabasca University Library's website and other online applications including Digital Reading Room (DRR), Digital Theses and Project Room (DTPR), and mobile friendly library websites. In 2006, Yang and her team won the Athabasca University's Sue and Derrick Rowlandson Memorial Award for Service Excellence.

Àngels Carles has a degree in librarianship, and is a bachelor in documentation and master of contemporary history. She has worked at the library services of Universitat Autonoma de Barcelona (UAB) since 1985. She is currently Head of the Medical School Library at the UAB.

Ana Castellano completed studies in biology and computer engineering. She has worked at Computer Services, Universitat Autonoma de Barcelona (UAB) since 1989. She is currently Chief of the UAB's Medical Resources Center.

Ruth Charlton is a social science graduate with a postgraduate diploma in librarianship and has worked most of her life in academic libraries, mainly as a subject librarian. Her current post is Senior Subject Librarian for the Faculty of Health and Social Work at the University of Plymouth, and her main role is to co-ordinate health library provision over four University library sites in Plymouth, Exeter, Taunton and Truro. In addition she is responsible for liaising with partner colleges and teaching their staff how to make best use of the Library's electronic resources. She is also involved with setting up library provision for the new Dental School. She currently works with two of the University CETL (Centres for Excellence in Teaching and Learning) projects: Placement Learning and Higher Education Learning Partnerships.

Billy Cheung has been working with Athabasca University, Canada, for six years. He first started as Instructional Designer in 2001, and became Instructional Media Analyst in 2003. He has been actively involved in developmental projects and currently researches on learning technologies and distance education. He co-authored and presented papers in the IEEE International Workshop on Wireless and Mobile Technologies in Education Conference (WMTE), 2005, and IADIS International Conference on Mobile Learning, 2006. He is currently attending the MSc Program in the School of Interactive Arts and Technologies at Simon Fraser University.

Robert Davies is a qualified librarian and an independent project manager, consultant and researcher. He has worked on the development of ICT deployment in public library services for many years, having co-ordinated a number of major European initiatives.

Susan Eales began her career in the FE sector where she worked for over eight years. In the last three years, she was leading on introducing the potential of e-learning to teaching staff. She then moved to JISC, where she was appointed Collections Manager for FE and Learning Materials. She then moved on to manage the Exchange for Learning and Digital Libraries in the Classroom Programmes as well as the Jorum national learning materials repository and an IPR consultancy for JISC. She was appointed Electronic Services Development Manager at the Open University in June 2006. Based in the Library, her main duties are to lead on the development of a new Library website and work as part of the OU VLE Programme to develop a federated search system. Susan has had papers accepted for Libraries Without Walls (2003 and 2005), ALT and the Coalition for Networked Information (CNI) and written articles in numerous publications, including The Times Higher Education Supplement, CILIP Update and

ALISS, on work to exemplify and embed the repurposing of learning materials in the further and higher education sectors.

Colin Elliott has worked for two years at Athabasca University in Canada. He is a digitization specialist in the AU library and has worked on a wide variety of projects. These include the Mobile Library and Mobile ESL projects.

Cain Evans is a Senior Lecturer in pervasive computing at Birmingham City University. He is a Chartered Scientist with the Science Council and a Chartered IT Professional with the British Computer Society. He is a member of the BCS, IEEE and ACM. He has worked in the UK IT industry as a systems engineer with blue-chip companies. He travelled and worked in the Far East for several years before returning to the UK. Cain is currently researching M-Business, Pervasive Computing (Mobile Commerce), E-Business, Internet Computing and Mobile Systems Integration.

William Foster was formerly Co-ordinator for Information and Library Management courses at Birmingham City University. He taught information management and aspects of electronic library development for over twenty years. He is currently Knowledge Manager for the National Library for Health Specialist Library in Genetic Conditions and works for the National Genetics Education and Development Centre in Birmingham.

Dr Ivan Ganchev received his engineering and doctoral degrees from the Saint-Petersburg State University of Telecommunications in 1989 and 1994 respectively. He is an Associate Professor at the University of Plovdiv and currently a lecturer and Deputy Director of the Telecommunications Research Center, University of Limerick, Republic of Ireland. His current and previous activities include being a founding partner and member of ANWIRE (Academic Network for Wireless Internet Research in Europe), the EU FP5 Thematic Network of Excellence, IST-38835, 2002–2004, and a member of two European 'COoperation in the Field of Science and Technology' Research Actions (COST 285 & 290). Previous posts held include those of Senior Lecturer in the University of Plovdiv, part-time Senior Lecturer in the University of Shumen, and Telecom Expert at Bulgarian Telecom. His research interests include wireless networks, mobile computing and new m-learning paradigms. Ivan has served on the Technical Program Committees (TPC) of a number of international conferences and workshops. He was Track Co-chair of the

65th IEEE VTC2007 Spring conference and TPC member of the IEEE Globecom 2006 conference.

Peter Godwin is currently working as Academic Librarian at the University of Bedfordshire in Luton. His main focus is on information literacy in academic libraries and in particular the impact of Web 2.0 on information literacy in all information sectors. He has recently co-edited a book on this topic (Godwin, P. and Parker, J. (2008), *Information Literacy Meets Library 2.0*, Facet Publishing). He draws on many years' experience in academic library management and has presented at conferences in the UK, Europe and the USA.

Fernando Guerrero has a degree in Education Sciences, and has a bachelor's degree in documentation. He has worked at Computer Services, Universitat Autonoma de Barcelona (UAB) since 1987. He is currently Chief of the UAB's Medical Computer Services.

Jim Hahn is Orientation Services Librarian in the Undergraduate Library at the University of Illinois at Urbana-Champaign, USA. His work is centered on helping students in transition find success at the University. He develops and delivers instructional workshops and services. He earned his MS in Library and Information Science from the University of Illinois at Urbana-Champaign in May 2007.

Anne Hewling is e-Learning Specialist at the Open University Library and Learning Resources Centre. She endeavours to bridge the cultural spaces presently occupied by new technologies, information professionals, learning developers and faculty by developing training events and offering case-by-case support. The development of mobileSafari has been another concrete outcome of this work. She also facilitates culture change activities with colleagues in the Digilab – a hands-on university 'play space' for faculty and staff who want to integrate new technologies into teaching and learning practice but lack confidence or experience with the latest tools. In her spare time she teaches online courses in e-learning and international development and writes poetry.

Maureen Hutchison is Manager, Learning Services of Athabasca University's Centre for Innovative Management (CIM) in Canada. Her work bridges the operational and academic elements of course development, production, and deployment for the Centre's business courses and programmes. Her career with CIM began as a Course Production Coordinator, working closely with CIM faculty in the development, editing, and production of online MBA courses. Maureen holds a BA (with distinction) in English literature from the University of Western Ontario and a Management Development certificate from the University of Alberta.

Dr Adesina Iluyemi is a dentist by training with almost three years postgraduate working experience in a teaching hospital in Nigeria. Dr Iluyemi participated in all aspects of clinical dentistry and was involved in the management of patients in oral and maxillofacial surgery, and in multidisciplinary management of clinical cases with general and specialist medical and surgical teams. He also participated in clinical and community health researches and programmes, and worked as a research assistant in the setting up of a community dental clinic, a continental-wide journal for oral health in Africa and a multi-centre survey of dental education in Nigeria. He also has experience in implementing and evaluating small-scale mobile ICT projects in the UK. He is currently undertaking a PhD research degree programme exploring policy and change management issues in the implementation and use of mobile/wireless information and communication technologies (ICTs) in the health system's reform and development in Africa. Adesina's first and masters degrees theses were written on the use of ICTs in health services. He also has business and project management qualifications.

Dr Agnes Kukulska-Hulme joined the Open University in 1996. Prior to this she was a lecturer in French and computational linguistics at Aston University in Birmingham (1985–1995), researching the design of dictionaries for foreign language translators and technical writers, and later working on the design of user-centred indexes for technical documentation. Her PhD thesis (1993) proposed ways of dismantling terminological barriers preventing users from gaining essential knowledge about computer security. Prior to that, she worked as a computer programmer in Birmingham and as an assistant lecturer at the University of Warsaw in Poland.

Since 1996 she has been working in educational technology, conducting research and developing online courses in the OU's Masters in Online and Distance Education programme. Her book *Language and Communication: essential concepts for user interface and documentation design* (OUP, 1999) drew on experience of language teaching and terminology in exploring the language elements of user interfaces, help facilities and user documentation. It set a framework for her subsequent work on the usability of educational websites. Recent research and evaluation work has been in the areas of mobile learning, web and mobile usability, student experiences with e-books, and exploiting digital video resources for groupwork. Her co-edited book *Mobile Learning: a handbook for educators and trainers* (Routledge, 2005) presents an international collection of evaluated case studies of innovative learning with mobile devices, and she is continuing work in this area through funded projects on mobile learning in tertiary education. Agnes is particularly interested in how mobile devices will transform language learning, and how new forms of language learning might in turn change our approach to knowledge seeking and knowledge representation on the web.

Susan J. Lea is Professor of Applied Social Psychology and Director of the Centre for Excellence in Professional Placement Learning. She was awarded a National Teaching Fellowship in 2000 and has extensive experience of higher education, including holding key roles at department, faculty and university level. She is an active researcher in higher education pedagogy and in recent years has developed an interest in how mobile devices might be used to support student learning.

Joan K. Lippincott is Associate Executive Director of the Coalition for Networked Information (CNI) in the USA. CNI, jointly sponsored by the Association of Research Libraries and Educause, includes about 200 member organizations concerned with the use of information technology and networked information to enhance scholarship and intellectual productivity. Joan is responsible for programmes focusing on the use of networked information to transform institutions, including New Learning Communities, Working Together, and Assessing the Academic Networked Environment.

Jane Lunsford got her first degree and then her Masters in Open and Distance Education with the Open University, and has been a tutor on several technology courses. She now works in Learning Design & Technology, a section of Student Services at the OU that develops online advice and guidance for OU students. She has been working on a project in which OU tutors have been producing content for their tutor groups that is suitable for mobile access.

Margaret Markland was until recently a Research Associate in CERLIM, the Centre for Research in Library and Information Management at Manchester Metropolitan University. Margaret has worked on a number of research projects involving networked information environments, digital libraries, virtual and managed learning environments, institutional repository development, and scholarly communication.

Dr Buhle Mbambo-Thata is Executive Director of the University of South Africa Library. Prior to that, she was University Librarian at the University of Zimbabwe. She holds a DPhil in information science, and has extensive experience in international librarianship. She has been actively involved with IFLA, Eifl.net and the International Network for Availability of Scientific Publications (INASP). Her research interests are in ICT applications in libraries in developing countries, women and ICT, and information literacy.

Rory McGreal is a professor and Associate Vice President, Research, at Athabasca University. He graduated from McGill University with a joint honours degree in History and Russian. He has a Bachelor of Education from Dalhousie University, Halifax, NS in language teaching. His Masters degree from Concordia University, Montreal was in applied linguistics. His PhD degree in computer technology in education at Nova Southeastern University's School for Computer and Information Science was taken at a distance using the internet.

Previously, he was the executive director of TeleEducation New Brunswick, a province-wide bilingual (French/English) distributed distance learning network. Before that, he was responsible for the expansion of Contact North/Contact Nord (a distance education network in the remote region of Northern Ontario, serving remote native reserves and small mining towns). He has worked in Arctic Quebec teaching Naskapi Cree students. Rory was the founder of the world's first e-learning website for TeleEducation NB, and of one of the world's first metadata learning object repositories, the TeleCampus. He has been a leader in the development of the CanCore metadata implementation profile for implementing the IEEE LOM international standard for learning objects. In the past, he has worked in Canada, the Seychelles, the Middle East and Europe as a teacher, union president, ESL technological training co-ordinator, instructional designer, language and computer laboratory co-ordinator, and educational advisor. He has served on the Board of the TeleLearning Research Network of Centres of Excellence, the Commonwealth of Learning's Knowledge Management Group and the Education Steering Committee for CANARIE, Canada's broadband research network. In 2002, he was honoured as recipient of the Wedemeyer Award for Distance Education Practitioner. He has published numerous articles and book chapters on e-learning in Europe, the Americas, Asia and Australia.

Rory campaigned for the past five years to support Athabasca University's successful bid for membership of EDEN. He has a particular research interest in open educational resources and interoperability, more recently using mobile devices.

Damien Meere received his BSc degree from the University of Limerick, Republic of Ireland in 2005. He is currently pursuing his MEng degree, leading to transfer to PhD within the Telecommunications Research Centre at the University of Limerick. His research is focused on the provision of intelligent mobile services across a university campus area.

Keren Mills is a librarian with an interest in educational technology. She has a broad understanding of current trends in educational technology and their possible applications in adult education, particularly m-learning and games for learning. Her work includes supporting and encouraging communities of practice and knowledge sharing across the Open University.

John Naughton is Professor of the Public Understanding of Technology at the Open University where he has worked since 1973. He is an electrical engineer with an interest in complex systems and the use of computers and networks in teaching and learning. He is also an experienced and well-known journalist, author of *A Brief History of the Future: the origins of the internet* (Weidenfeld & Nicolson, 1999) and a Fellow of Wolfson College, Cambridge.

Gill Needham's current post is Head of Strategic and Service Development at the Open University Library. Since joining the Open University in 1998 she has taken a leading role in developing the Library's electronic services to its 200,000 students, has launched and developed an Information Literacy Strategy for the University and has been a major author on three Open University courses. Previously she worked for 15 years in the National Health Service, initially as a librarian and then subsequently as an R&D Specialist in Public Health, responsible for promoting evidence-based practice and public involvement in healthcare decision-making.

Dr Máirtín O'Droma received his bachelor's and doctoral degrees from the National University of Ireland in 1973 and 1978 respectively. He is a Senior Academic and Director of the Telecommunications Research Centre at the University of Limerick, Republic of Ireland. Current activities include being a founding partner of TARGET, a European Union Network of Excellence, IST-507893, 2004–8 (www.target-net.org). He is also a founding member of two European COoperation in the Field of Science and Technology Research Actions (COST Actions 285 & 290) focusing on simulation and network aspects of wireless communications. He was a founding partner of ANWIRE (Academic Network for Wireless Internet Research in Europe), a European Union Network of Excellence, IST-38835, 2002–4. Previous posts held include those of lecturer at University College Dublin and at the National University of Ireland, Galway, Director of Communications Software Ltd and of ODR Patents Ltd. His research interests include: wireless network and protocol infrastructural innovations and new paradigms; complex wireless telecommunication systems simulation and behavioural modelling, linearization and efficiency techniques in multimode, multicarrier broadband nonlinear microwave and mm-wave transmit power amplifiers; smart adaptive antenna arrays and MIMO channels; and new m-learning paradigms. Máirtín has served on the technical programme committees of many international conferences and workshops. He was Publications Chair and Track co-Chair of the IEEE VTC2007 Spring Conference.

Dr Mícheál Ó hAodha works as a librarian and a lecturer (part-time) at the University of Limerick, Republic of Ireland, where he teaches on a number of HPSS (history, politics and social studies) courses relating to the history of Irish migration. He has published around two dozen books including: *Irish Travellers: representations and realities* (Liffey Press, 2006) and *American 'Outsider': stories from the Irish traveller diaspora*, (Cambridge Scholars Publishing, 2008). He has a particular interest in the use of technology as a means to circumvent barriers in educational access for groups who have traditionally been unable to access third-level education.

Jo Parker manages the Library's Information Literacy Unit at the Open University. The Unit's current (and major) piece of work is the TU120 (Beyond Google) short course for the Open University which puts a new spin on IL. Other work includes developing learning objects and assessing the effectiveness of e-meeting software for delivering IL. She is a member of the Sconul Working Group on Information Literacy, and, when not promoting IL, can sometimes be found dabbling in Facebook.

Mariano Rico has been the project manager for the Open Library 2.0 information system, and, with the support of Hassan Sheikh and Susan Eales, has been the driving force to implement and provide the mobile version of this system. He is Learning and Teaching Technologies Officer at the Institute of Educational Technology (IET) where he worked with Hassan to develop the Open University's Knowledge Network, a web-based application that enables OU staff to share and explore the University's knowledge and research of teaching and learning, and for which he is content manager. With a background in information management and information sciences, Mariano has been working during the last eight years on the design, development and implementation of information systems for e-learning. His research interests currently focus on the use of social networking, Web 2.0 tools and mobile technologies for the support of mobile learning communities and of communities of practice.

Non Scantlebury is Learning Resources Development Manager at the Open University Library. Her particular interest is the more strategic discovery and reuse of digital library materials for learning and teaching. Projects Non has been involved in include the JISC-funded DEVIL (Dynamically Enhancing Virtual Learning Environments from within the Library); ReFLEX (Resources for Learning by Exploration); and Library Resources Integration with the Open University's Virtual Learning Environment.

Steve Schafer is Director of Library Services at Athabasca University (AU), Canada, where he has been (as both student and employee) since 1981. He earned his MLIS from the University of Alberta (1989), completing a thesis entitled 'An Investigation of Student Use of the Supplementary Materials List at Athabasca University'.

AU specializes in distance and online learning, offering programmes and courses at the undergraduate and graduate levels, and has been approved to offer its first doctoral programme, a EdD, expecting to take students in September 2008.

Dr Wathmanel Seneviratne is University Librarian, Open University of Sri Lanka. She has 23 years of experience in the LIS field and has national and international publications to her credit. Her research interests are community information access strategies, web-based information portal strategies and ODL behaviour.

Hassan Sheikh has been working as Strategic IT Systems Development Manager for the SSDG group within the OU Library and Learning Resources Centre. He is the technical lead on several internal and external projects including Open Library 2.0, collaboration with Athabasca University on mobile delivery systems, Digilab, Library Systems Strategy, JISC DYNIQX and VLE, ECMS and Open Library 2.0 integration. Hassan has several years of experience in programming and usability evaluations and worked at the Institute of Educational Technology at OU for four and a half years before joining the Library in October 2006.

Dr Stanimir Stojanov received his informatics and doctoral degrees from Humboldt University in 1978 and 1986 respectively. He is Associate Professor at the University of Plovdiv, Bulgaria, and currently Head of the Computer Systems Department and of the eCommerce Laboratory. His research interests include: service-oriented architectures, agents and multi-agent systems, e-commerce and e-learning applications. Stanimir is a member of a number of international conferences and workshops, including: PISTA'04, PISTA'05, PISTA'06, SOIC 2005, EISTA'05, EISTA'06 (USA), MENSURA2006 (Spain), and the 1st and 2nd Balkan Informatics Conferences.

Rhodri Thomas is OU Virtual Learning Environment's Mobile Learner Support project leader. He is involved in co-ordinating OU activities with a view to providing course support and materials for a mobile audience. Current areas of interest are podcasting, moblogging (user-generated content on the move) and widening access (to those with unreliable connectivity via offline approaches), having worked on research and development programmes in the Faculty of Education and Language Studies.

Tony Tin is Electronic Resources Librarian at Athabasca University Library, Canada. He holds a BA and MA in history from McGill University and a BEd and MLS from the University of Alberta. Tony maintains the Athabasca University Library's website and online resources, and is the Digital Reading Room project leader. He is co-ordinator of Athabasca University's Mobile Learning Project.

John M. Traxler is Reader in Mobile Technology for e-Learning and Director of the Learning Lab at the University of Wolverhampton. He is keen to look at innovative technologies to support diverse communities of students in the UK and explore ways of using appropriate innovative technologies to deliver education in developing countries, especially sub-Saharan Africa. He is jointly responsible for workshops on mobile learning for UK universities and similar workshops in Africa, Canada and India. He was invited to the Microsoft Mobile Learning Summit in Seattle and is advising a project for Kenyan farmers that uses blended web-based and phone-based technology. He is the conference chair for mLearn2008 in Ironbridge and also works with South Africa's Meraka Institute.

Emma Whittlesea is Research Assistant at the Centre for Excellence in Professional Placement Learning (Ceppl). With a Bachelor's degree in psychology and a Masters degree in health psychology she has a breadth of experience in both qualitative and quantitative research methods, which has been enhanced by research experience through her work at the Centre. Emma's role involves working closely with the Ceppl Research Fellow, Director, and development activity teams to facilitate the development of, and engage in research associated with, placement learning.

Freda Wolfenden is Senior Lecturer in Education and Development at the Open University (UK) where she directs the Masters in Education programme and is a member of the TESSA (Teacher Education in Sub-Saharan Africa) team. She has had extensive experience of teacher education and development nationally, within the UK, and internationally, working as a teacher, adviser and academic within public and private organizations. Her recent research has concentrated especially on open educational resources in the context of their use to support professional learning of teachers in Africa, presenting at a range of international conferences in Africa, Europe and the USA.

Foreword
Always on: libraries in a world of permanent connectivity

Lorcan Dempsey

Summary

Mobile communication has been more widely adopted more quickly than any other technology ever. It represents a diffusion of communications and computational capacity into a growing part of our research, learning and social activities. It has resonated with emerging youth behaviours, providing support for distinctive patterns of social interaction and group formation, information use and personal expression.

Diffuse networking changes how we co-ordinate our resources to achieve goals; for example, our use of time and space changes. Timeshifting is routine, as students are able to listen or watch lectures in the gym or on the train. The use of space to support *ad hoc* rendezvous and social learning is more important.

As networking spreads, we have multiple connection points which offer different grades of experience (the desktop, the cell phone, the xBox or Wii, the GPS system, the smartphone, the ultra-portable notebook, and so on). While these converge in various ways, they are also optimized for different purposes. A natural accompaniment of this mesh of connection points is a move of many services to the cloud, available on the network across these multiple devices and environments. This means that an exclusive focus on the institutional website as the primary delivery mechanism, and the browser as the primary consumption environment, is increasingly partial.

Students are results-oriented and value convenience. This emphasis, coupled with the design constraints on some devices, promotes a need to get to relevance quickly. Socialization, personalization and location awareness become very important.

Libraries have been working to develop network-ready services; mobile communication intensifies this activity and adds new challenges as they look at what it means to be mobile-ready. This has organizational implications as a shift of emphasis towards workflow integration around the learner or researcher creates new relationships with other service organizations on campus. It also has implications for how space is used, for library skills, and for how collections are developed. We can see the impact of mobile communication on services in two ways. First, services may be made mobile-ready, as with special mobile interfaces for library services, alerting services, and so on. Second, mobilization continues the restructuring of services, organizations and attention that networking has brought about. Think here of how to socialize and personalize services; how to adapt to collection and service use which spans personal, institutional, and cloud environments; how to position and promote the library 'brand' as services become atomized and less 'visible' on the network; and add more complex questions about what best to do locally and what to source with collaborative arrangements or third parties.

Introduction
A prelude

The US presidential campaign of 2008 is a milestone. I am not talking about the much discussed issues of race, gender or age. I am talking about the diffusion of digital networking. It is clear that Barack Obama has been remarkably successful in mobilizing people and money through the network. At his meetings, he has asked the crowds to take out their mobile phones and text their contact details to his campaign HQ. Whatever the result, the election will be remembered for how the combination of social networking techniques and the diffusion of connectivity through mobile and other devices allowed Obama's campaign to scale effectively.

Mobile communications, according to Manuel Castells, is the fastest diffusing technology ever. It is not surprising, then, that we can suggest rapidly accumulating milestones. Here is a random and very recent selection:

- the importance of crowd-sourced photographs at significant events
- the large volumes of votes to TV shows like *American Idol*
- the appearance of the Apple App Store
- the ability to deliver rich applications to an increasing number of devices or the appearance of versions of enterprise applications for mobile devices (for example, think of the Pandora app for the iPhone or SAP CRM on the Blackberry)
- the Blackberry, the iPod, the iPhone, and the Asus Eee PC.

Until recently, we have thought about the *mobile* in *mobile communications*; more important maybe is the general diffusion of *communications* capacity and its resonance with particular patterns of behaviour, consumer choices and lifestyles.[1] As network infrastructure becomes more widespread, communications and computational capacity diffuses through more of our research, learning and consumer behaviors. We are not only looking at increasingly permanent connectivity, but connectivity through devices that have rapidly improving storage and processing capability. People can store thousands of songs, take photographs, and even locate themselves on the earth's surface. In these remarks, I take mobile communications to refer to a general diffusion of networking capacity through the fabric of our lives. This changes our experiences and expectations as creators, sharers and consumers of information.

In this vein, I was struck by some remarks by Trip Hawkins, the CEO of Digital Chocolate and the founder of leading games publisher Electronic Arts, in an interview at the Web 2.0 Summit in 2007.[2] He is talking about games in a mobile environment, where Digital Chocolate is active: 'In my opinion traditional content is dead ...', he said, and he went on to characterize traditional content as 'about a playback and immersive experience and which involve a business model where you pay a fee for the privilege of escapism and checking out'. These traditional forms include reading and cinema experiences, and he suggests that participation in those media has leveled out. He contrasts this with a new type of content and associated experience, which is growing:

> . . . where the consumer is increasingly going to spend their money is on social value which is enabled by content where the content isn't for sale for its own sake – the content is there to enable improvements in your social life.

Digital Chocolate is a developer of games for mobile phones. Depending on your point of view or cultural formation, this characterization might be plausible or startling.

This type of divided response is common in our current environment, where there are so few settled assumptions about direction, and varied patterns of behaviour across generations, countries or economic groups.

One clear development is a blurring of our social, business, learning and educational lives as the pattern of our communication and interaction across time and space changes. For example, the Blackberry has raised the expectation of anywhere, anytime availability in some work environments. Think of this in institutional terms; this blurring raises interesting questions about how libraries are 'present' to their users, and how their users see the library. The position of the library as a functionally integrated, discrete presence, whether on the web or as a physical place, becomes diffused through various manifestations (a physical place to meet, a toolbar, a set of services in the course management system, a Facebook application, a set of RSS feeds, office hours in a school or department, and so on). It also changes the relation between the library and other service providers on campus, as organizational boundaries track less well to learning and research behaviours. As more activities move onto the network, and as the network becomes more diffused through mobile communications, then workflow and information management become pervasive issues which prompt interesting questions about how academic support services are best configured.

For example, in his book about VLEs (aka learning or course management systems) Martin Weller talks about the changing, and sometimes politically difficult, relationship between the library and e-learning developments.[3] This not only throws up questions about where resources are managed or what technical interfaces are required, but also about responsibility and purpose, and about contribution to broader pedagogical practice. A similar convergence can be seen as university research support systems interact with information systems (expertise databases, support for research assessment or publication profiles, advice about citation and presentation, data curation, repositories for research output dissemination, and so on). This involves greater interaction with research practice and behaviour.

This interaction with research and learning practice becomes at once more critical and more complex, as the 'formal' systems offered by universities jostle alongside the bricolage of personal environments that are created with social bookmarking tools, RSS aggregators, search engines, communication with colleagues, and so on.

In this way, a discussion about mobile communications, especially when seen in the context of the broader diffusion of network communications, soon touches on many fundamental issues: pedagogy and cognitive approaches; organization and structures; lifestyles and social preferences. However, in this introductory piece, my purpose is to be merely *suggestive* about *medium term* issues for *libraries*. I will say something about mobile communications and library services in very broad terms as a prelude to the specific treatments which follow in the rest of the volume.[4]

I will start in this section with some brief comments about two pervasive themes: generations, an inevitable topic, and networks, increasingly supporting the milieux of work and learning. I will then look at some of the ways in which our behavior is being reconfigured in a network environment, before closing with a short discussion of library issues.

A note on generations

In their global review of mobile communications, Manuel Castells and colleagues make a strong connection between younger generations and mobile communications, arguing that they 'reveal more quickly the potential uses of the technology compared to people of an older age'.[5] They further argue that there is a structural match between the characteristics of youth culture and the capacities of wireless technology, and that this resonance helps explain the rapid diffusion of the technology. They summarize by saying that youth culture has found in the mobile phone an appropriate tool to express its demands for 'safe autonomy', ubiquitous connectivity, and self-constructed networks of shared social practice'. Other characteristics they discuss are: networked sociability, where social relations are increasingly selective and self-directed; the formation of a collective identity alongside the strengthening of individual identity; the importance of consumerism; and the focus on entertainment, games and media.

'Safe autonomy' refers to their contention that while people are becoming more autonomous at a younger age, they retain financial, emotional and other dependencies on family and others. Mobile communications support this autonomy within an 'always on' communications safety net. In her book about changing student behaviors and the academic library, Susan Gibbons reviews the literature around the 'net generation'. Although her emphasis is a little different – on the sheltered and protected lives many children lead – she points to a similar conclusion. The mobile communications safety net makes parents continuously present to many students. She talks about 'helicopter parents', only a call away, and to the practice of turning to parents and others by phone for support with assignments. Interestingly, she suggests that for this reason they now focus more library induction efforts on parents.[6]

Connaway et al.[7] also note that some graduate students rely on parents as sources for advice about information resources. They also note the results-oriented focus of current students, their multi-tasking, their desire to figure things out for themselves, a focus on convenience, and a preference for current resources.

The focus on consumerism, entertainment and games in these discussions highlights another important transformation. This generation is familiar with Facebook, Flickr, the iPod, and the xBox or Wii. It is sometimes suggested that this will raise expectations when they go to college or to work environments. And in some cases it will. Equally interesting in the long term, however, is the shifting balance of innovation and investment as general retail and consumer consumption of hardware increases. As computing and communications diffuses into the general population, so does the demand for new products and services. For this reason, developments in the consumer and retail space will increasingly outpace those in enterprise or educational contexts, and many enterprise or educational services will have substitute or rival products in the consumer space.[8] Think, for example, of what is happening with e-mail, where people may use their Gmail account in preference to an institutional one. Or think of discussions around personal learning environments, where it is recognized that students now have a rich set of social networking, content management, co-oordination and other services available to them outside of the university environment. The university, library, or work environment can no longer expect to provide a more sophisticated digital environment than that which is available in the general consumer space; in fact, the formal learning or work environment may appear increasingly clunky beside the social networking and consumer sites which increasingly set our expectations.

This creates complex service and sourcing choices. For example, do you build an internal social network for new students? Or do you piggyback on one of the social networks they already use?

The diffusion of networking

This congruence between young behaviours and the capabilities of mobile communications has been a factor in accelerating diffusion. An increasing part of what we do is potentially network-aware, and much is potentially sharable and shared. Eric Schmidt, CEO of Google, discusses the shift:

> It's pretty clear that there's an architectural shift going on. These occur every 10 or 20 years. The previous architecture was a proprietary network with PCs attached to it. With this new architecture, you're always online, every device can see every application, and the applications are stored in the cloud. [9]

Our online activity is increasingly diffused across multiple applications and multiple devices. As Schmidt suggests, this pushes more applications and data to the cloud: in other words, to shared network services which are then visible across these devices. This broad vision is increasingly shared; for example, Microsoft's Live Mesh initiative aspires to provide a framework for synchronizing and sharing across devices, applications and files, locally and in the cloud. This diffusion and concentration is a general pattern on the network. As the network diffuses into general behaviors, we see more peer to peer communication, creation and sharing of data, blogs, wikis, feed aggregation, and so on. At the same time, we see the concentration of computational capacity and data in large network applications: Google, Wikipedia, Yahoo, Facebook, and so on – where network effects drive scale and gravitational attraction.

What does this mean? First of all, when the network is always available, or always potentially available, the boundary between 'mobile' and fixed dissolves into multiple connection points, each with its own grade of experience (the mobile phone, the desktop, the xBox or Wii, the Kindle, the media centre). These connection points may come to be more similar: consider how the iPhone has changed expectations (there were fifty times more web searches to Google from the iPhone than from any other mobile handset in 2008 up to April.[10] Or, again, consider the drive to move business applications to smartphones, the network-aware Kindle book reader, or the growth in popularity of ultra-portable notebooks. However, it is likely that different grades of experience will remain common, and for some interim period at least, quite important. A cellphone provides a different grade of experience to an xBox, or to a powerful desktop with a large screen. An experience which includes complex transactions and multiple choices is not easily transportable across consumption environments, and it is increasingly common for providers to develop parallel sites specialized for mobile users. It is also increasingly common to develop apps targeted at particular devices. Think of apps created for the iPhone or the BlackBerry, for example. Some interesting correspondences emerge here. For example, writing applications for mobile devices and for other 'service composition environments' (Facebook, Myspace, iGoogle . . .) imposes similar constraints: scope for interaction and screen real estate is limited; it is important to do a small number of things well.[11]

Secondly, much of our current model of network information and communication behaviour is based on the desktop as a consumption target and the organizational website as the delivery target. However, it appears that the desktop (or laptop) and the website may no longer be the sole focus of attention, and a model which focuses almost exclusively on them looks increasingly partial in a world of diffuse network capacity, on the one hand, and cloud-based resources, on the other. We increasingly have a 'mesh' of entry points: PC and phone, of course, but also DVRs, cameras, navigation systems, consoles and so on. We increasingly use a range of shared network level 'cloud' services: for search, for social networking, for content and information, for communication. Providing service in this environment is very different than in one where the model assumes a personal desktop or laptop as the place where resources are accessed and used and the institutional website as the place where they are delivered.

And thirdly, this has an impact on how we build applications. The organizational website is also changing: rather than a destination in itself, it is a container which combines and processes resources and makes them available to multiple consuming devices. The BBC has a nice characterization of direction from the website point of view:

> From a conceptual point of view, the widgetization adopted by Facebook, iGoogle and netvibes weighed strongly on our initial thinking. We wanted to build the foundation and DNA of the new site in line with the ongoing trend and evolution of the Internet towards dynamically generated and syndicable content through technologies like RSS, atom and xml. This trend essentially abstracts the content from its presentation and distribution, atomizing content into a feed-based universe. Browsers, devices, etc therefore become lenses through which this content can be collected, tailored and consumed by the audience.[12]

Syndication, synchronization and feed-based integration are important patterns in this environment. Consider for example the synchronization across iTunes, a desktop and an iPod, or the podcasting experience, or the increasingly pervasive use of RSS or various alerting services.

Some reconfigurations

Communication

As mobile communications diffuse networking into more of what we do, it reconfigures our relationship with time, space and other people, just as earlier networks did. Affordable air transport shortened the distance between home and college; now they are a phone call or text apart. Selective social networks live alongside face-to-face interaction in new ways. For example, individual students may participate in multiple communicating groups: short-term as in a particular class on a particular day, or longer term as with family or old school friends.

Continuous connectedness supports a sort of incremental social synchronization as plans, schedules, arrangements, locations and progress can be shared and co-oordinated across these communicating groups. Arrangements to meet, decisions about what to buy, discussion about shared work can happen on the go and at any time, as colleagues and friends are a phone call or a text away.

This continuous communication means that communication occurs while people are in particular places, also interacting in face-to-face ways with people around them. And we are seeing variable tolerance for the interference of settled behaviors by newer behaviors, as when people talk on their mobile phones in the supermarket aisle, theatre, or train. We do not have clear norms here, meaning that expectations may need to be managed, as happens in some cases on trains with a quiet carriage (or in the library).

As network communication becomes more pervasive, and takes place on a variety of devices, we see higher level services emerge. For example, we see services like Dopplr which help co-oordinate travel, and we see a variety of niche and general social networking activities which support selective networking, communication and co-ordination. Some of these are currently niche – Twitter or Jaiku, for example – and may or may not fade. Some that we cannot now predict will emerge. At the same time, new communication and content services aimed at mobile users continue to appear. There is a major push by sites – the BBC, Facebook, Google, for example – to provide access to current mobile devices, and to prepare for a mobile world. And new services proliferate: see MusicID from AT&T, which provides a service that identifies music for you based on a 15-second sample. New businesses are emerging based on integration or co-ordination needs in this reconfigured environment. Examples are Boopsie and Rave Wireless. Boopsie indexes content from providers and makes it available in mobile-friendly ways. Rave Wireless provides services to meet communication needs across whole campus populations through various infrastructure services. These include alerting, security, and various information services (video, shuttle bus locations . . .).

However, although communications capability is diffusing, it does not result in a uniform communications environment. An institution cannot necessarily rely on one vehicle – e-mail or texting, for example – to reach everyone in a timely way. This accounts for the title of a recent article by Rave Wireless's Raju Rishi in *Educause Quarterly*: 'Always connected but hard to reach'. He talks about how students will choose the communication channel that best suits them 'in the moment', and this will vary with situation and communication group:

Understanding the impact that time-and-place shifting has on students' preferred communication channels and their priorities will help colleges and universities claim space on their students' busy communication radar.[13]

And it raises unexpected pragmatic issues. Gibbons, for example, notes the increased expense of communicating with students: they often have to communicate using long distance calls, because students do not change their mobile's 'home' since they still regularly communicate with family and friends from their 'home' environment.[14]

Pattern of creation and consumption

I opened with a quote about changing patterns of consumption. It highlighted three developments for me. First, the growing range of resources targeted at mobile users: games, certainly, but also music, videos, and so on. Video and audio generally are more important. People *listen* while commuting or exercising. They *listen* and *watch* when travelling. Again, time and space shifting are noticeable, as where a desire to listen to or view a lecture in the student's own time – on the train or in the gym – creates an interest in video and podcasts.

Secondly, recent discussion of social networks has highlighted the importance of 'social objects': the shared interests around which people affiliate, such as photographs, movies, music, and holiday destinations.[15] Social objects become integral to communications activity, and providers think about how their resources might benefit from social engagement. Where resources are abundant and attention is scarce, the filtering that social approaches (and the use of analytics) provides becomes more valuable. Pervasive networking supports this trend.

This leads into a third issue. A recent report from Microsoft Research discusses the concept of value in relation to human–computer interaction. In some interesting examples drawn from mobile communications, it discusses how usability may be a less important value than the augmentation of real experiences. For example, they talk about how taking pictures can enrich an experience:

Other studies show that, just as capturing images can enhance the moment, so mobile phones are being used as a new means of sustaining, embodying and creating social networks. ... What mobile phones allow for is the creation and sharing of new 'digital currencies' that bring people together.[16]

Here are some general observations:

- *Media*: Communication patterns alter consumption patterns. Mobile consumption may be focused on situationally relevant resources – facts or answers to questions; video or audio; the ability to manipulate resources on cloud services, to save, share, bookmark. In the desktop model, the user could look for resources, navigate, move around,_explore, move between multiple menus. And we have become used to this when thinking about presenting resources. As the interaction experience moves to multiple kinds of device, the challenge is different: the expectation is to get to relevance more quickly, to do a small number of things well, to understand individual needs. Convenience is key. In this context, resources will be increasingly socialized, personalized, and location-aware, and the mobilization of usage data (analytics) is a growing focus.
- *Socialized*: People connect and share themselves through 'social objects' (music, photos, video, links, or other shared interests) and it has been argued that successful social networks are those which form around such social objects. We are becoming used to selective disclosure and selective socialization through affinity groups within different social networks. Together, these experiences have created an interesting expectation: many network resources are 'signed' in the sense that they are attached to online personas that we may or may not know, whose judgement and network presence we may come to know. Think of social bookmarking sites or Amazon reviews, for example. People are resources on the network, and have become entry points and connectors for others.[17]
- *Analytics*: Of course, people's behaviour is important in another way also. We leave traces everywhere, and these traces are increasingly being mobilized to rank, relate and recommend based on shared interests and behaviours. This trend is intensifying, because the ability to present relevant or personalized materials is valuable. Think of the importance, for example, to Netflix of making good recommendations: it turns directly into dollars.
- *Personalized:* While personalization is a general trend, it is probably

more critical in a mobile environment given the need stated above to get to relevance quickly. This points to the importance of creating and sharing profile information (let me tell you what I am interested in), analytics (collecting data about my choices and behaviors), and socialization (crowd-sourcing relevance judgements, and mining associations and relationships).

- *Location-aware:* An infrastructure for location-aware services is being put in place. The combination of geotagged resources (whether these are restaurants, libraries, or physical items) and location-aware devices is making a range of services possible. An obvious case is search results organized by proximity to the searcher.

- *Synchronization and syndication*: Resources are received, created and shared across multiple environments. Think again of music or photographs, which may move in different directions between services in the cloud, the desktop, and multiple devices.

- *Cloud*: All of this discussion points to more services in the cloud. Collection and social services of course, but also content transformation or other services which facilitate use in this environment. Increasingly, it does not make sense for institutions to replicate functionality that is best sourced with specialist providers.

- *Changing attention patterns*: The network style of consumption – particularly mobile consumption – calls forward services which atomize content, providing snippets, thumbnails, ringtones, abstracts, tags, ratings and feeds. All of these create a variety of hooks and hints for people for whom attention is scarce. It has even been recently suggested that this pattern of consumption is rewiring our cognitive capacities.[18] Regardless of the longer term implications, it is clear that people need better clues about where to spend their attention in this environment, and that this is one incentive for the popularity of social approaches. This attention scarcity is apparent also in the academic environment where a bouncing and skimming style of consumption has been observed.[19] Carole Palmer talks about actual 'reading avoidance'. Researchers may survey more material, but spend less time with each item, relying on abstracts and other content clues to avoid reading in full.[20]

Space and time

As a pervasive network provides support for communication and shared working, these can be lifted out of physical shared space, and pursued when convenient. Shared space is important, but may need to be available in different ways: consider the role of Starbucks as a form of on-demand space for *ad-hoc* rendezvous. Connectivity is also important as a way of reclaiming time: consider the provision of wireless network by Google on buses ferrying employees from San Francisco to work in Mountain View, or the bursts of activity in airports or in other enforced intervals. Here is *The Economist* quoting William Mitchell:

> The fact that people are no longer tied to specific places for functions such as studying or learning, says Mr Mitchell, means that there is a huge drop in demand for traditional, private, enclosed spaces such as offices or classrooms, and simultaneously a huge rise in demand for semi-public spaces that can be informally appropriated to ad-hoc workspaces. This shift, he thinks, amounts to the biggest change in architecture in this century. In the 20th century architecture was about specialized structures – offices for working, cafeterias for eating, and so forth. This was necessary because workers needed to be near things such as landline phones, fax machines and filing cabinets, and because the economics of building materials favoured repetitive and simple structures, such as grid patterns for cubicles.[21]

Social/work/leisure

Participation in a shared communications space blurs boundaries between work, social interaction and leisure. This is related to our altered relationship to time and space, as it becomes possible to engage in different types of activity wherever we are and at whatever time. This may be both liberating and stressful, and poses interesting questions for service providers tied to 'office hours'. If assignments are prepared at two o'clock in the morning, should reference services be available at those times?

Some issues for libraries

Introduction

So, what about libraries, and academic libraries in particular? Think of the library as an articulation of four elements: *place, collections, people and expertise*, and *systems and services*. In a pre-network age, these were very much vertically integrated around the collection. Place existed to house the collection and permit its use. Expertise existed to organize and interpret the collections, and systems existed to process, store and make them available. These contributions continue to co-oevolve in a network environment, but there is also some unbundling as different trajectories are pursued.

For example, as the role of physical collections changes, and as university needs shift, the library is looking at how library spaces can support flexible, socially-directed working styles of mobile communicators, providing configurable spaces which support learning and rendezvous. Interestingly, as discussed above, their communication patterns are changing how students think about space and how they use university social spaces.

Or think of collections. The library is used to providing rather than adapting: resources are provided pretty much as they are published. The library may aggregate and filter, but it has tended not to atomize, recombine or reformat. Of course, the short loan or reserve collection has moved in this direction, providing materials which are more adapted to particular learning needs. As VLEs or course management systems have emerged, other campus partners have also been providing materials – in various ways – which are adapted for particular courses: links, chapters, and so on. This puts some pressure on the library to move up the value chain, and to provide materials which are more specifically adapted to learning requirements. This would be, of course, in addition to continuing to provide collections which support more open-ended exploration and discovery.

Here are five general observations before some more specific discussion:

- *Services*: As a growing proportion of library use is network-based, the library becomes visible and usable through the network services provided. On the network, there are only *services*. So, the perception of quality of reference or of the value of particular collections, for example, will depend for many people on the quality of the network services which make them visible, and the extent to which they can be integrated into personal learning environments. Increasingly, this requires us to emphasize the network as an integral design principle in library service development, rather than thinking of it as an add-on. The provision of RSS feeds is a case in point. Thinking about how something might appear on a mobile device is another.

- *Switch*: This network service orientation highlights the switch role of the library. This is in line with general industrial trends. For example, Prahalad and Krishnan talk about a new business dynamic to drive innovation. On the one hand they suggest that a focus on a standard product for an undifferentiated consumer is being replaced by a personalized experience and cocreation of value with the consumer. In addition to emerging network services, they point to numerous other examples, such as Unilever's Pond Institute. On the other hand, they point to the vertical disintegration of companies and the sourcing of critical components from many suppliers. In fact, effective supply chain management has emerged as an important competitive competence. They argue that the personalization of experience and the ability to effectively source capacities with multiple resources is central to the ability to innovate.[22] This dynamic is familiar to libraries, but it is interesting to see it highlighted in this way. Increasingly, the library will have to meaningfully synthesize a range of products and services from multiple sources, specialize them for particular users and uses, and then mobilize them into a personalized, socialized individual user experience.[23] There are not routine ways of doing much of this now. The library faces increasingly complex sourcing decisions, while at the same time it is not clear at what level socialization/personalization should happen.
- *Sourcing*: Sourcing decisions are getting more complex as the service environment diversifies. For example, I asked above if an institution should look at building a social network to support new students, or should it use an existing service. Here, as in so many other cases, we are in a transitional phase. How much will the library need to build, how much can be sourced by the library from third parties, and where will alternative services emerge which can be directly consumed by students or academics? Should a library begin to try to specialize collections of electronic resources for particular courses? Or build profiling and other infrastructure to support better personalization? Or should they wait and see what the market provides? Or look to JISC or others to create collaborative services?

Or try to build specialized services on top of Flickr, or Facebook, or Delicious?

- *Socializing and personalizing*: Libraries have experimented with socializing services, inviting tagging, reviews and other contributions. The library may not be the best level for this as they may not have appropriate volumes of use, or users may not perceive the incentives that motivate participation in other environments. There has also been some experiment with personalized library environments. In each case it is likely that approaches which mesh with broader initiatives, at campus level, or within some larger service level, will be more common. The University of Minnesota provides an example of the former where the library is working with student records systems to develop a concise representation of student academic interests (e.g. course enrollments, degree programs) which can then be automatically matched with relevant resources and services.[24] An example of the latter is where institutions are beginning to expose images on Flickr to benefit from the community Flickr has built.
- *Expectations*: Unlike other organizations, the library has limited flexibility in what it offers: it supports the research and learning needs of its institution with whatever materials are requested. It cannot simply turn off categories of provision (print materials or e-books) because it would rather not deal with them anymore or they present particular delivery challenges. This means that there will always be challenges of provision. These are highlighted in a network environment, as it is not possible to provide many things network-ready, and it is not possible to provide even more things mobile-ready. There are also variable expectations. Students are results driven; they want relevant, tailored, and fit-for-purpose materials; they may want to easily copy and share. The library wants to meet these expectations, as well as supporting other needs.

Services and systems

Service issues are discussed extensively throughout this volume. We can think of two ways in which this discussion is framed. First, how do you 'mobilize' existing services to work better with the variety of network consumption patterns which are emerging? And second, how does this changing network environment restructure some of the ways in which we think about and provide service? I will consider each of these in turn.

Here are some of the ways in which we see libraries already adapting with mobile-ready services. Kroski provides examples of some of these and other services.[25]

- *Reference/enquiry*: Libraries are offering services through the range of communication vehicles available: chat, instant messaging, texting, e-mail, and so on. Should the reference desk take phone calls from people in meeting or study space in the library? Data from an ongoing study of virtual referece services indicate that even where people are physically in the library they may prefer to use chat reference than seek out a face-to-face encounter.[26] Again, convenience and workflow integration are important.
- *Collections to go*: Audio- and e-books are made available in various ways. As discussed already, user lifestyles make these attractive. In some cases, devices are lent to hold the material.
- *Presentation and visibility*: Videos and podcasts describing or promoting particular library services, covering library events, and so on are becoming more common. Often, these are made available on network level sites – YouTube, iTunes – where they are more visible.
- *Alerting*: RSS is becoming pervasive. Text message and e-mail alerts are also more common. People may be told about events, about the status of their interactions/requests, about availability of staff, and so on. I quoted Raju Rishi above on the difficulty of reaching students through one channel. This is another interesting example of new service providers emerging to address needs in this reconfigured environment.
- *Syndication*: Libraries have begun to push applications and content into the diffuse network environment of their users. RSS feeds, widgets, and Facebook applications are becoming more common.
- *Mobile sites*: Some libraries are specifically designing for mobile access. This imposes an interesting and valuable discipline. The mobile site needs to be much simpler than the typical library site, and it is a useful exercise to think what is best to present there. Here is an example from North Carolina State University.[27] Note the status of

MobiLIB Home
1. Catalog Search
2. Computers
3. Library Hours
4. Campus Directory
5. Contact Us
6. Links
7. Wolfline Status

the bus again (Wolfline status). The 'computers' link lets you know the availability of computers in different areas of the libraries.

- *Communications and referral*: We are now familiar with staff in retail environments being 'wired up' for constant communication. Such micro-co-ordination support may also be useful for library staff.
- *Booking*: Rooms, equipment, and consultation may be booked over the network. Availability may be checked. This becomes more important in the 'micro-co-ordinated' lifestyle described earlier.
- *Note taking*: Cameras are now common, and can potentially be used in a variety of approved and unapproved ways. Rather than writing down the details of an item found in the catalogue, a photograph of the screen can be taken. Photographs of pieces of text or images may save copying or writing, and can be shared quickly. In time, of course, this type of activity will become more sophisticated as cameras can read encoded data associated with items and allow more sophisticated services.

So, how does an environment where networking is diffusing through research, learning and communication behaviors potentially reconfigure services in the near future? Here are some thoughts:

- *Institutional resources and timeshifting*: There has been a growing emphasis on managing institutional assets: learning and research materials, e-prints, and other research and learning outputs. We can see this interest now being extended to audio and video resources, capturing lectures, events and induction materials to cater to mobile users. This matches general timeshifting behaviors where watching lectures on the train or listening to a talk in the gym are routine. Managing the capture, accessibility and continuity of these resources over time is not yet a routine activity, nor does it have a clear organizational home. It seems like a natural library role.
- *Synching and portable collections*: The iPod and related devices have accustomed us to carrying large collections around and periodically docking to synch up between devices and services. People now load textbooks, theses, books, video, and music onto drives of various types. We also have reserve collections for particular courses. A model in which a student receives a collection tailored for their courses and periodically synchs it either with an institutional service

or a service in the cloud is increasingly feasible. Again, the balance between personal, institutional and cloud is one that crops up in various places.

- *Engaging with personal collections*: People use a growing array of services to manage their digital lives. Although some are local to their devices, a growing number are on the network. Think, in different contexts, of Zotero, Delicious or Connotea; Flickr, YouTube or Slideshare; Google Docs, Scribd or Zoho. Microsoft, Google and Yahoo, as well as others, will continue to aim to provide a framework within which people manage their resources, communicate, and build their online identity. Two thoughts come to mind. One I have already mentioned: some of these resources may be important to the institution, which may want to provide backup services to ensure their continuity. The other is increasingly interesting: how do library resources play in these environments? Can I link to individual catalogue records, journal articles or e-books? Can I mix library resources with those in my personal collections? Are library resources RSS-ified?

- *Specializing*: Resources will become more specialized for particular uses, users and user environments. This is a general trend: it is heightened by the convenience and relevance requirements of variously networked users. There is a growing expectation that resources should match the context of use: a particular course, for example. This may involve content atomization, into chapters, images and so on. Resources benefit from declaring more about themselves: what they are about, what they are suitable for (level of treatment, intended audience, etc). This is especially important in a mobile environment and points to the importance of abstracts and other evaluative information, as well as to the potential benefits of personalization or socialization. And resources may need to play on certain devices, to be linked to, or be subject to other requirements. They may need to be 'ready' to participate in whatever learning environments are used on campus.

  Such specialization represents a general issue in an increasingly networked learning environment. It also raises more specific questions around the intersection between the library and the generation of learning materials.

Collections

Access to collections was discussed above, as access is increasingly a network service issue. What about management of collections? I will highlight three issues here.

First, there is the issue of management of print collections. The related issues of network use and repurposing of space have heightened awareness of the opportunity cost of managing print collections: what is not being done because effort and resources are going into a library resource which is releasing progressively less value in active research and learning practices? This is prompting more thinking about 'collective collection' issues: how do you begin to think about managing at the aggregate or group level (consortium, state, country . . .)? We can see this thinking coming through in mass digitization initiatives, shared off-site storage, and initiatives like the UK Research Reserve, which are seeking to reduce the overall volume of materials held by considering what is required at a systemwide level (in this case the national level). This is a major issue with interesting policy and service ramifications.

Second, there is the issue of licensing external collections. As the types of things that we want to do with collections diversify, such as providing reserve collections, or consolidating and adapting resources, rights issues become more complex. This is an area where we may see more services emerge, both to clear rights and to provide value-added combinations. And as libraries subscribe to such services, or to streaming media and other services, it raises the question of what, if anything, the library actually 'adds' to its collection.

Third, there is the issue of the continuity of personal and institutional collections. There are two issues here. One, what about those resources which are managed outside the library or institutional ambit? So, if a department begins to use SlideShare to make presentations available, does the university want to copy them to some persistently managed university environment? The same issues arise with classes which use Flickr to manage pictures as part of their coursework. Or what about the collection of university podcasts on iTunes? And two, how does the institution assure continuity over time of its own digital assets as these proliferate? The continuity of the electronic journal literature, which libraries typically license rather than buy and locally manage, and individual library responsibilities towards that continuity is a matter of active debate. The issue comes up in relation to other resources: for example, does the library now pay extra to store local copies of materials from a streaming service? This leads us to a broader question, which goes beyond my intentions here: what is the library collection in an environment where licensed, personal and institutional collections mingle in use?

Space

Library space has been a major preoccupation in recent years as institutions have thought about how best to cater for social learning, to accommodate related endeavors (writing centres, centres for digital scholarship, specialist advisory services), and to deal with print collections.

Spaces increasingly cater for *ad hoc* rendezvous, for flexible meetings, and for communication alongside more traditional 'study' space. In addition, there is a need for facilities for recharging, for synching with the cloud, for copying/sharing media. Access to specialist or high-end equipment also becomes a potential service, as does lending of accessories or laptops.

People: presence

In some ways, the challenge for libraries is to make themselves invisible, by delivering services into user workflow in networking environments. We also know that users of library services on the network do not always associate them with the library as provider.[28] However, libraries must also demonstrate value in the context of growing competition for resources. This suggests that as their network services grow in sophistication it is important for the library itself, its people, to be more visible. Here are some examples:

- *Marketing*: Library services are going to have to continually adapt to evolving network practices. This makes marketing a central activity, not understood narrowly as promotion, but rather as the evolution of products and services based on a structured investigation of changing needs. Assessment is also critical, to understand how well services meet changing needs.
- *Physical presence*: As users interact with services on the network, library staff need to be more personally visible. This is partly a matter

of being accessible in the variety of ways people communicate (e-mail, texting, etc). And it is partly a matter of personal engagement in the life of the university: on committees, in teaching, in collaboration. It is interesting to see a growing interest in librarians taking office hours within departments, so that they are visible on the ground in the physical flow of conversation and casual encounter.

- *A 'signed' network presence*: As I noted above, we are used to seeing 'signed' resources: reviews, ratings, social networking profiles, bookmarks. People have become entry points on the network, and signature is important. Think of library websites. They tend to be anonymous. Often, it is not straightforward finding appropriate contact points: there may not be photographs, or communication options are limited (office hours, IM, texting, e-mail, phone). Library services are not always associated with people. How often do subject pages, for example, carry a name and contact information who can be consulted?

    Connaway and Radford note how students are sometimes reluctant to use virtual reference because they do not want to interact with somebody who remains anonymous or who they do not know, even if it is a library service.[29]

    Being present in a student's network environment requires tact. Not all intersection points are equal: it may be less appropriate for the library to use some channels than others. Libraries are exploring, for example, how best to use social networking sites. They want to be available in important venues, while avoiding the 'parents at the party' syndrome.

- *Expertise*: Libraries are broadening their expertise as they develop a better understanding of how to cultivate a network presence which is valued by their users. This extends to greater engagement with learning and research practice, an appreciation of how to construct network resources, dealing with marketing and assessment issues, and an understanding of the balance between university and publisher interests in IPR. An area of growing interest is support for reputation management as the network identity of individuals and institutions becomes more important. This intersects with research skills (citation, consistent naming) and search engine optimization.

Conclusion

I have discussed mobile communications in the context of the broader diffusion of networking into the research, learning and social lives of our users. This resonates with communication and group behaviours of students. And it reinforces the general emphasis on convenience: as resources become more abundant we see that students and researchers are concerned about how they 'spend' their attention. This poses challenges in how current services are provided, but also points to a reconfiguration of these services to better co-ordinate library resources in support of new patterns of information behaviour. Examples are the use of physical space; working across personal, institutional and 'cloud' environments; and the mobilization of services into where users organize their digital experiences.

Much of my discussion has been open-ended, looking into the medium-term, and I have not suggested answers for many of the questions I posed. Here are some examples:

- I have discussed how the emergence of network consumption across a variety of devices and environments, coupled with a user desire for convenience and relevance, presents a challenge for current service infrastructures. This is in an environment of abundant substitute or alternative information resources and scarce attention. The library cannot expect its users to build their workflow around the library; it must reach out into the workflows its users are creating on the network. This means providing a higher level of network- and mobile-ready services than now exists. This presents significant challenges for library systems and collection regimes. Currently, they are providing a thin layer over two sets of heterogeneous resources. One is the set of legacy and emerging systems, developed independently rather than as part of an overall library experience, with different fulfilment options, different metadata models, and so on (integrated library system, resolver, knowledge base, repositories . . .).[30] Another is the set of legacy database and repository boundaries that map more to historically evolved publisher configurations and business decisions than to user needs or behaviors (for example, metadata, e-journals, e-books, and other types of content, which may be difficult to slice and dice in useful ways). How much work should the library do locally to address needs (adding tagging systems, mobilizing sites, atomizing and remixing content, personalization, etc.)?

- This leads into a second issue. It is always tempting to talk about transition. However, this is misleading as it suggests a stable end-state. It is probably more reasonable to talk about continuous change. In such an environment it is important to focus effort where it will have most impact, and not to needlessly duplicate effort or to work on solutions which may be overtaken by other work. What should be managed or developed by the library? What should be sourced collaboratively with other libraries? What should be secured from third parties? Related to this is thinking about how best to leverage other campus environments (VLE, student record systems . . .) or external network services used by students and researchers (Flickr, Zotero, Facebook . . .).

- The library has a visibility and brand challenge. On the one hand, services need to be available which integrate well with personal and other work environments, and, consequently, may be less visible to the user. At the same time, the continued competition for resources means that the library needs to be as visible as possible. This is not easy and calls for heightened marketing engagement and local political skills. The library needs a brand which is meaningful and engaging, which communicates its value, and which transcends the caricatural impression many have based around the building and print collections.

- Users increasingly expect socialized and personalized environments. As I have discussed, it is not clear what role individual libraries should have here, nor how some of this might be achieved.

We are still working on organizational and technical responses to these and other questions. I hope that readers will find good directions in the assembled contents of this volume.

Acknowledgements

Thanks to my colleagues Lynne Silipigni Connaway and Brian Lavoie who commented on this piece while it was in draft, and to Gill Needham for her patience and encouragement!

References

1 This point is also made by Manuel Castells in: Castells, M. (2007) *Mobile Communication and Society: a global perspective; a project of the Annenberg Research Network on international communication*, The Information Revolution & Global Politics, Cambridge, Mass, MIT Press. I have found this volume helpful in developing the general remarks here. I have also benefited from 'Nomads at Last', an *Economist* special section, 12 April 2008, as well as the useful review of trends in Gibbons, S. (2007) *The Academic Library and the Net Gen Student: making the connections*, Chicago, American Library Association.

2 *Edge: gaming*, moderated by Morgan Webb with Trip Hawkins and Robert Kotick. From Web 2.0 Summit, San Francisco, CA, 18 October 2007, http://blip.tv/file/441160.

3 Weller, M. (2007) *Virtual Learning Environments: using, choosing and developing your VLE*, London, Routledge.

4 For more detail about current technologies, mobile services, and some discussion of library applications (with a US focus) see: Kroski, E., On the Move with the Mobile Web: libraries and mobile technologies, *Library Technology Reports*, 44 (5), July 2008.

5 Castells (op. cit.), 167.

6 Gibbons, S. (2007) *The Academic Library and the Net Gen Student: making the connections*, Chicago, American Library Association.

7 Connaway, L. S., Radford, M. L., Dickey, T. J., Williams, J. D. and Confer, P. (2008) Sense-making and Synchronicity: information-seeking behaviors of Millennials and Baby Boomers, *Libri*, 58, 123–35.

8 Stokes, J., Analysis: IT consumerization and the future of work, *Ars Technica*, http://arstechnica.com.

9 Vogelstein, F. (2007) Text of Wired's interview with Google CEO Eric Schmidt, *Wired* [Online], 9 April 2007, www.wired.com/techbiz/people/news/2007/04/mag_schmidt_trans?currentPage =all.

10 Nomads at Last, *Economist* special section, *Economist*, 12 April, 2008, 5.

11 I owe this observation to my colleague Bruce Washburn.

12 Titus, R. (2007) BBC Internet Blog, 'A lick of paint for the BBC home page', 13 December 2007, www.bbc.co.uk/blogs/bbcinternet/2007/12/a_lick_of_paint_for_the_bbc_ ho.html.

13 Rishi, R. (2007) Always Connected, but Hard to Reach, *Educause Quarterly*, 39 (2), 2007.

14 Gibbons (op. cit.).

15 The following has links to relevant work: Dempsey, L., 'Some thoughts about egos, objects and social networks', Lorcan Dempsey's weblog, 6 April 2008, http://orweblog.oclc.org/archives/001601.html.

16 Harper, R. et al. (eds) (2008) *Being Human: human-computer interaction in the year 2020*, Cambridge, Microsoft Research Ltd.

17 I owe the phrase 'people are entry points' to Dan Chudnov. See also this interesting presentation at the CIC Library Conference, Minnesota, March 2007, which reinforced for me the importance of 'signature': Hanson, C., *Next Generation Librarians: visions of our future*, http://codyhanson.com/CodyHansonCIC032007.ppt.

18 Carr, N., Is Google Making us Stupid?, *Atlantic Monthly*, July/August 2008, www.theatlantic.com/doc/200807/google.

19 Nicholas, D., Huntington, P., Jamali, H. R. and Dobrowolski, T. (2006) Characterising and Evaluating Information Seeking Behaviour in a Digital Environment: spotlight on the 'bouncer', *Information Processing and Management*, 43, 1085–1102.

20 Palmer, C. L., Cragin, M. H. and Hogan, T. P. (2007) Weak Information Work in Scientific Discovery, *Information Processing and Mangement*, 43 (3), 808–20.

21 The New Oases. In Nomads at Last, *Economist* special section, *Economist*, 12 April, 2008.

22 Prahalad, C. K. and Krishnan, M. S. (2008) *The New Age of Innovation: driving cocreated value through global networks*, New York, McGraw-Hill.

23 The expression 'synthesise-specialise-mobilise' is Robin Murray's: Murray, R., Library Systems: synthesise, specialise, mobilise, *Ariadne*, 48, 30 July 2006, www.ariadne.ac.uk/issue48/murray/.

24 Personal communication from John Butler, AUL for Technology, University of Minnesota Libraries, 4 August 2008.

25 Kroski (op. cit.) has an overview of mobile-ready services in libraries, with examples.

26 Personal communication from Lynne Silipigni Connaway (29 July 2008) based on unpublished analysis of telephone interviews in the 'Seeking Synchronicity: evaluating virtual reference services from user, non-user, and librarian perspectives' project, www.oclc.org/research/projects/synchronicity/default.htm.

27 North Carolina State University Libraries, mobile site, www.lib.ncsu.edu/m/.

28 Connaway, L. S., Prabha, C. and Dickey, T. J. (2006) *Sense-making the Information Confluence: the whys and hows of college and university user satisficing of information needs. Phase III: Focus Group Interview Study,* Report on National Leadership

Grant LG-02-03-0062-03, to Institute of Museum and Library Services, Washington, D.C. Columbus, Ohio, School of Communication, The Ohio State University, http://imlsproject.comm.ohio-state.edu/imls_reports/imls_PH_III_ report_list.html.

29 Connaway, L. S. and Radford, M. L. (2007) 'Service Sea Change: clicking with screenagers through virtual reference'. Presented by Lynn Silipigni Connaway and Marie L. Radford at the Association of College and Research Libraries 13th National Conference, 'Sailing into the Future – Charting Our Destiny,' 29 March–1 April 2007, Baltimore, Maryland (USA), and *forthcoming* in the conference proceedings. Pre-print available online at www.oclc.org/research/publications/archive/2007/connaway-acrl.pdf (.pdf: 68K/19 pp.).

30 Dempsey, L. (2008) *Reconfiguring the Library Systems Environment Portal: libraries and the Academy*, 8 (2), www.oclc.org/research/publications/archive/2008/dempsey-portal.pdf.

Introduction

Mohamed Ally

As learners and citizens of the world become more mobile, they will need to access information while on the move. As a result, mobile libraries (m-libraries) will play a significant role in learning in the future. M-libraries are libraries that deliver information and learning materials on mobile devices such as cell phones, PDAs, palm top computers, and smart phones to allow access by anyone from anywhere and at any time. There are many benefits of m-libraries to people who are on the move and those who live in remote locations where there are no libraries. For example, individuals will be able to access health information to improve their health, hence enhancing quality of life. Students living in remote locations can use mobile technology to access electronic library materials to facilitate their learning. Students and workers who are travelling can make use of m-libraries to learn while on the move.

This book is innovative since there are limited published documents or conferences on m-libraries. The first international conference on m-libraries was held recently at the Open University in the United Kingdom (OUUK). The conference attracted delegates from 26 different countries indicating the global interest in m-libraries. This book will have global benefits since there is significant growth in the use of mobile technology by people around the world, especially in developing countries. The citizens of the world can use mobile technology to access information from libraries. The challenge is for librarians and educators to design information for delivery on mobile devices so that people on the move can access information as needed.

Intended audience for this book

This book can be used by anyone who is interested in the use of m-libraries in learning. Librarians can use the book to plan the delivery of information on mobile technology. Universities and colleges can use it as a textbook in a library or information systems programme. Researchers can use it to plan and guide research on m-libraries, to become informed about current research and initiatives on m-libraries and to learn best practice on the use of mobile technology in libraries.

Organization of this book

The book consists of four parts. The first part explores the changing landscape in terms of mobile technology and information and sets the stage for the other sections in the book. This part discusses libraries in a networked society, the new generations of learners, knowledge in the mobile age, meeting the needs of people on the move, and how mobile technology is affecting libraries, education, and society. The second part of the book deals with mobile technology for development. It explores the development of mobile information for delivery on mobile devices. The third part of the book presents current initiatives and innovations on m-libraries around the world and discusses challenges on the use of mobile technology in libraries. The fourth part of the book presents current practice from around the world on the use of mobile technology in libraries.

Part 1: The changing landscape

The first part of the book consists of six chapters. The chapter by John Naughton discusses the role of libraries in a networked society and argues that future communication will be through networks. He suggests that technology is the prime mover of social development. The chapter by Joan K. Lippincott describes some of the characteristics of the current generation of learners and examines the role that technology, and specifically mobile devices, could play in learning. The chapter also explores the services that libraries should provide for learners who are frequent users of mobile devices. The chapter by Agnes Kukulska-Hulme discusses encyclopedic knowledge in the mobile age and the changing nature of all-encompassing collections of represented knowledge, how knowledge may be socially constructed and shared, and whether perspectives may be shifting due to greater mobility and travel. The author claims that the proliferation of portable and pervasive technologies is introducing many changes in knowledge construction and sharing that we are only just beginning to understand. The chapter by Mohamed Ally explores the role of mobile technology for information access by nomads. The author suggests that libraries must deliver library materials in electronic format so that people on the move can access information for 'just in time' use from anywhere and at any time. The chapter by John M. Traxler discusses the use of mobile technology for mobile learning and mobile library in a mobile society. The author claims that the mobile library occupies a similar and possibly overlapping territory with mobile learning, and that the challenge for both m-library and mobile learning is to deliver educational experiences to new or un-reached communities of learners in economically, socially or geographically remote or disadvantaged situations. The chapter by William Foster and Cain Evans discusses how pervasive technology is allowing information providers not only to offer information services outside the confines of the traditional physical space, but also to allow information recipients to receive this information via a variety of devices wherever they are located. The authors suggest that public libraries clearly need to exploit these pervasive technologies if they are to survive as mainstream providers of information.

Part 2: Mobile technology for development

The second part of the book consists of four chapters. The chapter by Freda Wolfenden discusses the use of mobile technology for teacher education in Africa. The author describes two projects that were implemented in Africa to explore how new technologies can be deployed to support the development of teachers working in communities across sub-Saharan Africa. The chapter by Buhle Mbambo-Thata discusses the convergence of computing and telecommunication technology and how this convergence can benefit libraries. The author also discusses the challenges that libraries face when using mobile technology to deliver information anywhere and at any time. The chapter by Adesina Iluyemi describes how mobile technology can be used to train community health workers and other health professionals in remote locations in developing countries. The chapter by Yang Cao, Mohamed Ally, Tony Tin, Steve Schafer and Maureen Hutchinson describes the development of an effective mobile-friendly digital library to support mobile learners, and reports on the evaluation that was done on the project.

Part 3: Initiatives, innovations and challenges

The third part of the book consists of ten chapters. The chapter by Lynne Callaghan, Susan J. Lea, Ruth Charlton and Emma Whittlesea describes an initiative that investigated the use of mobile technology to access library materials by students on placement. The chapter by Geoff Butters, Margaret Markland and Robert Davies discusses strategies that can be used to develop learners' creative potentials. The chapter by Jane Lunsford describes a project that is being used to provide support to students studying at a distance. The project implemented mobile technology to help support learners at a distance. The chapter by Ivan Ganchev, Máirtín O'Droma, Damien Meere, Mícheál Ó hAodha and Stanimir Stojanov describes the establishment of an innovative collaborative project between two universities. The authors describe a centre that provides m-learning and m-teaching facilities by allowing electronic access from virtually any device. The chapter by Tony Tin, Hassan Sheikh and Colin Elliott describes a collaborative initiative between two open universities that illustrates how sharing of resources and expertise between organizations can benefit both organizations. This chapter shows the benefits of thinking globally when developing library systems. The chapter by Hassan Sheikh, Susan Eales and Mariano Rico discusses how mobile technology is helping an 'open library' to provide support to students studying at a distance. The chapter by Jim Hahn examines metadata for learning objects: the Learning Object Metadata (LOM) standard, the IMS Access for All Specification. It investigates cell phone picture data annotation as a means for presenting and making accessible user-generated content. The chapter by Anne Adams looks at digital libraries in healthcare and reports on a study that investigated the use of mobile technology in the clinical domain. The chapter by Mohamed Ally, Rory McGreal, Steve Schafer, Tony Tin and Billy Cheung describes and presents the result of a project that used a digital library to develop English-as-a-second-language lessons for delivery on mobile phones. The chapter by Keren Mills, Non Scantlebury and Rhodri Thomas describes an innovative initiative called Digilab, designed to get faculty and tutors involved in the use of mobile technology in course delivery. The Digilab allows staff to obtain hands-on experience with emerging technology so that they can adopt the technology in course delivery.

Part 4: Practice perspectives

The fourth part of the book consists of four chapters. The chapter by Àngels Carles, Ana Castellano and Fernando Guerrero describes a project that used PDAs to provide access to information by students in clinical placement. The chapter by Jim Hahn presents an exploratory case study on library orientation. The project used a way-finder video on a librarian's cell phone to better guide students through the physical library space. The chapter by Wathmanel Seneviratne describes a plan to provide mobile service connectivity for the library system at the Open University of Sri Lanka. The chapter by Peter Godwin, Anne Hewling and Jo Parker describes a project that investigated the potential of using mobile technology to help students with information literacy.

In summary, since this is one of the first books on m-libraries, it will benefit librarians and educators by offering guidelines on how to design and deliver information on mobile technology and how to provide support to learning using the mobile technology. The book moves from the general to the specific: the first part of the book looks at the changing landscape, the second part explores technology and development, the third part looks at some initiatives and innovations in m-libraries, and the fourth part presents some specific case studies.

Since m-libraries allow individuals to access information and learning materials anytime and from anywhere, this will have a positive impact on all sectors of society and will benefit people in any location. Learners, educators, trainers, and workers will be able to use mobile technology to access information as needed for 'just in time' application. People in remote locations will not have to spend time and resources to go to a different location or to a physical library to access information.

Humans have the right to access information to improve their quality of life regardless of where they live, their status, and their culture. Increasing the level of education globally will improve quality of life and make the world a better place to live. M-libraries will empower the people of the world to learn and to access information to meet individual needs.

Part 1

The changing landscape

1

Libraries in a networked society

John Naughton

Introduction

There's an old Chinese curse: 'May you live in interesting times.' Well, we do. In particular, we live in a period when our communications environment is being transformed. And a big question is what this change might mean – both for society and for those of us who work professionally with data, information and knowledge and what one might loosely call the media business.

Most librarians would bridle at the notion that they are in the media business. But in a sense we're all – academics and librarians alike – in it. I don't mean that we are part of the circus of popular culture – which is what journalists mean by the term 'media business'. I mean it in a more profound sense, for 'media' is the plural of 'medium', a word with an interesting etymology.

The conventional interpretation holds that a medium is a carrier of something. But in science the word has another, more interesting, connotation. To a biologist, for example, a medium is *a mixture of nutrients needed for cell growth*. And that's a very interesting interpretation for my purposes.

In biology, media are used to grow tissue cultures – living organisms. The most famous example, I guess, is Alexander Fleming and the mould growing in his Petri dishes which eventually led to the discovery of penicillin.

What I want to do is to borrow that idea and use it as a metaphor for thinking about human society – to treat society as a living organism which depends on a media environment for the nutrients it needs to survive and develop. Any change in the environment – in the media which support social and cultural life – will have corresponding effects on the organism. Some things will wither; others may grow; new, mutant organisms may appear. The key point of the metaphor is simple: change the environment, and you change the organism.

Which leads me to my central question: what is changing in our media environment, and what does that mean for us?

Our media environment

This way of thinking is not new. I picked it up originally from the late Neil Postman, a passionate humanist who taught at New York University for more than 40 years and was an unremitting sceptic about the impact of technology on society. In a series of witty and thought-provoking books he described how our societies are shaped by their prevailing modes of communication, and fretted about the consequences.

From my perspective, Postman's most interesting book is *The Disappearance of Childhood*. In it, he argues that the concept of 'childhood' – as a special, protected phase in a person's life – is an artefact of communications technology. It was, he claims, a by-product of the evolution of a print-based culture.

Before print, Postman maintained, adulthood began the moment a young person was deemed to be competent in the prevailing communications mode of the society. In the oral culture which pre-dated Gutenberg, a child therefore became, effectively, an adult around the age of seven. This, he maintains, is why you never see children *per se* in the paintings of Breughel – you merely see small adults; and it is why the Catholic church defined seven as the 'age of reason' – after which an individual could be held accountable for their sins.

But the invention of printing changed all that. Why? Because – Postman argues – in a print-based culture, it takes longer (and requires more education, some of it formal) to attain the kind of communicative competence needed to function as an adult. So the concept of 'childhood' was extended to 12 or thereabouts – and this remained the case from the 19th century to the middle of the 20th.

The title of Postman's book – *The Disappearance of Childhood* – comes from his contention that the arrival of broadcast television represented the first revolutionary transformation of our communications environment since Gutenberg. Just as print had transformed society – undermining the authority of the Catholic church and stimulating the Reformation, enabling the rise of modern science and the growth of a new intellectual class – Postman argued that the dominance of TV had a correspondingly dramatic impact.

In particular, it had effectively lowered the age of reason. In a society dominated by the idiocies of such a medium, it didn't take long for a child to master the basics. Postman cited research which allegedly showed that American children were 'competent' TV viewers – in the sense that they understood genres and could follow narrative threads – by the age of three. This explained, he said, why, although there were remedial classes in reading in every American public school, he had never seen a remedial class in TV viewing! (It also explained, he contended, why adults were increasingly dressing like children, and vice versa.)

I'm not sure what to make of Postman's view about education, but his general point – that changes in the communications environment bring about cultural change – is, I think, spot on. He made a convincing case for it in another book – *Amusing Ourselves to Death* – which is in part a devastating analysis of the impact that broadcast television had – and continues to have – on American politics. What he argued was that we live in a polity which has been shaped by a single communications medium. Most of us have grown up in such an environment. It seems as natural to us as the air we breathe. And yet it is changing under our noses.

Media ecology

In seeking a language in which to talk about change, I've borrowed another idea from Postman – the notion of *media ecology*, that is to say, the study of media as environments. As with 'medium', the term is appropriated from the sciences, where an ecosystem is defined as a dynamic system in which living organisms interact with one another and with their environment. These interactions can be very complex and take many forms. Organisms prey on one another; compete for food and other nutrients; have parasitic or symbiotic relationships; wax and wane; prosper and decline. And an ecosystem is never static. The system may be in equilibrium at any given moment, but the balance is precarious. The slightest perturbation may disturb it, resulting in a new set of interactions and movement to another – temporary – point of equilibrium.

This seems to me a more insightful way of viewing our communications environment than the conventional 'market' metaphor more commonly used in public discussion, because it comes closer to capturing the complexity of what actually goes on in real life.

Just to illustrate the point, consider what has happened when new technologies have appeared in the past. When television arrived, it was widely predicted that it would wipe out radio, and perhaps also movies and newspapers. Yet nothing like that happened. When the CD-ROM appeared on the scene, people predicted the demise of the printed book. When the web arrived, people predicted that it would wipe out newsprint. And so on. These 'wipe-out' scenarios are a product of a mindset that sees the world mainly in terms of markets and market share. Yet the reality is that while new communications technologies may not wipe out earlier ones, they certainly change the ecosystem. The CD-ROM did not eliminate the printed book, for example, but it altered for ever the prospects for printed works of reference. Novels and other books continued to thrive.

The 'organisms' in our media ecosystem include broadcast and narrowcast television, movies, radio, print and the internet (which itself encompasses the web, e-mail and peer-to-peer networking of various kinds). For most of our lives, the dominant organism in this system – the one that grabbed most of the resources, revenue and attention – was broadcast TV.

This ecosystem is the media environment in which most of us grew up. But it's in the process of radical change, mainly because broadcast TV is in apparently inexorable decline. Its audience is fragmenting. In particular, it's being eaten from within: the worm in the bud in this case is narrowcast digital television – in which specialist content is aimed at specialized, subscription-based audiences and distributed via digital channels. The problem is that the business model that supports broadcast is based on its ability to attract and hold *mass* audiences. Once audiences become fragmented, the commercial logic changes.

Note that when I say that broadcast TV is declining, I am *not* saying that it will disappear. Broadcast will continue to exist, for the simple reason that some things are best covered using a few-to-many technology. Only a broadcast model can deal with something like a World Cup final or a major terrorist attack, for example – when the attention of the world is focused on a single event or a single place. But broadcast will lose its *dominant* position in the ecosystem, and that is the change that I think will have really profound consequences for us all.

Life after television?

What will replace it? Answer: the ubiquitous internet.

Note that I do not say the web. The biggest mistake people in the media business make is to think that the net and the web are synonymous. They're not. Of course the web is enormous; but it's just one kind of traffic that runs on the internet's tracks and signalling (to use a railway metaphor). And already the web is being dwarfed by other kinds of traffic. According to data gathered by the Cambridge firm Cachelogic, peer-to-peer (P2P) data exceeds web traffic by a factor of between two and ten, depending on the time of day. And I've no doubt that in ten years' time, P2P traffic will be outrun by some other ingenious networking application, as yet undiscovered.

What's happening is that we're moving from the era where the platform – the PC – was the computer to the point where *the network is the computer*. And that's where the foreseeable future lies. We're moving to what is sometimes called 'cloud computing' – where we get many of our 'computing' services (e-mail, messaging, document creation and management, multimedia asset storage, presentations, calendar services, etc.) from the internet 'cloud' rather than from our PCs.

The point of all this is that while *we* grew up and came to maturity in a media ecosystem dominated by broadcast TV, our children and grandchildren will live in an environment dominated by the net. And the interesting question – the point, in a way, of this chapter – is, what will that mean for us, and for them?

From push to pull

In thinking about the future, the two most useful words are 'push' and 'pull' because they capture the essence of where we've been and where we're headed.

Broadcast TV is a 'push' medium: a relatively select band of producers (broadcasters) decide what content is to be created, create it and then *push* it down analogue or digital channels at audiences which are assumed to consist of essentially passive recipients.

The couch potato was, *par excellence*, a creature of this world. He did, of course, have *some* freedom of action. He could choose to switch off the TV; but if he decided to leave it on, then essentially his freedom of action was confined to choosing from a menu of options decided for him by others, and to 'consuming' their content at times decided by them. He was, in other words, a human surrogate for one of B. F. Skinner's pigeons – free to peck at whatever coloured lever took his fancy, but not free at all in comparison with his fellow pigeon perched outside on the roof.

The other essential feature of the world of push media was its fundamental *asymmetry*. All the creative energy was assumed to be located at one end – that occupied by the producer/broadcaster. The viewer or listener was assumed to be incapable of, or uninterested in, creating content; and even if it turned out that s/he was capable of creative activity, there was no way in which anything s/he produced could have been published.

The web is exactly the opposite of a push medium: it's a *pull* medium. Nothing comes to you unless *you* choose it and click on it to 'pull' it down onto your computer. You're in charge.

So the first implication of the switch from push to pull is a growth in consumer sovereignty. We saw this early on in e-commerce, because it became easy to compare online prices and locate the most competitive suppliers from the comfort of your own armchair. The US automobile industry has discovered, for example, that a majority of prospective customers turn up at dealerships armed not only with information about particular models, but also with detailed data on the prices that dealers elsewhere in the country are charging for those models.

But the internet doesn't just enable people to become more fickle and choosy consumers. It also makes them much better informed – or at least provides them with formidable resources with which to become more knowledgeable. It's also become much harder for companies to keep secrets in a net-centric world. If one of your products has flaws, or if a service you provide is substandard, then the chances are that the news will appear somewhere on a blog or a posting to a newsgroup or e-mail list. My conjecture is that nobody who offers a public service will be immune from this aspect of a ubiquitous net.

Some years ago, I participated in a seminar at Addenbrooke's hospital in Cambridge on the future of information technology and how it might affect the health service. One memory that sticks in my mind from the event is of a statement made by a medical researcher from the National Institute of Health. The biggest challenge general practitioners will face in 2010, he said, was 'how to deal with the internet-informed patient'.

The emergence of a truly sovereign, informed consumer is thus one of the implications of an internet-centric world.

Another implication is that the asymmetry of the old, push-media world will be replaced by something much more balanced.

Remember that the underlying assumption of the old model was that audiences were passive and uncreative. What we're now discovering is that that passivity and apparent lack of creativity may have been more due to the absence of tools and publication opportunities than to intrinsic defects in human nature. Certainly, that's the only explanation I can think of for what's been happening on the net since the beginning of the 21st century.

Blogging and the public sphere

Take blogging – the practice of keeping an online diary. There are currently approaching 100 million bloggers across the globe. Many blogs are, as you might expect, mere dross – vanity publishing with no discernible literary or intellectual merit. But many thousands of them are updated regularly, and many contain writing and thinking of a very high order. In my own areas of professional interest, for example, blogs are often my most trusted sources, because I know many of the people who write them, and some are world experts in their fields.

What is significant about the blogging phenomenon is its demonstration that the traffic in ideas and cultural products isn't a one-way street – as it was in the old push-media ecology. People have always been thoughtful and articulate and well informed, but up to now relatively few of them ever made it past the gatekeepers who controlled access to publication media. Blogging software and the internet gave them the platform they needed – and they have grasped the opportunity.

The result is a reversal in the decline of what Jürgen Habermas calls 'the public sphere' – an arena which facilitates the public use of reason in rational–critical debate and which had been steadily narrowing as the power and reach of mass media increased. In recent years, the political implications of this re-energized public sphere have begun to emerge, notably in the debates among Democrats in the US about how to challenge Republican political ascendancy and the Bush presidency.

The explosive growth in blogging has prompted a predictable outburst of what John Seely Brown calls 'endism' – as in questions about whether the phenomenon marks the end of journalism. Yet, when one looks at it from an ecological perspective, what one sees is the evolution of an interesting parasitic/symbiotic relationship between blogging and conventional journalism. Several case studies – for example the Harvard study of the Trent Lott case, and the *60 Minutes* saga (which led to the premature retirement of TV news anchorman Dan Rather) – have delineated the contours of this relationship.

What has happened, I suggest, is that a new organism has arrived in our media ecosystem and existing organisms are having to accommodate themselves to the newcomer, and vice versa. Interesting, complex – and essentially symbiotic – relationships are emerging between the new medium of blogging and more conventional print journalism. My conjecture is that this is beneficial to both.

Digital imagery

Another remarkable explosion of creativity comes from digital photography. Since 2005 an enormous number of digital cameras has been sold – and of course many mobile phones now come with an onboard camera. So every day, millions of digital photographs are taken. Until the advent of services like PhotoBucket, Flickr.com and Kodak Gallery, an understandable response to this statement would have been 'so what?' But these services allow people to upload their pictures and display them on the web, each neatly resized and allocated its own unique URL.

Flickr is the service I use. It now stores over two billion photographs. For me, the most interesting aspect of it is that users are encouraged to attach tags to their pictures, and these tags can be used as the basis for searches of the entire database. When writing this I searched for photographs tagged with 'Ireland' and came up with 1,018,825 images! Of course I didn't sift through them all, but I must have looked at a few hundred. They were mostly holiday snaps, but here and there were some memorable pictures. What struck me most, though, was what they represented. Ten years ago, those holiday snaps would have wound up in a shoebox and would certainly never have been seen in a public forum. But now they can be – and are being – published, shared with others, made available to the world.

Audio and video

And then there's YouTube. Think of it as Flickr for video clips, many of them home-made. It too is growing almost exponentially, in true internet fashion. And it has an astonishingly wide range of content – from stuff that is unbelievably crass, to examples of wit and talent that take one's breath away.

YouTube deserves an essay to itself – but space precludes that. I just want to highlight two aspects of it that seem, to me, significant.

First, 9/11. In September 2007, as the anniversary loomed, I suddenly wanted to check what the video coverage of the day had been like. In the old, push-media ecosystem, there would have been no way I could have satisfied that need. *Broadcasters* were the ones who controlled that stuff and decided whether or not to make it available. But all I had to do was go to YouTube and perform a simple search. And there, sure enough, were recordings of all the CNN, ABC and Fox News coverage of the day, streamed across the net to my study in Cambridge. And they're available 24/7, as current marketing speak puts it.

Then my RSS reader turned up an entry on a blog by a journalist whose work I admire – Jeff Jarvis. He had been at Ground Zero on the day – and survived. A few days later, he recorded his experiences and posted them in six MP3 files to his blog. So I followed the link and spent about half an hour listening in the dark to an eyewitness account of the horror he had lived through.

These two experiences – of being able to find the multimedia records I sought and pull them down onto my computer – capture something of the essence of the new media ecosystem.

The second significant aspect of YouTube is the way it illustrates the extent to which we are moving into a remix culture. Lots of the material on the site is created by users who take products originally generated by old media like broadcast TV and then rework them in some satirical way.

What links all these things is a phrase that in our old media ecosystem would be regarded as an oxymoron – a contradiction in terms. The phrase is 'user-generated content'. In the old push-media world, users weren't seen as capable of generating anything. They were passive recipients of what *we* decided to create. And even if, by some miracle, they did succeed in creating something, well, there was no way they were going to get it published, because they would never get past the gatekeepers who controlled access to publishing media.

That world is coming to an end. The media which nurture and support our social and cultural lives are changing. And that means that our culture – and our economies – will change too. It also means that we will change in response to what has happened to our environment. Well, perhaps *we* – in the sense of my (baby-boomer) generation – will not change that much, because we haven't experienced the full force of the changes that I've been describing. But our children and grandchildren will. And they're the ones who will shape the future – and use its libraries. (Or not, as the case may be.) So we need to think about them.

Digital immigrants and digital natives

In October 2006, in a presentation to the New York Library Council, Lee Rainie – Founding Director of the Pew Internet and American Life Project – drew a useful distinction between adults and children. The former, he said, are 'digital immigrants' – i.e. recent and somewhat tentative arrivals in cyberspace – whereas children are digital natives, people who have lived there all their lives.

The first cohort of true digital natives has now graduated from university and entered the workplace. So let's look back at the media and technology environment in which they grew up.

Today's 23-year-olds were born in 1985. The internet was two years old in January that year, and Nintendo launched 'Super Mario Brothers', the first blockbuster game. When they were going to primary school in 1990, Tim Berners-Lee was busy inventing the world wide web. The first SMS message was sent in 1992, when these children were seven. Amazon and eBay launched in 1995. Hotmail was launched in 1996, when they were heading towards secondary school.

Around that time, pay-as-you-go mobile phone tariffs arrived, enabling teenagers to have phones, and the first instant messaging services appeared. Google launched in 1998, just as they were becoming teenagers. Napster and Blogger.com launched in 1999 when they were doing 16+ examinations. Wikipedia and the iPod appeared in 2001. Early social networking services appeared in 2002 when they were doing 18+ examinations. Skype launched in 2003, as they were heading for university, and YouTube launched in 2005, as they were preparing for graduation and the workplace.

These young people have been socially conditioned in a universe that apparently runs parallel to the one inhabited by most of us in the education business (and perhaps some even in the library business). They've been playing computer games of mind-blowing complexity *for ever*. They're resourceful, knowledgeable and natural users of computer and communications technology. They're true digital natives – accustomed to creating content of their own – and publishing it.

In his portrayal of this generation, Lee Rainie drew attention to what he described as six 'new realities' about the native inhabitants of our emerging media ecosystem:

1 Media and gadgets are ubiquitous parts of everyday life. This means that the media environment in which these young people have been socialized is immeasurably more complex than it was in the decade before they were born.
2 New devices allow them to enjoy media and carry on commun-ication anywhere. Mobile phones are a key element in this.
3 The internet is at the centre of the revolution – and mobile devices increasingly provide a window onto the network.
4 Multi-tasking is a way of life, and digital natives live in a state of 'continuous partial attention'.
5 Ordinary citizens have the chance to be publishers, movie-makers, song creators and story-tellers.
6 Everything will change even more in coming years!

Implications for the future

We need to beware of the dangers of technological determinism, that is to say the belief that technology is the prime mover of social development. The relationship between a society and its technological infrastructure is a complicated and interactive one; technology pushes, certainly; but society pushes back. And much of the time, the factors that determine which technologies become mainstream have relatively little to do with the properties of the technology itself – which is why most new technologies fail, because consumers refuse to adopt them, or the legal or social obstacles facing them are too high to be surmounted at a given moment.

Second, there is the fatal temptation to extrapolate current trends – to delude ourselves that the New New Thing (to adapt Michael Lewis's title) is what will determine the future. The truth is that, in historical terms, we have just embarked on the networking revolution and we have no idea of what it's long-term impact will be. But from what we've seen so far, it's clear that:

- The internet will become ubiquitous and a central component of our information ecosystem.
- The ecosystem will be immeasurably more complex than anything that has gone before in terms of numbers of publishers, density and range of interactions between audiences and publishers, and speed of change.
- The technologies which triumph are those which meet a major human need or satisfy a significant desire. The automobile was one such technology – which is why it has become such a pervasive force in our societies. The mobile phone is another such technology, because it represents a transition from a world in which telephones were tethered, like goats, to a wall, to a world where communication is always possible.
- Young people who grow up in the new ecosystem will have different competencies, coping strategies and expectations from those of earlier generations. Most of our traditional 'information sector' doesn't currently meet those expectations. The future is likely to be particularly acute for institutions that have hitherto regarded themselves as intermediaries between clients and services. Like travel agents. And libraries.

These are inferences drawn from my observation of what's happening. You may object, quite reasonably, that they are based on what are effectively just straws in the wind. But the whole point of straws is that they indicate which way the wind is blowing. What I want to suggest is that it's blowing in a direction that many of us, professionally conditioned as we were in an older ecosystem, may well find unsettling or downright uncomfortable. And the $64 trillion question for librarians is: how will they avoid the fate of travel agents?

Bibliography

Battelle, John (2005) *The Search: how Google and its rivals rewrote the rules of business and transformed our culture*, Nicholas Brealey Publishing.

Brynjolfsson, Erik and Smith, Michael (2000) Frictionless Commerce? A comparison of internet and conventional retailers, *Management Science*, 6 (4), 563–85.

CacheLogic Research, February 2004, www.cachelogic.com/research.

Carr, N. (2008) The Big Switch: our new digital destiny, Norton.

Clapham, W. B. (1973) *Natural Ecosystems*, Macmillan.

Economist (2005) Crowned at Last, *Economist*, Volume 375, Issue 8420, Special section, (31 March), 2005, 3–6.

Fallows, J. (1996) *Breaking the News: how the media undermines American democracy*, Pantheon.

Postman, N. (1971) *Teaching as a Subversive Activity*, Delacorte Press.

Postman, N. (1985) *Amusing Ourselves to Death: public discourse in the age of show business*, Penguin.

Postman, N. (1993) *Technopoly*, Vintage.

Postman, N. (1995) *Disappearance of Childhood*, Vintage.

Skinner, B. F. (1974) 'Superstition' in the Pigeon, *Journal of Experimental Psychology*, **38**, 273–4.

2

Libraries and Net Gen learners: current and future challenges in the mobile society

Joan K. Lippincott

Introduction

If we were creating academic libraries today from scratch, what might they look like? Would we create grand edifices packed with weighty tomes, like the Bodleian Library at Oxford, where students and faculty could sit at large tables and read great books in dim light? Or would we design libraries similar to the spaces being developed in many universities in the late 20th and early 21st centuries, often referred to as information commons or learning commons? Such spaces include the Learning Grid at the University of Warwick in the UK, the learning commons at North Carolina State University in the US, and many others. In those spaces, students can work together in areas designed for collaboration and have at their fingertips the kinds of hardware, software and network connectivity they need to produce digital projects for their courses. They have access to the library's licensed digital resources, additional materials on the web, and the library's print collection, often housed on adjacent floors of the building. Or would we design libraries that had only a virtual presence, perhaps a combination of Google Book Search meets iTunes, with a dash of virtual reference service thrown in? In these virtual digital libraries, students would have access to university-licensed content, additional materials on the web, and whatever types of services – online tutorials, chat reference, recommender services, etc. – that the library (or others) made available. However, in this 'm-library' model there would be no physical library.

While higher education institutions today are not seriously considering disbanding the current library model and starting from scratch, it is still incumbent on information and library professionals to create new types of content, tools, services and environments for today's mobile students. These students, who have grown up with portable audio devices, phones without tethered handsets and, later, mobile phones and access to media 24/7, are accustomed to 'grab and go'. As heard on the US National Public Radio, 'Whoever said "you can't take it with you" is sooo twentieth century!' (NPR, 2007).

This chapter will describe some of the characteristics of the current generation of university students, examine the role that technology and, specifically, mobile devices could play in their learning, and describe existing or potential library services for students who are frequent users of mobile devices.

Net Gen students and learning

Much has been written about the current generation of college students, sometimes referred to as the 'Net Gen' (Oblinger and Oblinger, 2005). These students were born between 1982 and 1991 and grew up with computers and other media at home or in school from the earliest age. They often travel with multiple electronic devices, such as a mobile phone, MP3 player, digital camera and laptop, and easily move back and forth between devices. These hands-on learners not only access digital information, they produce it in many forms, such as videos, podcasts, blogs, websites and plain text documents. Increasingly, individuals use their small, mobile devices in ways that formerly would have been reserved for desktop computer or laptop production. For example, one interviewer for a US higher education publication commented:

> Aaron Swartz – who at the age of 21, has already helped create RSS (that was in his early teens), published a couple of computer science papers, and developed infogami, a system enabling his digitally clueless elders to set up their own websites (and is working on a new project) . . . I recently sent him a number of questions . . . Some of his answers were, it seems, typed into a mobile phone. (McLemee, 2007)

Some of the characteristics of Net Gen students map in interesting ways to some of the characteristics of 'deeper learning' identified in a number of studies (Carmean and Haefner, 2002). For example, active learning, where students 'own' their learning by creating new content, is a hallmark of deeper learning, as is social learning, where students engage each other in dialogue as well as interact in meaningful ways with faculty and professionals in their field of study. George Kuh, who has developed a survey widely used in US higher education, the *National Survey of Student Engagement*, writes about these types of factors that characterize deeper learning:

> faculty and administrators would do well to arrange the curriculum and other aspects of the college experience in accord with these good practices, thereby encouraging students to put forth more effort (e.g. write more papers, read more books, meet more frequently with faculty and peers, use information technology appropriately) which will result in greater gains in such areas as critical thinking, problem solving, effective communication, and responsible citizenship. (Kuh et al., 2005)

It is the challenge of information professionals to assist faculty and others involved in the teaching and learning process, to use technologies effectively to accomplish learning objectives.

When we consider the current population of students in higher education, some faculty and administrators express concern about the 'digital divide', that some students may be disenfranchised from technology-enabled learning experiences because they lack easy access to technology. However, most students today in developed countries are connected. For example, the 2007 survey by Educause reported that 73.7% of students on the campuses participating in the survey owned a laptop. Amazingly, more than half of the students surveyed owned four or five of these devices: computer (desktop and/or laptop), digital camera, music/video device, game device, wireless hub, PDA or smart phone. Students are heavy users of their hardware, spending an average of 18 hours per week using an electronic device. They are also heavy users of social networking sites, with 81.6% reporting using Facebook, MySpace and similar sites (Educause, 2007). In a study of youth in the UK, 70% of 11-year-olds reported owning a mobile phone and, on average, teenagers reported that they send or receive 9.6 text messages per day (Mobile, 2007). While not many undergraduates own PDAs or similar devices, it is likely that graduate students, especially those attending professional schools, will be early adopters of these devices. A survey at Harvard Medical School in 2007 showed that fully 52% of their medical (graduate) students owned a PDA. The application they most used (by 26% of respondents) was reference information; only 6% reported subscribing to podcasts (Panettieri, 2007). Net Gen students are also more versatile in the use of their devices and the use of the internet than older generations. For example, they listen to television and radio on the internet much more so than older generations as the survey carried out by Zogby International for the Congress and Internet Caucus Advisory Committee Annual State of the Net Policy Conference, Washington DC, 31 January 2007, makes clear (Zogby International, 2007). Information professionals need to expand their notion of what students may do or use on a mobile device *vs* a desktop device and plan services accordingly.

Many faculty and others involved in the educational process express concerns that Net Gen students are wasting their time with technology and that their use of technology may even hinder their learning. However, some research sponsored by JISC reported that students who are effective learners in the digital environment:

- use mobile phones, laptops, and PDAs to support their learning
- use software to create, manipulate, and present content
- seek peer support via informal networks of family by using e-mail, texting, chat, and Skype, 'an underworld of communication and information-sharing invisible to tutors'. (JISC, 2007)

Many Net Gen students think of their mobile devices as more than an efficient or convenient piece of hardware; they view the devices as integral to their daily lives:

> Many speak of their personal devices as individualized learning environments which, if possible, go everywhere with them. As a result, they express a need to integrate personal technologies with institutionally based systems – for example downloading podcasts onto a palmtop or uploading work from a storage device, such as a USB memory stick, to an institutionally based computer – to provide a seamless flow of study . . . Not being able to do so causes them frustration.   (JISC, 2007)

While many of our university students today use electronic devices with ease, their understanding of the academic resources accessible through such devices may be limited. For example, one part-time UK student stated that 'a central repository of information, approved by the university, would help learners locate online resources more efficiently, citing Wikipedia as an example of such a repository' (JISC, 2007). Many information professionals would suggest that a university library, particularly its online resources, could play exactly such a role in a student's life. Or, more specifically, guides to subject areas, prepared by librarians, could fulfil the stated need. However, this student was presumably unaware of the potential role of the digital library in his academic life.

While the studies cited above are important for understanding the student landscape today, it is even more important that information professionals and faculty understand the students in their own institutions. By using existing survey data, consulting with other institutional units to see what type of data they already collect and how they can partner with them, and supplementing existing quantitative data with qualitative data, through focus groups, interviews, or observations and field studies, one can develop a profile of students (or subgroups of students) in a particular university.

University libraries and mobile learners

As university library personnel begin to plan how they will address the needs of their clientele who use mobile devices, they should first clarify the meaning of 'mobile library users' in the context of their campus. Mobile users can be:

- students who study entirely at a distance
- blended learning students (students whose courses include online and on-campus components)
- learners in the field, e.g. clinical settings, professional internships
- learners using mobile devices such as clickers in the classroom
- learners using mobile devices for learning activities outside of the classroom.

It is likely that more than one type of use will be evident on any given campus. Since services for distance education students may have different characteristics from those for students who primarily use mobile devices in their classrooms and other campus buildings, each institution should gather data on the types of devices their students employ, the prevalence of distance education courses, and the use of mobile devices for on-campus courses. In addition, campuses need to have data on the types of mobile devices students own and whether they are using them for educational purposes. Some types of devices they may already be using are mobile/smart phones, PDAs, clickers/personal response systems, MP3 players/iPods and laptops/notebook computers. It is likely that new mobile devices will be coming onto the market, such as Livescribe's Smartpen (www.livescribe.com), with which a student can record notes from a lecture, upload them to a computer and also tap on the notes on paper and hear an audio recording of them.

As libraries consider their re-tooling for mobile users and mobile devices, they should examine the consequences of mobility and the opportunities for innovation in the areas of content, systems and tools, services, and environments, both physical and virtual.

Mobilizing content

What will library users want to access and actually read on mobile devices? What types of library users will be most likely to want to access content on mobile devices? At present, few libraries offer licensed content configured for mobile devices. An exception is in the medical field, where some libraries, such as the University of Alberta in Canada, offer an array of health science reference sources for their users.[1] The notion of offering authoritative reference sources to students and faculty in clinical settings seems a natural choice for a first offering of content tailored to mobile devices other than laptop or notebook computers. One can imagine offering reference sources for other researchers (students or faculty) in the field, such as those doing agricultural studies, environmental data collection, anthropological work, or social services outreach in the community. Such individuals may find ready access to directories, handbooks and the like to be of great use in the field.

Another aspect of content for mobile devices is the opportunity to make university-connected content available for downloading to MP3 players and other devices. At the Arizona State University, the Library Channel provides access to content such as podcasts and videos on information literacy and guest speaker lectures.[2] Libraries may want to consider how they could make some of the content in their institutional repository more available for mobile devices, if the content includes course lectures, podcasts or similar material.

Mobilizing systems and tools

Some university libraries have begun to make versions of their catalogues available for access on mobile devices. The North Carolina State University (NCSU) envisions its Catalog WS as a 'versatile discovery platform'. Their MobiLIB catalogue interface is optimized for mobile devices.[3] Through this interface, NCSU offers a mobile catalogue, opening hours, a campus directory, and other services. At the Athabasca University Library in Canada, the 'digital reading room' offers mobile services such as access to catalogue and patron records in formats for mobile devices and podcasts.[4] One can imagine that an adult student driving near the campus and weighing the decision whether to find a parking space and come into the library might find it very convenient to query the catalogue and check-out records of items from his or her mobile phone.

As higher education institutions increasingly use mobile devices for some courses, there may be opportunities for tie-ins with library content and services. For example, a company is offering English lessons with test preparation materials for use with cell phones; libraries could offer access to dictionaries or other language reference tools that would be cell-phone compatible. In some subject areas, students and researchers rely on quick-reference sources. Could the University of Pennsylvania business school library, which offers a Business FAQ linked to reference sources, be made compatible for cell phone use?[5] The Open WorldCat offers citation styles for many of its entries; students needing quick access to the correct citation format for the sources for their paper might find access to WorldCat by cell phone to be useful. OCLC is experimenting with what it takes to make WorldCat available to mobile devices, and even the possibility of downloading all of WorldCat to a mobile device (Dempsey, 2005).

Mobilizing services

Libraries have been providing reference services by phone for many years, and most higher education institution libraries also provide reference services by e-mail, instant messaging and chat. At least in the US, fewer are using text messages at this point. Some libraries already make available to mobile devices some factual information, including a patron's record of items checked out, the hours the library is open and directions to the library. As information resources in new formats for mobile devices are made available, the library may serve as a training centre for the devices and the use of the content; this has happened at the University of Alberta, which does the training for the campus use of PDAs for information resources (Adams, 2007). Some libraries, like Arizona State University mentioned above, are developing podcast tutorials for information literacy purposes. Libraries can also consider whether their users might benefit from simple tutorials on finding a periodical article or evaluating internet resources that would be mobile-phone accessible. As information professionals consider what types of services they might offer that would employ mobile devices or be accessed by users with mobile devices, they need to target specific user groups, such as students at a distance, field-based students, or students in professional programmes, e.g. health sciences, education, social work, or journalism. Some of these disciplines are rethinking their curricula so that they more realistically prepare students for the way professionals are working today. For example, at the Northwestern University journalism school, it was decided 'At a time when newspaper readership is steadily declining and many readers are bouncing from blogs to internet video to get their news, the new approach will send student reporters out into the field with video iPods and digital camcorders, as well as spiral notebooks' (Chronicle, 2007). There are probably some library resources configured for mobile devices that could also be part of these students' repertoire.

Mobilizing environments

The use of mobile devices also has implications for the physical spaces in libraries. For example, some libraries are loaning mobile devices, including iPods, video cameras and laptops. Service desks need to be configured to house this hardware and signage needs to convey the availability of the equipment. Use of all of this equipment has implications for the need for electrical outlets and network connectivity throughout the library facility. In addition, students who bring their own devices need access to electrical outlets in order to recharge their own equipment. At the Montesquieu Learning Center at Tilburg University in the Netherlands, some lockers with electrical outlets are available so that students can recharge their devices while they are off doing other things.[6]

Many libraries are developing new types of collaborative learning spaces when they renovate; these include group study rooms, multimedia production spaces, and rooms with equipment that enables students to practice giving a multimedia presentation. All of these types of space support students' use of mobile devices in creating content for their coursework. In addition, some institutions have centres that are oriented towards encouraging faculty to use technology effectively in their teaching. The Open University Library's DigiLab is an innovative facility that provides the latest technologies in an engaging physical space for faculty to try out new products and get advice from professional staff in the facility (http://digilab.open.ac.uk).

As students increasingly develop innovative digital content on their mobile devices, libraries should consider not only providing spaces or small rooms for collaborative work on projects, but spaces to display finished work. These could be posters, digital displays, or digital images mounted as screen savers on public computers. If universities want to highlight the type of work their students or faculty are doing in the field, it would be interesting to have the capability for some real-time streaming of data into a display in the library.

Conclusion

As information professionals conceptualize the 'm-library', they may think about updating or modernizing the traditional library, or they may think in terms of transforming the library. At present, some pioneering academic libraries are addressing mobile library issues in their planning processes. They are beginning to discuss with publishers and information providers the possibilities of licensing content configured for mobile devices. They may be part of an institution-wide group that is looking at the implications of mobility for learning and support of the user community. Within the library, planning needs to incorporate consideration of the library's role in:

- licensing information products for mobile devices
- hosting or pointing to institutional content intended for mobile devices, e.g. podcasts
- preserving new content types and formats
- providing instruction on the devices themselves, not just access to content
- providing space for new equipment and work styles.

Additional issues for consideration, not touched on in this paper but of relevance to the adoption of content and services for mobile devices, are authentication, privacy, theft and leakage of confidential or licensed information, standard platforms, and mobile devices and cheating.

As libraries plan to move into the mobile learning environment, they may want to consider establishing a task force or study group that involves individuals representing various sectors of the university. There are many considerations in planning (Wagner, 2007). The group may want to address:

■ specific goals and objectives for mobile content/services
■ the current state of uptake of mobile devices by campus sectors
■ target audience for anticipated content/services
■ stakeholders who should be involved in the detailed planning
■ a clear understanding of resources needed and funding streams
■ a plan for assessment of the effectiveness of the new content/services.

Libraries have established their presence in the internet environment and they have developed many innovative services for their user communities. However, attention to the issues of mobile users has yet to capture a high-visibility spot on many libraries' agendas. As our user populations increasingly rely on rapidly evolving mobile devices, libraries need to keep pace by providing compatible content and services.

References

Adams, Karen (2007) E-mail communication to the author, (9 August).

Carmean, C. and Haefner, J. (2002) Mind Over Matter, *Educause Review*, 7 (6), (1 November 2002), 26.

Chronicle (2007) *Chronicle of Higher Education,* (20 July), http://chronicle.com/daily/2007/07/2007072002n.htm.

Dempsey (2005) *Dempsey's weblog* (19 January), http://orweblog.oclc.org.

Educause (2007) *The ECAR Study of Undergraduate Students and Information Technology, 2007,* http://connect.educause.edu/Library/ECAR/ TheECARStudyofUndergradua/45075.

JISC (2007) *In Their Own Words,* www.jisc.ac.uk/intheirownwords.

Kuh, G. D., Kinzie, J., Schuh, J. H., Whitt, E. J. and Associates (2005) *Student Success College: creating conditions that matter*, Jossey-Bass.

McLemee, Scott (2007) *Inside Higher Education* (8 August), http://insidehighered.com/views/2007/08/08/mclemee.

Mobile Life (2007) *The Mobile Life Youth Report, 2007*, www.mobilelife2007.co.uk.

NPR (US National Public Radio) (2007) (23 August).

Oblinger, Diana G. and Oblinger, James L. (2005) *Educating the Net Gen*. Boulder, Colorado: EDUCAUSE, www.educause.edu/LibraryDetailPage/666&ID=pub7101.
This study was reported on in 'Waiting on the Wave,' Campus Technology, March 2007, http://campustechnology.com/articles/452441.

Panettieri, J. C. (2007) Converged Devices: waiting on the wave, *Campus Technology*, 3 January 2007, 1–4, http://campustechnology.com/articles/45244_3/.

Wagner, Ellen (2007) Mobility Matters: why learning professionals should care, *ELI Web Seminar* (20 February), http://connect.educause.edu/Library/Abstract/MobileMattersWhyLearningP/39419.

Zogby International (2007) 31 January, www.zogby.com/news/Read/News.dbm?ID=1244.

URLs

1   www.library.ualberta.ca/pdazone/index.cfm.
2   www.asu.edu/lib/librarychannel/.
3   www.lib.ncsu.edu/dli/projects/catalogws/.
4   http://library.athabascau.ca/drr/.
5   http://faq.library.upenn.edu/recordList?library=lippincott.
6   www.tilburguniversity.nl/services/its/mlc.

3

Encyclopedic knowledge in the mobile age

Agnes Kukulska-Hulme

A walking encyclopedia for the new generation?

'A walking encyclopedia' is an expression used from time to time to describe a very knowledgeable person. It seems to encapsulate the values of ready access and comprehensive coverage suggested by the terms of the expression, while also denoting a human presence that may enhance, or perhaps just differ from, what could otherwise be obtained from a book. Whether in print, on digital media or inside someone's head, exhaustive, all-embracing information easily accessible in one go has always been valued and continues to be so. On the web, the single portal is still the 'holy grail' (e.g. Schreibman, O'Brien Roper and Gueguen, 2008). The question arises as to whether mobile and pervasive technologies are set to make a difference.

At the start of the 21st century, the explosion of information and an increasing need to stay in constant touch with the latest developments has created new conditions and unfamiliar demands on individuals and organizations. It is now easier to be informed about events happening remotely or knowledge produced in a distant part of the world, but paradoxically, this creates an additional imperative to understand a different context. To fully appreciate the context, it may be necessary to understand some aspects of a foreign language and culture; even when the language is known, or a translation is available, incorrect assumptions and nonequivalence are commonplace. So while distributed information has become easier to access it can be difficult to interpret and assimilate into a person's current knowledge and understanding.

Human cognitive challenges include the capacity to take in a great deal of information, and the ability to make sense of it and to make further connections. The translation into English of Pierre Bayard's 'How to Talk about Books You Haven't Read' (2007) has highlighted common insecurities about extensive reading and how apparent shortcomings, such as not having finished reading a book, might even be reinvented as advantages. Writers have always had a good appreciation of this issue. The author Claire Messud describes a woman's apartment filled with books, some of which were 'acquired for courses and never read . . . but [. . .] suggested to her that she was, or might be, a person of seriousness, a thinker in some seeping, ubiquitous way' (Messud, 2006, 107). There is more than one way to use a book, and the environments where books are kept and talked about often have their own significance, providing a new context for these works and their associations with related writings and ideas. With new web publishing technologies such as blogs, the allure of sampling, commenting and making connections, without having spent much time on a single item, may be ever stronger.

A focus on encyclopedic knowledge should not be taken to imply that this type of knowledge is uniquely valuable; however, the aim of this chapter is to shed some light on the changing nature of all-encompassing collections of represented knowledge, how knowledge may be socially constructed and shared, and whether perspectives may be shifting, due to greater mobility and travel. As a publication, a general encyclopedia is also of special interest because it answers a variety of reader needs – for entertainment, informal learning and formal study – such as to find answers to questions in a light-hearted quiz, for general interest or for more serious study. As such, it tends to have a reputation for being interesting and useful as well as authoritative. New manifestations of encyclopedias on the web attest to the enduring appeal of gathering together and disseminating what is known about a broad range of topics. At the same time, the scale and nature of knowledge sharing on the web differs in many respects from traditional formats. The proliferation of portable and pervasive technologies is introducing further changes that we are only beginning to understand.

Travelling towards knowledge

Back in the age of the French Enlightenment, Diderot and d'Alembert worked with a circle of colleagues on an ambitious project to create an encyclopedia that would change 'the common way of thinking', through the expansion of knowledge and the development of critical thought. The 32 volumes of the encyclopedia made available during 1751–77 covered topics from the sciences and the arts as well as a great deal of technical knowledge, supplemented by no fewer than 11 volumes of beautiful illustrations that enhanced the encyclopedia's visual appeal and helped to communicate its ideas. As part of their mission, the encyclopedists were keen to emphasize the merits of travel; Jaucourt explained how, in the past, 'famous travellers [would go to Egypt] in order to profit from the conversation of the priests of the region, who alone possessed the reflective sciences' and went on to say that travellers 'develop and raise the level of the mind, enrich it through knowledge, and cure it of national prejudices'; 'such study cannot be replaced by books or by the tales told by others. Men, places, and things one has to judge by oneself' (Jaucourt, n.d.). So this was an exhortation to travel, but with the explicit aim of developing the mind and influencing society upon one's return.

Fast-forward to the beginning of the 21st century and a world in which encyclopedic knowledge has been represented countless times in a multitude of ways and on different media. In this world, books and libraries can sometimes seem outdated, yet we continue to develop our understanding of what they offer that is not always otherwise available in the digital era. In San Francisco, a city often associated with the high-tech Silicon Valley, there is a small research library which aims to demonstrate the fluidity of classification and the importance of social interaction in sustaining a living collection that continues to evolve through human contact, serendipity, and discussion in the aisles (Lewis-Kraus, 2007). The creators of the Prelinger Library explain on their website why their physical library is important:

> Now that many research libraries are economizing on space and converting print collections to microfilm and digital formats, it's becoming harder to wander and let the shelves themselves suggest new directions and ideas.   (Prelinger Library, 2008)

Items on the shelves are therefore organized so as to encourage discovery, principally by having maps, documents, books, periodicals and so on, all shelved together within subject headings. Someone looking for a book may accidentally discover a relevant map or a periodical located right next to it. Further, items to be found in this library have strong connections with local events and people: 'The library's flow of subject matter starts with where we are, with the local' (Prelinger, 2004, para. 7). This local context gives depth of meaning to items found in the library; but once they have gained local knowledge, library users are encouraged to take photographs of copyright-free materials to share with others on digital media.

Knowledge construction and sharing in the digital age

'A library is often assumed to be just a repository of information. But libraries are more than this, and there is a danger that in the rush to networked information we will lose the significant non-informational (what we call "situational") features of libraries', was a warning given by Reich and Weiser in 1993 (p.1). They had identified certain library functions that met essential human needs, in particular the needs of local communities. Looking ahead 20 years into the future, i.e. approximately 2013, they predicted that libraries might loan portable devices to members of the local community who want to follow some community activity, e.g. their local football team. The devices would be programmed to follow that activity and there would be no need to log on, know any commands, or do anything other than glance at the device from time to time. 'Networked posters' could serve a similar function, they suggested, being taken home and put up on the wall, remaining connected to a steady display of community information that was updated daily by the library.

Interestingly, Reich and Weiser (1993) advocated using physical proximity as a way to control access, so that some local information would be easily available only to locals, thereby protecting their sense of community. Further, they contended that 'the physicality of communities is part of their charm and value. The man who has never been more than five miles from home adds community value by the richness of his knowledge of those five miles, and by the reduced dilution of that knowledge from the outside' (Reich and Weiser, 1993). Do we see things differently today? The richness of local knowledge ought to be valued still. Technology has the power to change how it is captured and shared, but with personal handheld devices increasingly in the hands of the public, the idea of totally controlling how local knowledge is accessed may seem passé. Yet echoes of a protective attitude may be detected among those who today design digital services and systems allowing users to choose whom they wish to invite to be part of their online set of friends, community or local interest group. Completely open access (e.g. global) is not always appropriate, is not always the most effective for participants and is not necessarily preferred. Tensions between local knowledge and more widespread sharing must continue to be explored and resolved.

Not a Walking Encyclopaedia is the title of a blog whose author reviews books she has read as well as writing about her diverse interests and hobbies (Schultz, 2008). Like many other bloggers, she shares her everyday experiences with whoever cares to read about them, along with her perspective on life and some of her specialized and local knowledge. The incremental and sometimes unpredictable environment of a blog can be contrasted with highly organized web publishing activity such as Wikipedia (2008). Wikipedia has become a household name in the past few years, although it was not the first project of its kind and it is not the last. h2g2, 'an unconventional guide to life, the universe and everything', was launched in 1999 and has been hosted since 2001 by the BBC (h2g2, 2008); Citizendium was started by a Wikipedia founder and emphasizes 'credibility and quality, not just quantity', which includes the use of contributors' real names (Citizendium, 2008). In December 2007, the official Google blog reported that a new tool called 'knol' was being tested for collaborative knowledge creation, also stressing that knowing who wrote an article would help users make better use of web content (Manber, 2007).

Another popular way of sharing encyclopedic content on the web takes the form of questions and answers, for example within WikiAnswers (2008), which states on its home page that 'You don't need to be an expert. Thousands of people just contribute a few tidbits of new information, or improve spelling and grammar'. Other sites specialize in particular media formats, e.g. SuTree (2008), a site for instructional and educational video sharing which also encourages communities of interest and course creation. In yet another approach to collaborative knowledge generation, InnoCentive (2008) connects 'seekers' and 'solvers', with the offer of financial rewards for best solutions to open challenges in areas such as science and engineering.

Enabling cultural discovery

The web has opened up endless possibilities for collective knowledge representation and collaboration. I believe the next challenge is to see whether we can move towards a better appreciation of the diverse cultural contexts that give rise to different ways of describing and organizing knowledge. As suggested earlier in this chapter, distributed information has become easier to access but its interpretation still poses interesting challenges. People's Daily Online (2002) reported some time ago that the National Library of China is setting about digitizing the 'world's earliest and greatest encyclopedia', the great Encyclopedia of Yongle, dating from the 15th century. Assuming that this will one day be freely accessible online, understanding the contents will be no easy matter. The same applies to more recent creations: Baidu Baike (2006) is a Chinese-language web-based collaborative encyclopedia available since 2006. In terms of translation, the introduction by Google of language tools that allow users not only to request a translation for a web page, but also, significantly, to suggest how the translation might be improved, seems a notable stride forward. Potentially it can raise the quality of translation and also engage people by making use of their skills and knowledge; perhaps no less significantly, it can draw everyone's attention to the fact that translation is an act of interpretation and not a mechanistic process.

The issue of how technology can truly support people in getting to know other cultures and their perspectives on the world does not currently receive a great deal of attention. Mobile technologies are often used to perpetuate the view that a handful of phrases in another language, along with practical information for travellers, is all that is needed. Business travellers can often access such information on their handheld computers (e.g. Discover Hong Kong, 2008). As has been pointed out by Jaokar and Fish (2006), the mobile phone is fast becoming a 'security blanket' (p. 87) and, in the future, mobile users may be able to generate queries that will trigger multilingual information retrieval and natural language processing technologies to return relevant information in the user's native language.

Conclusion

Themes emerging from this reflection centre on ready access to knowledge, but combined with a deeper understanding of the contexts in which it is created and with an emphasis on the human, local and community perspectives mediating all knowledge. Mobile access to encyclopedic web content has not yet had a significant impact on the nature of what is represented and how communication takes place among contributors or community participants. Travel – whether physical or virtual – represents a unique opportunity to engage with another culture. Automatic translation both facilitates that engagement and obscures the differences that direct knowledge of another language and culture can reveal. This is a difficult paradox that needs to be noticed and analysed so that it can be properly addressed and reflected in the design of environments for knowledge creation and sharing.

References

Baidu Baike (2006) http://baike.baidu.com.

Bayard, P. (2007) *How to Talk about Books You Haven't Read*, trans. J. Mehlman, Granta.

Citizendium (2008) The Citizens' Compendium Website, http://en.citizendium.org/wiki/Main_Page.

Discover Hong Kong (2008) Website for Business Travellers who have PDAs, http://discoverhongkong.com/eng/travelneeds/business/pda/index.jhtml.

H2g2 (2008) *The Hitchhiker's Guide to the Galaxy*, www.bbc.co.uk/dna/h2g2/.

InnoCentive (2008) www.innocentive.com.

Jaokar, A. and Fish, T. (2006) *Mobile Web 2.0*, Futuretext.

Jaucourt (n.d.) Travel, an article from Diderot's Encyclopédie, trans. N. S. Hoyt and T. Cassirer, http://quod.lib.umich.edu/cgi/t/text/text-idx?c=did;cc=did;rgn=main;view=text;idno=did2222.0000.169.

Lewis-Kraus, G. (2007) A World in Three Aisles – browsing the post-digital library, *Harper's Magazine* (May 2007), http://harpers.org/archive/2007/05/0081511.

Manber, U. (2007) Encouraging People to Contribute Knowledge, *The Official Google Blog*, posted 13 December, http://googleblog.blogspot.com/2007/12/encouraging-people-to-contribute.html.

Messud, C. (2006) *The Emperor's Children*, Picador.

People's Daily Online (2002) *China to Digitalize World's Earliest Encyclopedia*, http://english.peopledaily.com.cn/200204/18/print20020418_94330.html.

Prelinger Library (2008) Prelinger Library website, http://home.earthlink.net/~alysons/library.html.

Prelinger, M. S. (2004) *On the Organization of the Prelinger Library*, www.home.earthlink.net/~alysons/LibraryOrg.html.

Reich, V. and Weiser, M. (1993) Libraries are more than Information: situational aspects of electronic libraries, *Libraries and Information Resources*, Xerox Palo Alto Research Center, www.ubiq.com/weiser/SituationalAspectsofElectronicLibraries.html.

Schreibman, S., O'Brien Roper, J. and Gueguen, G. (2008) Cross-collection Searching: a Pandora's box or the Holy Grail? *Literary and Linguistic Computing*, Issue 1, 23 April, 3–5.

Schultz, C. (2008) *Not a Walking Encyclopedia*, blog, www.not-a-walking-encyclopedia.blogspot.com/.

SuTree (2008), www.sutree.com/.

WikiAnswers (2008), http://wiki.answers.com/.

Wikipedia (2008), www.wikipedia.org.

4

Nomadicity and information access: the mobile digital library for people on the move

Mohamed Ally

Introduction

According to Collier (2006), digital libraries have dominated libraries' strategic plans since the year 2000. Digital libraries have primarily catered for learners and individuals on site, learners having to come to the library or to be at specific locations to access information. Libraries need to be on the move, taking digital access one step further by enabling access for nomads and individuals, anywhere and anytime, using mobile technology. Nomads are individuals or groups of people who travel from one place to the next to work, trade, or to seek food and shelter. Hence, mobile technology for nomadic access anywhere and anytime should be part of the strategic planning of libraries so that they can meet the needs of those users who are not presently being reached because of their nomadic lifestyle. Kleinrock (1996) defines nomadicity as providing the required system support to meet the needs of nomads. The goal of nomadic access is to enable a consistent experience for users anywhere in the world as they travel from one place to another. The infrastructure should allow easy access to information in a convenient form as the nomad moves from place to place. The nomadic environment should be transparent to users, regardless of location, the device and platform they are using, the available bandwidth, and whether or not they are on the move at any given time (Kleinrock, 1996). This information access environment should be implemented in both rural and urban areas, since users move from place to place in major cities.

In the past the library was a specific place where learners, workers and citizens physically went to access information and learning resources. Now, libraries provide electronic access to information and learning resources using desktop and notebook computers. Future libraries must cater for users who are constantly on the move, so that they can access information from anywhere and at any time, depending on their lifestyles. In addition to accessing information from libraries, people today search the internet for information, participate in wikis, talk to others through social networking sites, and use technology to go directly to the expert (OCLC, 2005). People on the move are looking for answers to questions as they work and study, rather than looking for books or journals. They want to use the capability of the computer and search engines to find information rather than reading through a book or a journal to find a specific piece of information. Hence, libraries must plan to meet the needs and the style of people on the move. In this chapter the term 'library' refers to different types of libraries, including libraries in educational institutions, governments, organizations and businesses.

Information access and nomads

As people on the move use mobile technology, they will demand that library services be provided for access by that technology. This demand is being driven by the proliferation of mobile devices around the world, with the biggest growth being in the developing countries. Use of mobile technology has surpassed the use of desktop computers. At present, approximately 16% of the world's population have access to desktops and laptops to connect to the internet. At the same time, 38% have access to mobile technology (Breck, 2007). As the number of mobile subscribers increases, the communication cost is reduced, making it affordable to access the internet and digital resources. At the same time, governments in developing countries are investing in the infrastructure to improve access from remote locations. Governments see access to information as a strategic initiative, since enabling citizens to access information will improve their lives and well-being. This will increase competitiveness and quality of life in developing countries. Financial organizations are allowing citizens around the world to use their mobile technology to conduct business – referred to as 'a bank in every pocket' (*The Economist*, 2007). As other sectors of society start using mobile technology to conduct business and to access information, libraries will be forced to deliver information on mobile technology – 'a library in every pocket' – so that people on the move can learn and access information anywhere and at any time. This will have an impact on how libraries operate in the future.

Libraries have a major role to play in the digital world, with the rapid explosion of information and the ongoing demand for education and training. In the 21st century, access to quality information and learning materials is required for nomads around the world to be productive citizens. There are many reasons why nomads need timely access to information wherever they are located. The following sections describe those different reasons and how libraries can facilitate transparent and easy access.

Formal learning

Nomads who live in remote locations have limited access to formal education because of lack of resources. Formal education is needed to enable citizens of different countries to be competitive in a global environment. Hence, nomads need to be educated with the latest course content and need to apply information in their own contexts to make the learning more meaningful. Applying information in familiar contexts allows learners to personalize that information, leading to the creation of knowledge which becomes part of the learner. As the learner applies that knowledge, new knowledge is created which promotes skill development and wisdom.

To facilitate the remote delivery of digital information and learning materials that result in specific learning outcomes, libraries must start thinking in terms of learning where interaction is built into the information. In the digital world, libraries have to play the role of providers of learning materials in addition to being providers of information. This is because information without built-in learning strategies results in students being passive, which is not an efficient way to learn. Information for access by mobile technology should also take the form of learning objects which are stored in electronic repositories. Storing information and learning materials in open electronic repositories would allow nomads to access the materials anywhere and at any time (Ally, 2004).

Using mobile technology to send content to nomadic learners and to people in different regions in the world would help to achieve major global goals such as the United Nations Millennium Development Goal to 'achieve universal primary education' (UN Millennium Development

Goals, 2007). For different regions of the world to acquire a high standard of primary education so that students are prepared to move on to higher levels of education, access to appropriate primary educational materials is needed. If the curriculum for primary education is digitized and formatted properly, nomads in any part of the world will be able to access learning materials from electronic repositories, using mobile and computing devices. In addition, students on the move will be able to use the communication capabilities of the computing device to connect with tutors anywhere in the world.

Informal learning

Informal learning is learning that is not tied to a programme of study and occurs on an ad hoc basis. Nomads who want to access information to improve their daily lives are participating in informal learning. For example, a nomadic farmer who is experiencing a problem with crops can use a mobile technology to access information to learn about the problem and identify solutions. A fisherman who is about to go fishing can use the mobile device to access the latest weather conditions before going out to sea. Or, while at sea, he can monitor the weather using the mobile technology. Informal learning is important for nomads since, as they move around, they want to find information about their changing environment. Informal learning can be used to help the UN to achieve the following Millennium Development Goals.

Eradicate extreme hunger and poverty

Hunger and poverty result from natural disasters such as drought, flooding, etc. or nomads not having the knowledge and skills to acquire the resources to prevent hunger and poverty. Nomads should be able to access information from their remote areas using mobile technology so as to learn both what to do when disasters occur and how to plant crops and run a farm to prevent hunger and poverty. People in remote locations cannot afford to go to major urban areas to obtain information on how to improve their quality of life. They need to access information using their available digital technologies. Libraries have a role to play in ensuring that information is accessible in remote locations via digital technology.

Reduce child mortality

Nomadic parents should be able to access information anywhere and at any time on how to raise their children, so that the child mortality rate is reduced. For example, parents can learn how to prevent diseases, and the proper diet to follow so as to prevent malnutrition.

Improve maternal health

One of the most important preventative measures in healthcare is to make sure that the mother's and child's health are taken care of during pregnancy. Mothers in some regions of the world do not have information on healthy pregnancy. The use of mobile technology in remote locations to access information about healthy pregnancy is critical for quality of life. Libraries need to make digital information available for access anywhere and at any time to ensure that nomadic mothers can access proper information on healthy pregnancy.

Combat HIV/AIDS, malaria and other diseases

Nomads need access to information on the prevention of disease and what to do when they have a disease. People in remote locations do not have access to medical facilities and information on disease prevention and cure. Libraries have a role to play in ensuring that nomads and people in remote locations have access to information on disease prevention and cure.

Disaster situations

Major destruction and deaths occur in natural disasters because people do not know that the disaster will occur, they do not know how to deal with it, and they do not know what to do after it has happened. Nomads in remote disaster locations can use their available mobile technology to access early warning information on disasters so as to take the necessary preventative measures. They can also use mobile technology to access information from libraries on what to do during and after a disaster, and to locate family members and others after a disaster.

Changing role of the library to cater for nomads

According to Winston and Quinn (2005), libraries have a major role to play in world crises and can take a leadership role by enhancing positive social change around the world through opportunities for information access, education and enhanced citizenship. Mobile wireless technology will allow libraries to reach people with digital information in different parts of the world regardless of location. Use of this technology will allow users to communicate with different communities, to share information and to learn from each other (Long, 2005). Hence, the feeling of isolation will be something of the past. The following sections describe the changing role of libraries in meeting the needs of nomads.

Any time and anywhere access

As people move from one place to the next to live, learn or work, they require access to information so as to learn and to improve their quality of life. For nomads, the information system must be transparent and allow access regardless of location, time, hardware, software and connection type and speed. Nomads have existing mobile devices and telecommunications infrastructures that they would like to use to access information. Information systems should be built to enable nomads to connect using their existing technology anywhere and at any time. The new generation of nomadic users require direct access to information (Jurewicz and Cutler, 2003). Libraries must make the shift from being physical libraries to being virtual libraries, where information is in electronic format and is tagged for easy access by users to meet their individual needs.

Provide meaningful information

Information must be meaningful, so that nomads can apply what they learn in a constructive way to help improve themselves. Users must be able to adapt information to meet their needs. A good example of how this can be done is illustrated in a project by the Commonwealth of Learning (COL), where the creative commons approach is used to allow users to adapt learning materials to meet their contextual needs (Farrell and Shafika, 2007). People will use a constructivist approach to develop knowledge, using the information they access to improve their knowledge and skills. According to Choy (2007), libraries should provide information within an appropriate context so as to help transform it into knowledge that is personal to the individual. Hence, no one but the individual can create the knowledge.

Keep up with innovations in technology

Constant innovations in both hardware and software technology are driving the way information is formatted and accessed. The mobile computing devices are multipurpose, where the user can use the device to do many things. For example, some new mobile devices can be a computer, a telecommunication device, a camera and a social device. The hardware is getting smaller but more powerful, resulting in computing and information access being in people's hands rather than on the desktop or the laptop. Input and output devices are becoming virtual, so that mobile technology users will be able to have input and output capabilities similar to those of a desktop computer. Users are becoming more mobile because of smaller computing technology. The goal of libraries should be to have 'a library in every citizen's pocket'. Computing is also becoming ubiquitous, enabling people to learn and work from anywhere. At the same time, there is considerable growth in social networking, which is allowing students and workers to create, access and share information easily. For example, Wikipedia allows users to contribute information that anyone can access. Podcasting allows users to post audio and video files on the internet for everyone to access. Since 2005, there have been many initiatives on the use of virtual space in education and training. In a virtual world, users will be able to access a virtual librarian as they learn and interact in the virtual world. The virtual librarian could be an avatar that is created by the user, based on individual preferences.

Conclusion

Librarians have an important role to play in the exciting future of mobile digital libraries for access by nomads. The most important contribution librarians can make to the nomadic world is to assist nomads to access the right information at the right time and to make sure that the information has high integrity. Librarians need to work with computer professionals to build intelligent agents that will customize information for specific users and mobile technology so as to make information access seamless and transparent anywhere and at any time. Intelligent agents can play many roles including: (1) providing electronic information services to customize information for individual users; (2) collection development and acquisition; (3) classification of library materials; (4) indexing and abstracting; (5) circulation; and (6) providing automated reference services (Lohani and Jeevan, 2007).

To meet the needs of nomads, libraries must form consortia so that users can access information anywhere and any time regardless of time zone and location (Collier, 2006). Different libraries could each concentrate on one aspect of information and content and form a network to create a super-library, a worldwide network of all libraries. For example, individual libraries could concentrate on different functions such as research, learning, training, etc. or on different content areas such as medicine, engineering, education. To be efficient in terms of storage, libraries should not store duplicate information. Libraries should be networked so that users can access information from a single source. According to Dempsey (2006), it may not make sense for every institution to invest in a complete storage and preservation solution. If different libraries can link their individual repositories to create a global repository for access by anyone, anywhere and at any time, this super-library will eliminate duplication of information between libraries, resulting in efficient storage and access. Awre and Swan (2007) present an aggregation model for linking repositories for users to access, which is one model for linking repositories. To help educational organizations with limited resources, Drury (2007) suggests regional repositories.

Information access and education for nomads and others around the world are basic human rights. With the technology of today, governments, businesses, communities and educators can work together to facilitate universal access of information and learning materials regardless of location and culture. One benefit of remote access to information would be less damage to the environment, since citizens of the world could access information for their own locations rather than having to travel to major cities. Also, nomads would save time and resources, since they would be able to access just-in-time information and learning materials from any location.

References

Ally, M. (2004) Designing Effective Learning Objects for Distance Education. In McGreal, R. (ed.), *Online Education Using Learning Objects*, RoutledgeFalmer, 87–97.

Awre, C. and Swan, A. (2007) Linking Repositories: scoping the development of cross-institutional user-oriented services, *OCLC Systems and Services: International Digital Library Perspectives*, **23** (4), 372–81.

Breck, J. (2007) Education's Intertwingled Future, *Educational Technology*, (May–June), 50–4.

Choy, F. C. (2007) Libraries and librarians: what next? *Library Management*, **20** (3), 112–24.

Collier, M. (2006) Strategic Change in Higher Education Libraries with the Advent of the Digital Library During the Fourth Decade of Program. In Tedd, L. A. (ed.), *Celebrating 40 Years of ICT in Libraries, Museums, and Archives*, Emerald Group Publishing, 65–76.

Dempsey, L. (2006) The (Digital) Library Environment: ten years after, *Ariadne*, 46, www.ariadne.ac.uk/issue46/dempsey/intro.html.

Drury, C. (2007) Building Institutional Repository Infrastructure in Regional Australia, *OCLC Systems and Services: International Digital Library Perspectives*, **23** (4), 395–402.

Economist (2007) *Mobile Banking: a bank in every pocket*, 15 November, www.economist.com/opinion/displaystory.cfm?story_id=10133998 [accessed 28 January 2008].

Farrell, G. and Shafika, I. (2007) *Survey of ICT and Education in Africa: a summary report, based on 53 country surveys*, Washington, DC: infoDev/World Bank, www.infodev.org/en/Publication.353.html.

Jurewicz, L. and Cutler, T. (2003) *High Tech, High Touch: library customer service through technology*, Washington, DC, American Library Association.

Kleinrock, L. (1996) Nomadicity: anytime, anywhere in a disconnected world, *Mobile Networks and Applications*, 1, 351–7.

Lohani, M. and Jeevan, V. K. J. (2007) Intelligent Software Agents for Library Applications, *Library Management*, **20** (3), 139–51.

Long, S. A. (2005) NorthStarNet: libraries harness the internet to build communities, *New Library World*, 106 (1216/1217), 395–415.

OCLC (2005) *College Students' Perception of Libraries and Information Sources*, OCLC www.oclc.org/reports/2005perceptions.htm [accessed 29 January 2008].

UN Millennium Development Goals (2007) www.un.org/millenniumgoals/ [accessed 2 January 2008].

Winston, M. D. and Quinn, S. (2005) Library Leadership in Times of Crisis and Change, *New Library World*, 106 (1216/1217), 464–6.

5

Use of mobile technology for mobile learning and mobile libraries in a mobile society

John M. Traxler

Introduction

Mobile learning – sometimes called m-learning – is increasingly familiar. Since the early 2000s, across every sector and in many parts of the world, there have been mobile learning pilots and projects. It is sufficiently mature and diverse to have a major textbook (Kukulska-Hulme and Traxler, 2005), a dedicated journal, the *International Journal of Mobile and Blended Learning*, and a variety of prestigious international conferences. The development of mobile learning has frequently been driven by pedagogic necessity, technological innovation and funding opportunity, and has often worked within relatively narrow educational and pragmatic discourses. The m-library concept, still probably an emergent concept, occupies a similar and possibly overlapping territory with mobile learning; a territory where technology expertise meets academic expertise, where 'know' meets 'know-how' and where clearly defined communities of practice are just starting to emerge. The relationship between these two communities is itself interesting since the mobile learning community and the m-library community collaborate to deliver or support some types of learning and also each deliver or support other types of learning alone. The mobile learning community has a focus on teaching and interaction, whereas the m-library community has a greater focus on services and content. Nevertheless the challenges for both communities will prove to have much in common; first, to deliver educational experiences to new or unreached communities of learners in economically, socially or geographically remote or disadvantaged situations (under banners such as inclusion, regeneration, participation, development, assistivity, opportunity etc.), and second, to enrich, extend and transform what is understood by the concepts of education and learning (perhaps as situated, authentic, context-aware and personalized experiences). The success and durability of both communities may depend on their ability to think through these unique characteristics and then to align them to national and international policy objectives and funding agendas.

The purpose of this chapter is not, however, to explore the interactions of education and technology within or between these communities but to look outwards, at the society around them.

Mobility, knowledge and learning

Technology and society are intimately and dynamically connected, each shaping the other. Education and society are also intimately and dynamically connected, each leading the other. Technology shapes much education, though, sadly, education does not often seem to shape technology. Mobile technologies are widespread and increasingly involved in education. They have led to the development of mobile learning, but with insufficient recognition of the wider social changes catalysed by these technologies. This chapter will draw attention to these wider social changes and explore their implications for the m-library concept. We will concentrate on the most relevant changes, those of the ideas of knowledge and learning, but there are others. These are increasingly documented in the literature of mobilities (see for example Plant, 2000, Katz and Aakhus, 2002, Ling, 2004 and Brown and Green et al., 2002).

Mobile technologies are redefining the relationships between knowledge, learning (and that includes libraries), education and society partly by the way they redefine the nature and significance of knowledge, partly by redefining society's expectation and requirements in relation to learning and partly by the way they redefine access to knowledge and learning.

Libraries have historically been the physical and institutional custodians of knowledge on behalf of society, or at least the culturally dominant part of society. Libraries have been the banks for accumulated intellectual capital. Mobile technologies are now widely owned, accepted and understood through all sectors and levels of our society and challenge this state of affairs in a variety of ways.

One is relatively trivial and purely technical. Mobile technologies represent a dramatic increase and diversification of the information assets and resources that must be managed. Mobile technologies also mean, however, that knowledge can be accessed without recourse to physical or institutional premises. Again, this may be purely technical and just the consequence of personal mobile technologies providing anywhere/any time access to knowledge in specialist resources like Wapedia (Wikipedia reversioned on-the-fly for WAP) and MobilED (Wikipedia queried by SMS and delivered back by text-to-speech) and in generalist resources like Google, YouTube and Flickr (as the functionality, connectivity and usability of the world wide web delivered on mobile devices continues to improve and business models develop). It may, however, also challenge libraries' (and more so, universities') roles as gatekeepers to knowledge and technology. Previously these institutions and their premises have enabled the less well-off to access technologies, in the form of networked computers, and to access knowledge, in the form of books or courses, but only in quite circumscribed ways. The technologies were those specified, provided and procured by the institution, and constrained in terms of functionality, time and place; knowledge was accessed on similar terms, in courses and in libraries; and both were constrained by access to buildings at specified times for specified people. Mobile technologies have redressed this imbalance and access to both technology and knowledge is becoming far less constrained.

So mobile technologies deliver the promise of anywhere/anytime access to knowledge, learning and information but they also provide just-in-time/just-for-me/just-here access. This may be the basis for contextualization and personalization, where knowledge and learning are customized to the user's location, preferences, history and requirements; it may also be the start of a drift towards fragmented, highly individualized and isolated learning – the so-called 'neo-liberal nightmare'. This undermines the widely held view that education and learning are somehow about some common body of knowledge, a canon or 'core curriculum', that everyone needs to know. This is perhaps an old-fashioned and essentially liberal definition of education. The alternative and utilitarian view is that education is about training and servicing the economy. This too is undermined as mobile technologies deliver 'just-in-time' training and 'performance support' to remote and peripatetic workers and to a generally more mobile workforce, thereby transforming the requirement for vocational training, especially 'just-in-case' vocational training.

Of course, mobile technologies are transforming many parts of our economy, creating new forms of transaction, artefact, consumption, commodity, business organization, economic activity and asset, and this means that a model of education based on servicing the economy must change too. Mobile technologies also transform aspects of work itself, among other things blurring the divisions between the times and spaces devoted to work, home and commuting, and the division between supervision and surveillance.

Mobile technologies are also transforming aspects of our artistic, social, spiritual and political lives, creating now forms and new formats, and any view of the role of education and learning must recognize and respond to all these transformations.

Mobile content

The role of libraries and the nature of the m-library concept will be significantly affected by the growth of 'user-generated content' and the Web 2.0 technologies of wikis, blogs, RSS feeds etc. and their migration to mobile technologies. This is happening in two ways. First, users will be able to consume personalized and privatized knowledge on the move entirely under their own control but second and more importantly, they will be able to produce and transmit it too. This will mean that the whole cycle of production, transmission, storage, retrieval and consumption of information can take place while on the move but, furthermore, without recourse to or control by any of the centralized networks, organizations or agencies. Increasingly, as we have said, Wikipedia (in the form of Wapedia), Flickr, YouTube, Google and similar tools are being accessed on mobile devices, and now these services are becoming context aware and location specific - Google on mobiles, for example, offers improved 'local search experience', based on the belief that mobile search is more often used to find area information such as cinema listings – leading to the possibility that knowledge itself is location specific.

Another significant instance of this is citizen journalism, where members of the general public, usually using camera phones, capture images of breaking news and post it straight to shared file space such as

Flickr or YouTube. Journalism is sometimes called the first draft of history, and here we see it generated without the intervention of professional journalists or centralized and controlling organizations. The role of libraries in this new world of user-generated content is not clear, but developing the idea of m-libraries is a response to this changing environment. One obvious tension between the Web 2.0 phenomenon and user-generated content on the one hand and earlier notions of knowledge on the other will be around ownership and intellectual property. The spread of mobile technologies amplifies this tension, and the idea of m-libraries is somewhere in the middle.

The transformations of knowledge and learning that we have outlined above are unlikely to be the only ones. Mobile devices deliver knowledge 'chunked', structured and connected in very different ways from the lecture, the web and the book. Knowledge is not purely abstract, unaffected by how it is stored, transmitted or consumed. In its earliest forms, knowledge and learning came from lectures, a substantial linear format from an authoritative 'sage-on-the-stage' with no facility to pause or rewind, and from the book, also authoritative, substantial and linear but segmented and randomly accessible. The delivery of knowledge and learning by networked computers using the world wide web meant a break from linearity (with the introduction of hyperlinks) but new heuristics of usability described how knowledge and learning should be 'chunked' and presented. With mobile technologies, usually using a small screen and a limited input medium, the usable 'chunks' become much smaller but the navigational overheads become much, much larger. In essence, small pieces of knowledge and learning can be easily presented but their relationship to anything else may be difficult to understand. One view of this would be to say that mobile technologies trivialize knowledge and learning by turning them into small, isolated facts. A less extreme view would be to say that managing, organizing and presenting knowledge and learning for mobile technologies are likely to be significant challenges.

Mobile time, space and society

The emerging literature of mobilities is starting to reveal the minutiae of people's use of mobile technologies, both individually and as social groups. One aspect of this is the characterization of learning on mobile devices as being opportunistic, spontaneous, informal and private, and another aspect is the extent to which mobile technologies take knowledge and learning out of the clearly demarcated times, spaces and places of earlier types of learning and weave them into the mainstream of people's lives. There is a growing body of work that talks about the way that mobile technologies transform space, place and time. Mobile technologies are eroding established notions of time as the common structure. Plant (2000) talks about the 'approx-meeting' and the 'multi-meeting', Sørensen et al. (2002) about 'socially negotiated time' and Ling (2004) about the 'micro-cordination of everyday life' alongside the 'softening of schedules' afforded by mobile technologies. Mobile technologies are also eroding physical place as a predominant attribute of space. Gergen (2002) talks about 'absent presence' and Plant notes that mobile phones have created 'simultaneity of place': a physical space and a virtual space of conversational interaction, and an extension of physical space, through the creation and juxtaposition of a mobile 'social space'. 'Developments in mobile communications are leading to changes in the spatial and temporal ordering of social practices as increasingly fragmented "time-space maps" are disconnected from many of the constraints of "regionalisation" or "presence-availability"' (Sheller, 2004). Clearly, one challenge for m-libraries is that of physical and temporal locatedness.

Mobile devices facilitate users' direct experience of ('messy', 'noisy') reality and so challenge the reductionism and foundationalism that underpin the ways that knowledge and learning have been classified and managed in order to expedite their storage and consumption in libraries and universities.

Another aspect of the relativity of knowledge and learning is the observation that they may only have value in the eyes of specific communities. Mobile technologies are defining new communities and transforming old ones. Rheingold (2002) and others describe some of these communities 'swarming' and his book *Smart Mobs* he describes 'thumb tribes' and 'the power of the mobile many'. 'Flash-mobs' are an obvious example; others are various political movements and issues-based groups catalysed by mobile technologies.

Social networking, the use of network software systems designed and built to increase the sense of community among groups of like-minded people, is rapidly migrating to mobile devices and each of these services defines a new community. Twitter is one such service, providing free social networking and micro-blogging and allowing subscribers to send updates (140-character text-based posts called 'tweets') to the Twitter website by SMS or instant messaging. These updates are displayed on the subscriber's profile page and instantly delivered to users who have signed up to receive them. The sender can restrict delivery to users in their circle of friends. Subscribers can receive updates via the Twitter website, instant messaging, SMS, RSS, e-mail or through an application. Twitter is popular in North America, whereas in Europe Jaiku, another micro-blogging site, is the comparable phenomenon; this one lets subscribers' friends know not only what the subscribers are doing but also where they are (their 'presence') via the mobile component.

Each of these communities has its own norms, protocols, ethics, expectations and values, and each perhaps generates and validates local and specific versions of knowledge and learning. At the same time, Gergen (2002) and others describe how mobile technologies trouble or undermine physically co-located communities – the family, the town, the university. In the utilitarian sense, these transformations must be recognized if libraries are to continue to identify emergent communities, albeit sometimes virtual and transient ones, and to serve them, perhaps with the m-libraries approach. In a deeper sense, mobile technologies challenge the relatively stable view of learning and knowledge that has been embodied and embedded in libraries and universities.

Mobile learning

We return finally to the relationship between mobile learning and m-libraries. There is much potential synergy and overlap between the mobile learning community and the m-library community. We have generally talked about knowledge and learning in the same breath. However, in various contexts there are differences. Many in the wider community access learning and knowledge that are not mediated, managed or delivered by educators and their institutions but solely by libraries and their staff. Much of this is based around the individual or around social groups; it is not necessarily assessed or organized and, compared to educator-based learning, there may be little or no concern for pedagogy or meta-cognition and in the various contexts learning has different connotations. Both communities must understand how mobile technologies transform learning as well as knowledge, but there is little consensus on this. Some researchers talk about a transition from behaviourism and constructivism to navigationism (Brown, 2005) or connectivism (Siemens, 2005), where the location and evaluation of knowledge becomes more important than its storage and recall; others recognize how mobile technologies are transforming the ideas of discourse and dialogue upon which some models of education and learning rest (Laurillard, 2007).

Conclusion

This chapter has talked in terms of broad trends and diverse and varied changes. These may not continue, and they may not happen in the ways we anticipate. Their implications for the meaning and value of learning and knowledge are uncertain. The concept of m-libraries will evolve in the context of these global and social changes but also in the context of local factors. The same is also true of mobile learning. Both concepts and their communities face the challenges of developing internal coherence and rigour while recognizing the significance of their wider environment.

References

Brown, B. and Green, N. et al. (2002) *Wireless World – social and interactional aspects of the mobile age*, Springer.

Brown, T. H. (2005) Beyond Constructivism: exploring future learning paradigms, *Education Today*, issue 2 of 2005, Thames, New Zealand, Aries Publishing Company.

Gergen, K. J. (2002) The Challenge of Absent Presence. In Katz, J. E. and Aakhus, M. (eds) (2002) *Perpetual Contact*, Cambridge University Press.

Katz, J. E. and Aakhus, M. (eds) (2002) *Perpetual Contact – mobile communications, private talk, public performance*, Cambridge University Press.

Kukulska-Hulme, A. and Traxler, J. (2005) *Mobile Learning: a handbook for educators and trainers*, Routledge.

Laurillard, D. (2007) Pedagogic Forms of Mobile Learning: framing research questions. In Pachler, N., *Mobile Learning – towards a research agenda*, Institute of Education, University of London, 153–77.

Ling, R. (2004) *The Mobile Connection – the cell phone's impact on society*, San Francisco, CA, Morgan Kaufmann Publishers.

Plant, S. (2000) *On the Mobile. The effects of mobile telephones on social and individual life*, www.motorola.com/mot/documents/0,1028,333,00.pdf.

Rheingold, H. (2002) *Smart Mobs: the next social revolution*, New York, Perseus.

Sheller, M. (2004) Mobile Publics: decoupling, contingency, and the local/global gel, *Environment and Planning D: society and space*, **22**, 39–54.

Siemens, G. (2005) Connectivism: a learning theory for the digital age, *International Journal of Instructional Technology & Distance Learning,* (January), www.itdl.org/Journal/Jan_05/article01.htm.

Sørensen, C., Mathiassen, L. and Kakihara, M. (2002) Mobile Services: functional diversity and overload. Presented at *New Perspectives on 21st-Century Communications,* 24–25 May, 2002, Budapest, Hungary.

6

Exploiting mobile communications for library service development: technical possibilities and cultural implications

William Foster and Cain Evans

Introduction

At the launch of Framework for the Future (Department for Culture Media and Sport, 2003a), the UK government's ten-year public library strategy, Baroness Tessa Blackstone (Department for Culture Media and Sport, 2003b) said that:

> Public libraries in the 21st century should be open when people want to use them, including evenings and weekends, and offer family-friendly facilities like cafes and crèches. And ideally, library users should be able to get easy access to any book – whether or not it is still in print – with others getting expert help on everything from basic literacy to setting up their own community websites and taking part in the ICT revolution.

She clearly envisaged the public library continuing to provide a physical space in which to feed users' recreational and information needs, albeit increasingly based on an ICT infrastructure. However, today's pervasive technology is allowing not only for information providers to offer information services outside the confines of the traditional physical space, but also for information recipients to receive this information via a variety of devices, wherever they are located. Public libraries clearly need to exploit these pervasive technologies if they are to survive as mainstream providers of information. A number of libraries are using text messaging facilities such as SMS for renewals and reservations and this approach could be used to advertise events, new books and information services more widely.

However, public library services need to develop a broader strategy to decide how best to develop their services for an increasingly IT-literate population; particularly the net generation, who have grown up with computers and a range of portable devices since their early years. Mobile technology is central to the lifestyle of the modern young. Texting is increasingly the first means of communication for young people, and mobile phones, iPods, MP3 players and video consoles are all widely used by the younger generation for some form of multimedia information delivery. However, public libraries support a wide range of users and, as Garrod (2004) has said, 'striking a balance between the traditional and the new is a difficult task and trying to provide something for everyone, irrespective of age or social group, is a hard task'. An OCLC survey in 2005 of nearly three and a half thousand users from six countries revealed that although 96% of those surveyed had visited a public library in person, only 27% had visited the website of the public library (OCLC, 2005, 20). For the United Kingdom, that figure is just 9%, demonstrating that whatever new services UK public libraries offer in the future will require considerable marketing and promotion. Enabling people to search for information using large touch screens from outside the library as some libraries have done is one attempt to increase website use, but one that still requires a user to go to the physical library building. A more imaginative, location-independent approach is clearly needed for long-term, sustainable information delivery.

Public libraries and IT

The IT revolution in UK public libraries has been ongoing since the beginning of the 21st century. The People's Network was the largest project in UK public libraries and has been a major success in attracting new customers to the public library service. Unfortunately not all of these new customers have become borrowers and many continue to enter the library merely to make use of the personal computers (PCs). Teenagers and young adults, in particular, have been attracted into an environment that they have traditionally considered old fashioned by the introduction of personal computers and the prospect of free internet access at generally acceptable speeds. However, these users will increasingly be expecting the library to provide much more than just PC and internet access. Public libraries now need to consider how they can build on the success of the

People's Network and retain the interest of not only this younger population but also others who do not normally use library services but have been
or could be tempted to use the public library for computer-based services.
They need to consider how they might develop their electronic services in
more innovative ways. This will be necessary not only to keep these new
customers but also to demonstrate that libraries can continue to be at the
forefront of technological use. However, significant service developments
will depend upon libraries' ability to secure additional and sustainable
funding for replacement hardware, new software and increased connectivity
and to get maximum value from the investment.

Potential for new technologies

One of the key issues for the public library is the continued centrality of the
traditional Library Management System (LMS) as the main ICT driver. LMS
have been around for over 40 years, yet their functionality has remained
largely unchanged during that time. Most of them evolved before the
internet was widely available and certainly before web-based interfaces were
developed. In the 21st century university libraries have moved away from
system centrality by linking the LMS with related systems such as the Virtual
Learning Environment (VLE) and the digital repository. This has led to the
development of new educational functionality, delivering a broader range
of service for users. Public libraries generally have not had appropriate secondary or tertiary systems available with which to integrate in order to
develop appropriate additional functionality and enhanced service delivery.
The public library LMS has traditionally been based on proprietary software,
making collaborative ventures difficult. Talis, in its *Project Silkworm* white
paper (Leavesley, 2005, 3), has suggested that library suppliers should collaborate in order to help libraries deliver better services. This would
facilitate:

- sharing and community over duplication and isolation
- reuse over reinvention
- openness and interoperability over exclusivity
- experimentation over certainty.

Miller (2007) discusses the idea of the 'mashup' – a web-based application that combines information content from several different sources to

create a brand new service, increasingly based on Web 2.0 technologies. He discusses Talis's 'Mashing up the library competition' established to 'create a safe and incentivized environment within which the whole sector can begin to give serious thought to what they actually want in the future'. Such an approach would be enormously beneficial to public libraries which need to build on the experience and gains of the government-funded digitization projects from earlier in the decade. One interesting example is the 24-hour museum, where RSS (Really Simple Syndication) aggregators are being used to pull together multiples sources into a single interface. Such developments are necessary, argues Pratty (2007), to 'keep readers on-site', a particular necessity not only for short-attention-span teenagers but also for elderly users with diminished powers of concentration.

The obvious area for exploitation, therefore, would appear to be the ever-developing mobile technology. Phone companies, commercial information service providers and web technology companies have all suggested ideas for information delivery via mobile handsets using third-generation technology embedded with Wireless Application Protocols (WAP). Introducing mobile applications into the public library environment will provide patrons with services that can be accessed by either a desktop PC or a mobile device. Tracking technologies such as RFID (radio-frequency identification) and GPS (Global Positioning System) will be central to this development. Portable devices could also be used to provide a delivery vehicle for those who are disabled or housebound and physically unable to travel to the library. Changes in disability legislation have already had an impact on the presentation of information, with libraries legally obliged to provide information in a range of alternative formats.

The term 'mobile' should be considered as referring not just to portable devices but also to a broader concept of portability that enables library and data services to be more pervasive. For more than a decade computer scientists have used the terms 'ubiquitous' or 'pervasive' computing to refer to the broad range of these pervasive technologies and their application, yet little is understood about how best to use this technology. Ubiquitous computing has steadily been introduced into the business world to support operational needs, and libraries could learn from their experience. Arya (1995, 230) has said that ubiquitous computing 'represents the most explicit attempt yet to move computing beyond the confines of tool usage towards a pervasive penetration of human activities, with potentially far-reaching effects'. He contended that without the infrastructure to provide a sense of closeness between the end user and technology, ubiquitous computing would not become a part of the next generation of technologies. However, he suggested that wireless information needed to be 'based on non-intrusive availability'. Public libraries need to address this issue in order that that users are fully aware of the range of resources and services that are available and can 'tap into them' at will, but are not overwhelmed by the potential unlimited choice set before them. Certainly, future user interfaces require developers to think about how patrons can best access and retrieve information. More research needs to be done on how to organize and 'chunk' information for portable devices to support public library information services. New services are initially likely to be based on existing mobile technologies, but the incorporation of enhanced retrieval and service interfaces using Web 2.0 technologies could radically alter the way public libraries deliver and present their services in the future. Web 2.0 in the library arena is increasing being referred to as Library 2.0.

We might call the technical infrastructure with a Library 2.0 interface PerLS (Pervasive Library System), to describe the environment offering the new range of library services. Figure 6.1 shows a conceptual model of PerLS with its component parts.

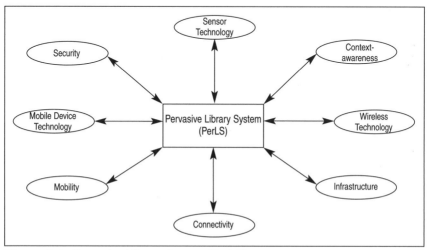

Figure 6.1 Pervasive Library System (PerLS) concept

A number of components need further explanation. Security of information and authenticating user accounts are two of the barriers to successful 'uptake' of a system. Roaming is fast becoming the norm when it comes to users accessing pertinent information from a public server. This approach requires an infrastructure to be in place that could support the PerLS, necessitating integration with catalogue servers, personal data servers as well as back-end systems that provide online/offline support. Before information can be 'pushed' to a mobile device the PerLS is required to ascertain the type of device being used to access its data. Obviously a user who is roaming from one place to another would prefer information shown on the PDA screen to be formatted in a style that is easily recognizable. Additionally, PDA devices which are formatting information need to be platform independent. Once the device is recognized and acknowledged, then the repository server can send the requested information to the device.

Location will increasingly be a 'common piece of context used in application development' (Abowd, Harvel and Brotherton, 2000), as will content relevance. Delivering appropriate content requires knowledge about the user's status within the environment. Evans (2007, 3) has suggested that 'a number of components are pertinent to content-aware applications such as: where is the user; who is the user; what is the user doing; when did the user access information; and how best to serve the needs of [their] end users'.

Information provision in the new environment

The exploitation of the book stock continues to be the central focus of most public libraries, although issue figures have been hit by competition from book sellers and others. An increasing number of libraries are using RFID to enhance access to information within library buildings. The traditional process of searching for and locating a title is time consuming, and RFID can enable the user to withdraw and borrow the book more quickly than would be possible under normal circumstances. A range of portable devices such as PDAs could be supported by the library to allow users to scan for books and their locations. However, although the technology provides a quicker path to finding a particular book, time and effort is needed by the library staff to set up and implement the technology, which requires tagging of the complete stock collection. Emberton

(2007, 1), though, has rightly argued that 'the benefits to the user and the organization will be lost if major barriers are not removed, such as traditional library attitudes and behaviour, outdated work practices and weak management'. Of course, in the context of pervasive computing an increasingly major irritation for many library users used to obtaining items online is that public library books cannot be loaned online, even though public library catalogues are readily available over the internet. One possible answer is the use of e-books, a concept that has been around for many years and which has been successfully taken up by many academic libraries. However, the hurdles for adoption are significantly greater for public libraries. Nevertheless, although older public library users may not yet be ready to replace the look and feel of the traditionally published volume, the culture hurdle should not be a problem for the net generation, already accustomed to gaining much of their information via technological devices. The latest e-book readers provide a reading experience that is closer to print on paper and if those readers are capable of supporting other functionality that could be provided this might provide a way for public libraries to get the younger generation using the book stock as well as the People's Network computers. Libraries would probably need to collaborate to establish themselves as an e-book hub, not only delivering complete texts but also using podcasting techniques to offer a range of related book-reading services. The decision to offer the 2007 Man Booker Prize shortlisted novels freely online was an interesting move in this direction (Alberge, 2007). It would be useful if libraries could automatically deliver texts of potential interest to users using the type of profiling techniques already exploited by companies like Amazon. Clearly there are many significant issues for public libraries with regard to e-book provision, but libraries could already be experimenting with out-of-copyright texts to test the water.

One major success for location-based information delivery is the use of GPS-based navigation systems for route navigation in cars. These provide access to comprehensive route information for those on the road, which takes the user from starting point to destination, providing detailed road information on the way. A similar approach to information navigation and location could be developed to provide tourists or holidaymakers with a database of information that would support and enhance their visits to destinations and also flag up potentially interesting places en route. This information could be a mixture of formal information, such as travel guides, and information contributed by other users of the system. Such a database would be an enhancement to the existing GPS database. If a local library provides WiFi capability (and many libraries are providing this at no cost to the end user (Civic Regeneration and Information Management Associates, 2006)), visitors could park (or stand) outside the library, and connect to local venues to check ticket availability for events. If the library is open, RFID (radio-frequency identification) could be used to gain access to more detailed information from the library about particular venues that is not accessible electronically.

There are a number of issues associated with such an undertaking: volume of data, currency and authority. Of course it might not be practical, nor desirable, to create a single information database for the whole country. It might be necessary, therefore, to divide the country between a number of databases, each covering a region or an individual local authority. There would be an issue of information currency. The information provided by such a database would be likely to change more frequently than highway information. However, data could be downloaded from public library web pages into a portable device that could be uploaded to the GPS in the car or on the mobile phone prior to departure. In the long term, one could envisage a distributed database networked in such a way that users were automatically switched to the relevant subset of information as they entered a different region of the country, using RDS (Radio Data System – a European communications protocol) techniques similar to that used for changing radio stations while on the move.

A third issue relates to authority. Who should have responsibility for maintaining such databases? Public libraries have a long history of creating and maintaining local community databases. However, as Mary Rowlatt (2007, 14) has said 'Libraries are finding it hard to attract traffic to their sites and to justify the resources required to maintain the information to their authorities'. On the other hand, the success of wikis and social networks such as MySpace, Bebo and Facebook could mean that some relevant material could be created less formally by local residents. As Miller (2006, 12) says, 'library 2.0 is about encouraging and enabling a library's community of users to participate, contributing their own views on resources they have used and new ones to which they might wish access'. However, there needs to be improved integration between the more formal information and resource provision that libraries have traditionally provided via their Library Management Systems and the Web 2.0 environment. The library service would also need to take responsibility for maintaining and co-ordinating the information content of the database, assuming any necessary final editorial control.

Implications for service provision

The scenario just outlined is highly system driven, essentially a reference service with little interactivity. What is needed is a comprehensive retrieval interface that takes the traditional library OPAC/website into the next generation. Certainly, public libraries and system suppliers need to work together in this area. Overall, service provision using state-of-the-art technologies needs to be accomplished in a seamless way, integrating appropriate retrieval interfaces with the available WAP technology, and necessitating the development of appropriate gateways and browser functionality to route information seekers to appropriate information, whether originating from the public library or not. Understanding how the mobile application is to work for the benefit of the user is paramount to its development and implementation. Dryer et al. (1999, 657) have made the obvious point that 'pervasive computers change our relationship not only with devices but with other individuals as well'. They have developed a simple but useful model of social impact which shows the interrelationship between the key four components of a pervasive computer system (Figure 6.2). Public libraries will need to consider the implications of each of these.

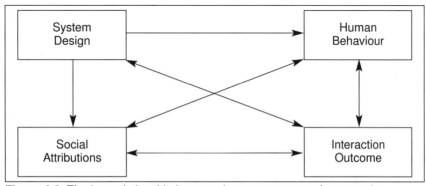

Figure 6.2 The interrelationship between key components of a pervasive computer system

This model needs to be set alongside the information experience that many information users are now expecting. Leavesley (2005, 4) has usefully summarized this experience as:

- all encompassing
- without walls
- immediate
- rich
- participative
- personalized
- fulfilling.

Some of these elements are already achieved through non-computerized activities performed by libraries, such as reading groups and children's activities such as 'bounce and rhyme'. However, they need to become part of the new, pervasive computing systems.

One of the critical issues for public libraries will be adapting to the range of library users that they support. Table 6.1 considers three age groups and their typical IT use.

Table 6.1 Typical library user groups and their IT use			
Age group	Age range	User group	IT use
1	11–25	Net Gen	Mobile devices
2	26–55	IT dependent	Laptops
3	56+	Silver surfers	Library only

Over the next ten to 20 years, those at the older end of age group 2 will be retiring, but they will not become traditional silver surfers. Many will be retired academic, company and office workers who have become used to having high-end specification machines on their desks with easy access to a range of subscription and non-subscription resources (Table 6.2).

Table 6.2 Typical future library user groups and their IT use			
Age group	Age range	User group	IT use
1	11–25	Pervasive generation	Embedded devices
2	26–55	Net Gen	Mobile devices
3	56–75	Retired IT dependents	Home and away IT
4	76+	Silver surfers	Library only

For libraries, this raises issues about how to deploy their staff to support the needs of these disparate user groups. It also raises issues of how much IT support to provide within the library itself. If new developments such as podcasting are to be used, then library staff will need to be sufficiently trained. This will require a new round of public library training beyond that envisioned in building the People's Network (Library and Information Commission, 1998).

Conclusion

Increasingly an ageing but highly IT-literate user community will expect the library to provide a wide range of services using ubiquitous computing technologies. Some of these services will be enhancements of existing services; others will be new and innovative, using Web 2.0 resource integration techniques 'remixed' to appropriate levels of user need and demand. Some of these services may need to be provided on subscription, which some users may be willing to pay, but public libraries will need to decide how best to deploy its resources to accommodate the increased demand that is likely to be placed on them. Public libraries will need to work more closely with other sectors, system suppliers, and indeed with each other, to develop ideas that can build on the success of the People's Network.

References

Abowd, G. D., Harvel, L. D. and Brotherton, J. A. (2000) Building a Digital Library of Captured Educational Experience, *International Conference on Digital Libraries: research and practice*, Kyoto, 13–16 November, 467.

Alberge, D. (2007) Every Novel on Booker Shortlist to be Available Free for Online Readers, *The Times*, (18 October), www.timesonline.co.uk/.

Araya, A. A. (1995) Questioning Ubiquitous Computing, *Proceedings of the 1995 ACM 23rd Annual Conference on Computer Science, Nashville, Tennessee, United States*, 230–7, ACM.

Civic Regeneration and Information Management Associates (2006) *Review and Evaluation of WiFi in Public Libraries: report to the Museum, Libraries and Archives Council*, MLA,
www.mla.gov.uk/resources/assets//W/wifipubliclibraries_10230.pdf.

Department for Culture Media and Sport (2003a) *Arts Minister Tessa Blackstone Unveils Government Library Strategy for the Next Ten Years*,

www.culture.gov.uk/Reference_library/Press_notices/archive_2003/dcms17_
2003.htm.

Department for Culture Media and Sport (2003b) *Framework for the Future: libraries,
learning and information in the next decade*,
www.culture.gov.uk/Reference_library/Publications/archive_2003/framework_
future.htm.

Dryer, D. C., Eisbach, C. and Ark, W. S. (1999) At What Cost Pervasive? A social
computing view of mobile computing systems, *IBM Systems Journal*, **38** (4),
652–76.

Emberton, F. (2007) Cost and Culture are Main RFID Challenges, *Library and
Information Gazette*, (2–15 November), p.1.

Evans, C. (2007) Intelligent Retail Business: location based services for mobile
customers, *International Conference on Pervasive Computing and Applications*, IEEE,
354–9.

Garrod, P. (2004) Public Libraries: the changing face of the public library, *Ariadane*,
39, (April), www.ariadne.ac.uk/issue39/public-libraries.

Leavesley, J. (2005) *Talis White Paper: project silkworm,* Talis,
www.talis.com/applications/downloads/white_papers/silkworm_paper_
13_06_2005.pdf.

Library and Information Commission (1998) *Building the New Library Network*,
(9 November), www.mla.gov.uk/resources/assets//N/new_lib_net_11771.pdf.

Miller, P. (2006) *Library 2.0: the challenge of disruptive innovation*, Talis,
www.talis.com/applications/resources/documents/447_Library_2_prf1.pdf.

Miller, P. (2007) What Happens when we MASH the Library? *Ariadne*, **50**,
www.ariadne.ac.uk/issue50/miller/.

OCLC (2005) *Perceptions of Libraries and Information Resources*,
www.oclc.org/reports/2005perceptions.htm.

Pratty, J. (2007) 24 Hour Museum: from past to future, *Ariadne*, **52**, (April),
www.ariadne.ac.uk/issue52/pratty.

Rowlatt, M. (2007) Time to Link up Place and Space, *PanLibus Magazine*, **6**, Talis.

Part 2
Mobile technology for development

7

Harnessing OERs, mobiles and other technologies for teacher education in Africa: the TESSA and DEEP projects

Freda Wolfenden

Introduction

Investment in human resources, in education and health, underpins economic and social development. Many African countries have made substantial progress towards the EFA goal of universal primary education (UPE) over the first years of the 21st century; across sub-Saharan Africa the number of children entering primary school increased by 40% between 1999 and 2005. But 33 million children remain out of school, fewer than two-thirds of the pupils who start grade 1 remain in school until the final grade and low pupil achievement is widespread (UNESCO, 2008). In addition, gender equity in education remains problematic. There is increasing recognition that meeting the EFA goals requires a sustained focus on teachers. The challenges are framed in terms not only of providing sufficient teachers for the rapidly expanding basic education systems in sub-Saharan Africa (an additional four million teachers will be required by 2015) but also of ensuring that both existing and new teachers have received appropriate high-quality training and support to ensure effective primary education and quality classroom practice. Currently a substantial proportion of teachers working in primary schools in the region have received very minimal or no training. These issues are most acute in rural areas, where over half the population lives. Teachers are frequently reluctant to accept such postings, remote from professional development opportunities and where they experience little engagement with professional communities. Teachers in rural areas, particularly in remote regions, are now as likely to be unqualified volunteers as trained teachers (Global Campaign for Education, 2006).

The scale of the need for teacher education demands innovative, scalable, cost-effective solutions for both pre- and in-service programmes. A number of reports and commentators have suggested that the focus of these new models should be the school (Moon 2000; UNESCO, 2005), acknowledging that traditional lengthy, campus-based training is unable to meet the scale of the need, and recognizing the imperative to develop teacher education curricula based on classroom effectiveness.

The immensity of the challenge makes it unlikely that such models can be delivered without exploiting the capabilities of new technologies and their abundance of tools, techniques, resources and mechanisms (Cawthera, 2001; DfID, 2001; Dladla and Moon, 2002; Leach, 2005; Unwin, 2005). Wireless and mobile technologies in particular, with their focus on interactivity and participation, offer perhaps the first opportunity for easy, regular engagement with teachers in communities lacking telecommunications infrastructure. Historically, developing countries have seen low uptake of new technologies, hindered by issues of finance, political and commercial commitment, and infrastructure, but this has not been true of mobile phone growth. Across sub-Saharan Africa an explosion of relatively low-cost devices, mainly but not exclusively the mobile phone, is occurring. Mobile technology is being applied to an increasingly large number of activities. The University of Pretoria, for example, is successfully using mobile phones to provide administrative and academic support to teachers on a range of programmes (Viljoen et al., 2005) while another project in Kenya is using SMS to aid school administration (Farrell and Shafika, 2007, 19).

A number of other influential developments are happening in parallel with the proliferation of mobile devices. The world wide web, for example, is clearly evolving from its early days as a source of information to incorporate the social characteristics seen in hugely successful sites such as Facebook – the 'social web'. Arising from the open source software movement we observe a growing advocacy for open content – the 'open educational resources' movement or OERs (UNESCO, 2007).

This coming together of mobility, social interactivity and OERs offers the potential for creative responses by teacher educators; new practices with extended reach to inspire, enthuse and educate teachers. An educator's 'toolkit', guided by principles of equity of access, seems likely, therefore, to include both mobile technologies and open educational resources. These can work in an integrated way to support new possibilities for communication, new locations for learning that can facilitate new and flexible styles of learning with access to knowledge (Brown, 2005). Production and sharing of educational materials relevant to the cultural context and heritage of each locality is beginning to become viable.

Such technologies are at the heart of programme design and delivery of the two collaborative programmes described here: the Digital Education Enhancement Project (DEEP, www.open.ac.uk/deep) and Teacher Education in sub-Saharan Africa (TESSA, www.tessaafrica.net). Co-ordinated by the OU (Open University, UK) each explores how new technologies can be deployed to support the development of teachers working in communities across sub-Saharan Africa, whether in isolated communities or in the increasingly large slums of the big cities across the continent. DEEP, which ran from 2002 to 2005, focused on the use of a number of mobile devices in urban schools in Egypt and rural schools in South Africa. The TESSA initiative (2005 and ongoing), working across nine countries of sub-Saharan Africa, is engaged in producing open educational resources which can be modified and assembled in ways to suit the local environment. TESSA aims fundamentally to provide the tools and resources to significantly improve existing teacher education programmes and rapidly expand such provision.

There has been considerable advocacy of the importance of new communication technologies for a range of development purposes, economic, social and educational, recognized in Millennium Development Goal priority 8 (www.un.org/millennium.org).

However, there has been some reluctance (mostly at the international donor level) to embrace these new concepts, while basic issues of sanitation, health and so forth remain unmet. Development is not a simple linear process and it seems extremely important to build on the emerging use of such technologies as quickly as possible. There is a need for experimentation and exemplification now so as to provide a sure foundation for expansion as access and connectivity improve.

The DEEP and TESSA projects are contributing to such research. While very different in scale and mode of partnership working, they are underpinned by the following shared principles and characteristics:

1 Teacher learning is conceptualized as being social, jointly constructed with pupil partners and peers.
2 The site of learning is the teacher's own school, ensuring that it is not dislocated from the everyday realities of life and paying attention to teachers' roles within their communities and their ability to act as agents of change, thus avoiding the need for teachers to relocate to colleges, depriving pupils of their teacher.
3 The focus is on the core professional classroom practices of the teacher – extending their understanding of the fundamental principles and accepted theories of effective learning and supporting their 'knowledge in' and 'knowledge of' practice – rather than on the technology.
4 The centrality of language and culture to the learning process is recognized, with content relevant to the needs of the teacher learners (little local content is available, particularly in local languages).
5 Consideration is given to the importance of the integration of pre-service and in-service training to provide career-long professional development.
6 A blended approach is used within the programmes, using a mixture of text and new and older technologies.
7 Collaborative networks are supported among both teacher educators and teachers.

The Digital Education Enhancement Project (DEEP)

Conventional orthodoxies around ICT and schools frequently focus on the provision of networked suites of computers and the development of ICT skills in both pupils and teachers. This project challenged these orthodoxies by exploring how small numbers of innovative 'cutting edge' mobile devices could support teachers' professional development in resource-starved schools.

Between 2002 and 2005 the DEEP project engaged with 50 teachers across primary schools serving disadvantaged communities in Egypt and South Africa, in partnership with local institutions (Leach, 2005). In the first phase teachers in the project undertook and evaluated a sequence of curriculum-focused classroom activities with their pupils, using a range of new technologies; handheld computers, laptops, cameras, projectors, scanners and printers offered flexible opportunities for professional activity – at school and at home, on field trips and at special events. Supporting resources included a range of digital materials (video clips, case studies, lesson plans), print materials and a project website with a discussion area for project participants. Many of the teachers had no prior experience with new technologies. The activities introduced teachers to a wide range of new teaching approaches and had two interrelated aims:

- the development of the teachers' professional knowledge
- improvements in the teachers' classroom practices.

Teachers in both countries very quickly began to use the technologies for a range of personal, professional and pedagogic purposes, experimenting, modelling and then generalizing. This challenging process was hugely powerful in developing their confidence. During the project teachers grew significantly in personal and professional confidence and motivation – far more rapidly than expected. Project evaluation revealed extensive use of the technologies to enhance teachers' professional knowledge and capability in four distinct areas:

- extending their subject knowledge
- enabling more efficient planning and preparation for teaching
- extending the range of their pedagogic practices
- supporting new forms of teacher-to-teacher interaction (Leach et al., 2005).

Teachers' subject knowledge represents an essential component of effective teaching. Crucially, in remote rural, information-deprived communities, this aspect of professional knowledge was considered by the project teachers to have been the most improved by participation in the project. Teachers within the project found authentic uses for the new technologies. The tools, and their uses, became embedded within their communities and formed part of a shared professional knowledge.

Teacher Education in sub-Saharan Africa (TESSA)

TESSA is focused on harnessing new technologies to support improvements in access and quality of teacher education. Rapid expansion of pre-service training and putting in place even the most rudimentary professional development programme for the millions of unqualified teachers requires planning and provision on a scale hitherto rarely contemplated. During the year following launch of the TESSA website almost half a million teachers who registered on programmes at partner institutions will have engaged with TESSA study materials.

TESSA exploits two recent developments: the philosophy of OERs – open content which is freely available for download, adaptation and mixing with other materials – and the interactive sharing technologies of Web 2.0. Through alignment of their capabilities TESSA is able to combine the efficiencies of scale achieved by an international effort with meeting local needs; TESSA seeks to maintain international standards while being sensitive to local cultures and conditions.

TESSA is an international consortium of 18 organizations: 13 higher education institutions from nine countries in sub-Saharan Africa (Ghana, Kenya, Nigeria, Rwanda, South Africa, Sudan, Tanzania, Uganda and Zambia) in partnership with the Open University (UK), BBC World Service Trust, Commonwealth of Learning, the African Virtual University and the South African Institute for Distance Education. Through a series of workshops and other activities, the consortium has worked with over 100 academics across sub-Saharan Africa to produce a large bank of original OER, in both text and audio format, building on local knowledge, materials and approaches. These materials are designed to support teachers' learning within their own classroom (school-integrated activities) offering innovative practices where they can have an immediate effect. There is a strong focus on the basics of the curriculum: literacy, numeracy, science, and social and personal education.

In parallel with development of materials, four interlinked strands of activity have taken place. It is pertinent to mention two here. The first is devising appropriate methods of technical delivery for the materials. Second, the consortium has put considerable effort and resources into working with institutions to devise strategies and practices for implementation of delivery and use of the materials. In the emergent world of OERs, take-up has thus far often been disappointing (Atkins et al., 2007). Given this experience TESSA activities have focused on take-up issues; adaptation of the resources for different environments, the development of 'learning pathways' through the materials and the best ways of supporting learners are being identified and explored. Each TESSA partner institution contributed to the overall strategy of the initiative but there was differentiated involvement in the concurrent strands of activity: technical (modes of delivery), research, pedagogic (design of materials), and take-up (integration into courses). Strands of activity are shown in Figure 7.1.

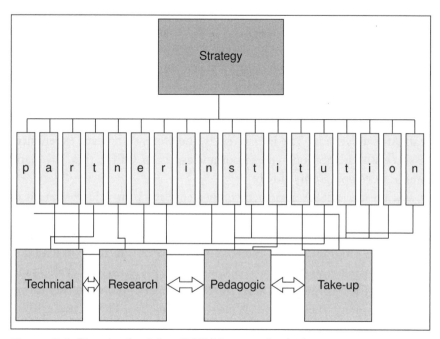

Figure 7.1 Strands of activity of TESSA partner institutions

TESSA OER content development to date has focused primarily on the creation of hundreds of text-based study units supported with short audio clips; dramas; documentaries; and teacher audio diaries. The study units have been developed in a highly structured template framework, each being designed to possess integrity and a high degree of autonomy. Centred on three learning outcomes for the teacher, each study unit comprises three activities, three case studies, a linking narrative and a maximum of six accompanying resources to support and extend the activities and case studies. Teacher learning is interwoven throughout the unit, up to and including the final activity.

Recognizing the extensive role that language, culture and mode of delivery have in mediating teaching and learning (Gaskell, 2007), the internal structure of the study unit template was designed to allow adaptation for different environments, or localization. *Activities* are written to be appropriate across a range of contexts, whereas *case studies* are specially selected or modified to reflect local conditions. Rather than taking the approach of mass production of identical artefacts, the TESSA model is perhaps closer to the manufacture of the thousands of Chinese soldiers in the Terracotta Army 2000 years ago, where each soldier has unique features but the production process was highly organized so as to maximize efficiency. Using this flexible template and working with academics from consortium institutions, TESSA has initially developed the study units in nine local country versions, including versions in four languages – Arabic, English, French and Kiswahili – and in a generic 'pan-African' version. The initiative has, therefore, significant experiences in successful adaptation – an important aspect of OERs, that, on many sites, is developing only slowly.

Within the TESSA approach teacher educators provide mediation of the materials for their students' building courses with attendant support and assessment around the materials, or incorporating them into existing courses and programmes. At the Kigali Institute of Education in Rwanda, TESSA materials form part of a continuing professional development programme for primary teachers; the Professional Diploma in Mentoring at the University of Education, Winneba, Ghana uses TESSA materials as a core component; the University of Fort Hare in South Africa has integrated TESSA materials into its BEd Primary programme. Initial feedback from the first programmes in Nigeria and Sudan to use the materials with teachers was highly encouraging, noting enhanced teaching and learning in classrooms and evidence of an extension in teachers' repertoires and self-confidence.

Two further significant features distinguish TESSA from many OER projects concerned with building repositories of online materials (Merlot is an example: www.merlot.org). First, TESSA is not focused exclusively on the development of materials for delivery within online courses. Across the countries in which TESSA is operating, a set of common factors coexist that limit access to use of online materials: lack of a reliable supply of electricity, deficient infrastructures and extreme high costs for internet access (*Economist*, 2007). The response in TESSA has been to develop a 'document transfer engine' within the TESSA website which transforms original text files into a variety of formats: web pages, MS Word format for educators to download and amend, and pdfs for printing. Institutional course developers are able to print materials in an attractively designed format as self-standing booklets or for easy integration with existing materials for students. Depending on the local environment, teachers engage with the materials in one of these different formats; at present the majority encounter them in printed booklet format, with the audio materials being used as teaching materials within tutorials and seminars.

Second, TESSA is not limited to making available new pedagogic materials, as in the MIT OpenCourseWare initiative (www.ocw.mit.edu) for example, but is equally concerned with creating the conditions in which even better ideas and materials can be developed and shared. Alongside multilingual forums, supporting communities of teacher educators, at both country and regional level, is an interactive tool, TESSAShare. TESSAShare enables users to create new materials in the TESSA template, adapt existing materials, and then submit them, as a collection, to the TESSA resource bank Other materials, in a wide variety of file formats, are also accepted. Submitted content is checked to ensure that it does not infringe any legal provisions. Peer assessment via a ratings and comments functionality provides further quality assurance. This opening up of opportunities for users to create and publish their own content, the principle of Web 2.0, is not the dominant discourse in the OER movement (dos Santos et al., 2007). In TESSA it is considered intrinsic to the notions of openness. There is an attempt to balance expertly written, robustly structured and highly quality-assured material with tools to enable educators to join the ranks of the Web 2.0 amateur production paradigm.

Next steps

It is anticipated that the immediate future will see connectivity spreading across the region, mobile devices becoming ever more available and sophisticated, and greater visibility of the OER movement as witnessed in the launch of the Cape Town Declaration (www.capetowndeclaration.org). In this environment the focus of the TESSA initiative moves towards exploring how these different tools can best be aligned within an educational model to support teacher development. The nature of the content and of the conditions in which many teachers are working makes it highly likely that we will see the adoption of hybrid modes of interaction, varying according to availability of technologies, cultural characteristics and needs of the teachers. To develop these effectively it will be increasingly necessary to refine and develop research models. Current scoping activity within TESSA embraces these strands:

- exploring integration of the TESSA materials into institutional virtual learning environments and access to these environments
- use of mobile devices to access specific aspects of the TESSA content preserving pedagogic structure while presenting content on a small screen
- development of audio materials – the availability and ease of use of voice on mobile devices suggest that there are huge opportunities for considering expanding its use to deliver educational experiences (Lee and Chan, 2007)
- understanding more deeply how collaboration can be fostered at both institutional and individual level within these virtual spaces
- widening participation through increasing the 'push' of local content from local people (UNESCO, 2007).

The aspiration is to integrate key understandings of teachers' effective use of mobile technologies with localized OER materials so as to support a range of locally owned, large-scale teacher education programmes. But ultimately, the value of these new technologies in enhancing professional learning will only be judged by the value they add for teachers on the programmes, both current and potential, by creating improvements in their classroom practices and increased levels of participation and achievement on the part of their pupils.

References

Atkins D. E., Brown, J. E. and Hammond A. L. (2007) *A Review of the Open Educational Resources (OER) Movement: achievement, challenges and new opportunities*, report to the William and Flora Hewlett Foundation.

Brown, T. (2005) Towards a Model for M-Learning in Africa, *International Journal of E-Learning*, 4 (3), 299–315.

Cawthera, A. (2001) *Computers in Secondary Schools in Developing Countries: costs and other issues*, Department for International Development.

DfID (Department for International Development) (2001) *Imfundo: partnership of IT in education inception report*, DfID

Dladla, N. and Moon, R. E. (2002) Challenging the Assumptions about Teacher Education and Training in Sub-Saharan Africa: a new role for open learning and ICT, *Pan-Commonwealth Forum on Open Learning*, Durban, South Africa, www.open.ac.uk/deep/Public/web/publications/core.html.

Dos Santos, A. I., McAndrew, A. and Godwin, S. (2007) The Discourses of OERs: how flat is this world? In *Proceedings of OpenEducation 2007; Localising and Learning*, Logan, UT, USA.

Economist (2007) *The Digital Gap*, (20 October), p.72.

Farrell, G. and Shafika, I. (2007) *Survey of ICT and Education in Africa: a summary report, based on 53 country surveys*, Washington, DC, infoDev/World Bank.

Gaskell, A. (2007) Open and Distance Learning on the Move: mobile learning, crossing borders, rethinking roles, *Open Learning*, **22** (3), 197–200.

Global Campaign for Education (2006) *Teachers for All: what governments and donors should do*, policy briefing, www.campaignforeducation.org.

Leach, J. (2005) Do New Information and Communication Technologies Have a Role to Play in Achieving Quality Professional Development for Teachers in the Global South? *The Curriculum Journal*, **16** (3), 293–329.

Leach, J. with Ahmed, A., Makalima, S. and Power, T. (2005) *DEEP Impact: an investigation of the use of information and communication technologies for teacher education in the global south*, Department for International Development, Researching the Issues, **58**.

Lee, M. J. W. and Chan, A. (2007) Pervasive, Lifestyle-integrated Mobile Learning for Distance Learners: and analysis and unexpected results from a podcasting study, *Open Learning*, **22** (3), 201–18.

Moon, R. E. (2000) The Open Learning Environment: a new paradigm for international developments in teacher education. In *The Routledge International Companion of Education*, Moon, B., Brown, S. and Ben Peretz, M. (eds), Routledge

UNESCO (2005) *EFA Global Monitoring Report 2005, The Quality Imperative.*

UNESCO (2007) *OECD Study of OER: Forum Report.*

UNESCO (2008) *EFA Global Monitoring Report 2008: Education for All by 2015. Will we make it?*

Unwin, T. (2005) Towards a Framework for the Use of ICT in Teacher Training in Africa, *Open Learning*, **20** (2), 113–29.

Viljoen, J. M., Du Preez, C. and Cook, A. (2005) The Case for Using SMS Technologies to Support Distance Education Students in South Africa: conversations, *Perspectives in Education*, 23 (40), 115–22.

Note

TESSA is funded by the Allan and Nesta Ferguson Charitable Trust and the William and Flora Hewlett Foundation.

DEEP was funded by the UK Department for International Development (DfID).

8

Libraries and mobile phones in Southern Africa: possible applications at the University of South Africa Library

Buhle Mbambo-Thata

Introduction

The convergence of computing and telecommunication technology facilitates transfer of data, text, images and voice over the same lines. Such developments have not been limited to fixed-line telecommunications but have also spread to mobile telephones. Data so transferred may be for social, business or educational uses and mobile devices have facilitated communication in ways unimaginable in the late 1990s. The technology has created opportunity and possibilities for individuals and organizations; what gets done with the technology is left for organizations to explore.

In Southern Africa the growth in mobile phone use has created opportunities for business transactions and business and social spaces have converged because of the increased usability of mobile phones. This same convergence creates a potential in education. Could higher education use similar technology to advance its goals? Could libraries, in particular, use mobile technology to reach distance learners?

Advances in mobile phone usage in Southern Africa

According to a report by International Telecommunications Union (ITU, 2006), growth in Africa's mobile phone use averaged 60% in the six years between 1998 and 2004. By 2004 there were 76 million mobile phone users in Africa and this growth has enabled Africa to access modern telecommunications. Table 8.1 illustrates the increase in mobile phone use in Southern Africa between 1998 and 2004. In most countries in Africa the increase exceeded 1000% in those years. It is estimated that there were over 96 million mobile phone users in Southern Africa in 2007 (Ford and Batchelor, 2007).

Table 8.1 Mobile telephones per country in Southern Africa

Country	Mobile phone density 1998	Mobile phone density 2004
Angola	2,000	25,800
Botswana	–	20,000
Namibia	3,500	82,000
South Africa	535,000	7,000,000
Tanzania	3,500	180,000
Zimbabwe	3,500	340,000

Source: (Ashurst, 2001)

Ford and Batchelor (2007) state that the technology itself has grown in sophistication. The process of sending a text message from a mobile phone has become not merely a telecommunication but the interaction of a computer, a server and a telecommunications process. It is through this convergence that mobile technology is opening up possibilities in Africa. The mobile phone has become a computing device, within the reach of most individuals in both remote and urban areas.

An emerging trend in Southern Africa is the ubiquity of mobile phones among students (Viljoen et al., 2005). This growing trend has been driven by demand, reforms in the telecommunication sector and ease of acquisition (Adomi, 2006). While an increasing number of students own mobile phones, Adomi also found in his study that students shared mobile phones: 'The majority of students used phones that belonged to relatives and friends' (Adomi, 2006, 4). The shareability of the device in itself widens access.

Another emerging trend in parts of Africa is mobile phone kiosks. Such facilities enable individuals, who may not own mobile phones, to purchase time slots. They can perform similar functions at the kiosk to those they would carry out on a phone of their own. However, kiosks have limited flexibility in that only the sender can initiate conversation or contact, and there is no possibility to receive calls or messages at random. In the case of students, for instance, they can only be online when they have hired the time slot; only they can initiate the communication. Therefore, anyone needing to contact a student cannot have the just-in-time engagement which they would have if the student owned a mobile phone.

What has made these developments possible? Deregulation of telecommunications in Southern Africa has certainly contributed. It has led to competition among service providers, and subsequently to reductions in the cost of telephone communication. Some of the specific developments which have led to expansion of access to telecommunications are described below.

Deregulation of telecommunication

Mobile phone access has far surpassed access to land lines in Africa (Adomi, 2006; Viljoen, et al., 2005). The advent of competition in most countries of the world has meant that there is more than one mobile phone company operating in the countries of Southern Africa (Mutula, 2006) and deregulation of telecommunications has opened up opportunities for many companies to provide telecommunications services. As a result, individuals can acquire mobile phone lines and thus avoid dependency on fixed lines. Penetration of fixed lines in Africa is a mere 0.3% (Adomi, 2006), as compared to 3% for mobile lines.

The ease of licensing creates several advantages for the user. First, it has made hand-held communication devices easily available in Africa. Second, in most countries there is more than one service provider, creating competition for customers and resulting in competitive pricing (Mutula, 2006).

Affordability

Relatively speaking, hand-held devices have become comparatively cheap, depending on what one buys. In South Africa they range from R400 for a basic handset that communicates text and voice, to R3000 for a handset that facilitates access to the world wide web. As communication devices become more available, prices will become further reduced.

Opportunity and potential uses in higher education

Mobile phone ubiquity presents several opportunities for reaching students, both for learning and for just-in-time access to information and communication.

Just-in-time communication

As indicated above, the availability and affordability of hand-held devices facilitates student access to mobile phones. Never before has there been an opportunity for just-in-time communication with students. Wherever there is a network anyone with a mobile phone is reachable; students and staff can be reached immediately. For distance education, this provides the ability to reach students wherever they are.

Appropriate content

Appropriate content is central to using mobile technologies in higher education, and in libraries in particular. What content can be piped down these devices? Libraries now have the facility to reach readers just in time with announcements and with information resources. Two distinct possibilities for libraries are SMS content and web-based content, including e-mail and articles. Research from the United States and the United Kingdom describes innovative use of hand-held devices in libraries (Balas 2006), including SMS announcements to clients and access to the OPAC and library web pages.

Social space and educational space

Web 2.0 and Library 2.0 have collapsed learning space and social space into multi-use space. Computers and mobile phones are no longer entirely different. Learning and play happen on both the computer and the mobile phone. There is an opportunity for learning to happen in the student's multitasking space.

Students who are technology enabled

The average student entering university is more technology enabled now than in the late 1990s. Most have e-mail accounts and mobile phones. Some have BlackBerry phones and Personal Digital Assistants (PDAs). Most have accounts on Facebook, and other social networking sites such as Bebo and MySpace. This offers opportunities to provide such students with content that is technology based, as their modus operandi is online.

Reaching remote students

Mobile phone technology enables us to reach remote students. In open and distance learning, students living in different geographical locations are no longer an issue. Mobile technology will enable us to reach on-the-move students, making them realize that the library can be part of their everyday learning life wherever they are located.

Prevailing use of mobile learning devices in libraries

Several universities in the West are using mobile phones in their libraries (Balas, 2006). There are also libraries which have policies prohibiting use of mobile phones in the library. Many libraries have notices that ask patrons to switch off their mobile phones while in the library (Lever and Katz, 2007). In a wide-ranging survey undertaken in the United States in 2005–6, Lever and Katz (2007) found that the majority of libraries surveyed had policies prohibiting mobile phone use. However, there is a growing trend towards prohibiting conversation on mobile phones within libraries, while encouraging text-based services to the mobile phones of library clients (Balas, 2006). Clients will thus be encouraged to use their phones in silent mode while in the library.

In the United Kingdom mobile technologies have been used for learning in the health sector (Walton et al., 2005). Walton et al. found that most medical professionals preferred to use PDAs, using them largely for accessing the internet. However, they indicated that access to university learning resources, including libraries, would be desirable. Medical students indicated that access to e-resources would be desirable.

In the United States use of mobile devices, particularly hand-held devices, is more frequent in university libraries. At Ball State University a project was implemented in 2004 to configure the pages of Ball State University's website to fit the screens of PDAs, BlackBerrys and mobile phones. The services that the library provided through mobile service were:

- general library information (opening hours, policies, departments and 'contact us' feature to which e-mails could be sent)
- connection to a list of journal holdings, with links where online subscription to an e-journal existed
- catalogue access through CardCat, with an interface enabling mobile users 'to search . . . display . . . and navigate among titles in the results' (West, Hafner and Faust, 2006, 105).

South Eastern Louisiana University uses SMS for a reference service. Students and staff send queries to a mobile phone number in the library (Sims Library, n.d.) This is part of the 'Ask a librarian service' and is open to students and staff of South Eastern Louisiana University. Reference librarians take turns to respond to queries.

In Nigeria, Adomi (2006) studied student use of mobile phones. While the students used their mobile phones for business and social communication, none of them accessed library services through their mobiles. Case study-based articles on usage of mobile devices in libraries in Southern Africa could not be found in the literature; however, Mutula (2006) indicated the possibility of mobile phone use in libraries. Since his article pre-dates much of the development in mobile phone technology, his predictions are limited to services that would have been based on voice and text. The article also indicates that availability of broadband in Southern Africa provided the infrastructure for expansion of the volume and type of data transferred on mobile phones. Two articles on studies of the use of mobile phone devices in education in South Africa were identified. Ford and Batchelor (2007) discuss an experiment on encouraging interactive learning through mobile phones in high schools. Viljoen et al., 2005) focus on the use of SMS to reach distance learning students. Both of these articles report on pilot implementations and are summative evaluations of large-scale projects. However, they provide useful indicators of the possibility of mobile phone applications in education in South Africa. However, neither of these studies includes applications in libraries.

The possibilities for the use and application of mobile phones in libraries in Southern Africa are many. They range from SMS communication with clients, through announcements, reference inquiries, catalogues and library pages, to mobile technology screens. The challenges, however, are many, ranging from the technical to the social and economic.

Challenges

A number of challenges have been identified which could deter the use of mobile phones in libraries in Southern Africa.

Library etiquette

All over the world, libraries are quiet places, traditionally renowned for providing space for quiet study. Devices, voices and activities that interfere with this are traditionally discouraged or banned. Mobile phones are perceived as nuisances in libraries. Could it be that librarians who do not see beyond the nuisance may fail to see the value of reaching clients with information just in time? Could it be that the technology convergence that has collapsed social space and learning space together, merged computer and phone and encouraged multitasking, will draw libraries away from this view, to see opportunity in this new, converged space?

Technical challenges
Financial prohibitions

In many parts of Africa R400 is a month's wage. A mobile handset is therefore not affordable to some students. Further, the cost of establishing the infrastructure for the service within a university could be prohibitive to underfunded universities.

Network coverage

While most countries may have more than one subscriber network, coverage may not reach all parts of a country, especially in rural areas. The service would therefore not be available to all clients.

Lack of knowledge

It may also be that technical skills relating to mobile services are not available in some university libraries. Thus, developing such services could be hindered by lack of skills.

Size of screen

Relatively cheap mobile phones have small display screens. The average screen is 120–240 pixels. This makes it difficult to display web pages, for example. Most students can only afford the cheap devices.

Limited memory

Memory on most mobile phones is limited, so only limited amounts of data can be stored. This makes it impossible to download and display graphics-intensive web pages, photographs, audio files and large texts.

Application at UNISA

The University of South Africa is an open and distance learning institute with about 250,000 registered students. The students receive their material on the world wide web via a learning portal called MyUnisa, by post and courier service or through regional services. The UNISA library uses the same services to send material to its clients. Two developments have galvanized the library to look for other ways of reaching clients, wherever they are. One was the result of the Commonwealth of Learning quality audit in 2007, which recommended that the library consider increasing service to remote learners rather than focusing on walk-in clients. The second was the university's drive to develop the Open and Distance Learning model that focuses on enhanced learner support. The library has thus sought solutions to supporting learners with information in ways that are within their reach.

The UNISA library has set itself a target to deliver two types of service to its user community: short message service (SMS) and the Online Public Access Catalogue (OPAC). Preparatory work has been done on setting up the service. The service provision via SMS is in the early stages of implementation. At a later date and at future conferences, more evaluative information will be available.

The SMS facility

The general framework is for the service to be provided to students and staff from UNISA. The library will be able to send bulk SMS and receive SMS from students. Raubenheimer (2007) indicates that the SMS facilities will include:

- notices regarding overdue items, item ready for pick-up, outstanding debts, etc.
- recall notices
- messages regarding withholding of examination results by the library

- urgent messages regarding changed service hours, disruption/unavailability of services, changed training schedules, etc.
- messages regarding lost items found in the library
- notification that search requests are ready
- reminders relating to training sessions, annual renewal of items issued to staff, etc.
- confirmation that information requests, reservation of a training session or study carrel have been received or that an appointment has been scheduled
- general messages regarding new books, special events, new databases, new services, availability of user documentation, availability of user support services, etc.

The library will also receive the following messages from its clients:

- requests for books, journal articles, etc.
- requests for the renewal of items
- requests for the cancellation of a requested item (hold), booked study card, reservation for training, etc.
- requests to use another university library
- requests to be registered as a supplementary member
- requests to book a study carrel
- requests for information searches, bibliographies, etc.
- requests for an appointment with a subject librarian or other information specialist
- requests for general information regarding services, payment of services, contact persons, where to find information
- general queries relating to issued items, outstanding debt, mailed items, etc.
- requests to change personal information, e.g. name, address, e-mail, telephone number
- queries or requests for assistance regarding pin numbers, inability to access electronic databases and information resources, inability to use the available electronic services: renewal of items, requesting of items, printing of full-text articles, etc.
- requests to terminate the use of a study carrel.

The SMS facility will not be limited to tasks listed in the previous section, and the type of services provided could be expanded, enhanced, or even reduced, according to client needs. The service will be run from the library's workflow management system LIBFLOW. Sending SMS will eliminate the need to manually print out notices and mail them to clients. Further, it will provide an alternative to e-mail alerting of clients.

OPAC

The second service the library will deliver is web service to its clients. The library has already acquired AirPAC from Innovative Interfaces at a cost of between $10,000 and $15,000. Erasmus (2008) states that the services will be:

> an additional OPAC solution for clients using alternative access technology such as cell phones or PDA (palm devices) with wireless capability. Clients will be able to search the catalogue and retrieve item information related to location, shelf number, real-time status and availability. Clients will be allowed to request an item, view loan record, renew items, check due dates for items, fines information and personal information. (p.1)

Conclusion

The availability of mobile phones in Southern Africa creates a potential to reach remote students and staff and provides the opportunity to reach clients just in time with library information. While some challenges have been identified, they can be overcome as there are examples of how they have been solved elsewhere. The cost of a mobile phone library service for the minority of students and for underfunded universities may be prohibitive. However, for institutions like UNISA with a client base that occupies the global village and in remote parts of South Africa that may not have any fixed-line telecommunications, the ability to communicate with clients via SMS and web-based internet technology opens significant opportunities to communicate with clients. While UNISA library is only starting with this service, the framework laid by the university to focus on reaching remote students and enhancing support to learners wherever they are, provides the foundation for success.

References

Adomi, E. A. (2006) Mobile Phone Usage Patterns of Library and Information Science Students at Delta State University, Abraka, Nigeria, *Electronic Journal of Academic Librarianship and Special Librarianship*, 1 (1), 1–10.

Ashurst, M. (2001) Africa's Cell Phone Boom, *Newsweek*, (27 August), 14–18.

Balas, J. L. (2006) What's in Their Pocket? *Mobile Electronics, Computers in Libraries*, 26 (4), (April), 32–4.

Erasmus, A. (2008) Air Pac Usage at UNISA (Internal working documents).

Ford, M. and Batchelor, J. (2007) From Zero to Hero – is Mobile Phone a Viable Learning Tool for Africa? *Third International Conference on Social and Organisational Informatics and Cybernetics: SOIL 2007 Orlando, USA, 12 July 2007*.

ITU Report (2006) *What is the State of ICT Access Around the World?*, www,itu.int/ITU-D/icteye/Reporting.

Lever, M. L. and Katz, J. E. (2007) Cell Phone in Campus Libraries: an analysis of policy responses to an invasive mobile technology, *Information Processing and Management*, 43, 1133–9.

Mutula, M. Stephen (2006) The Cellular Phone Economy in the SADC Countries: implications for libraries, *On Line Information Review*, 6 (2), 79–81.

Raubenheimer, J. (2007) *Department of Library Service SMS Requirements*. Internal working document.

Sims Library (n.d.) Text a Librarian, www2.selu.edu/Library/ServicesDept/referenc/textalibrarian.html.

Viljoen, J. M., Du Preez, C. and Cook, A. (2005) The Case for Using SMS Technologies to Support Distance Education in South Africa, *Perspectives in Education*, 23 (4), 115–22.

Walton, G., Child, S. and Blenkisopp, E. (2005) Using Mobile Technologies to Give Health Students Access to Learning Resources in the UK Community, *Health Information and Libraries Journal*, 22 (9), 51–65.

West, M. A., Hafner, A. W. and Faust, B. D. (2006) Expanding Access to Library Collections and Services Using Small Screen Devices, *Information Technology and Libraries*, (June), 103–7.

9

Mobile information access for community-based health workers in developing countries

Adesina Iluyemi

Introduction

A case study of community health workers and m-learning will be presented in this chapter to illustrate the issues for its adoption by health workers in developing countries. M-learning is the delivery of e-learning regardless of the time and space orientation of the learners. That is, it involves technology such as mobile/wireless information and communication technologies (ICTs), end-users (learners, students and workers), organization (developing and packaging the learning applications) and environment (context where learning and application development take place). Capturing this global 'meaning' of m-learning could provide an understanding of how the potential benefits of m-learning can be made available to the growing populations of developing countries. As widely reported, mobile ICTs provide the most appropriate means of bridging the 'digital' and 'information' divides in these parts of the globe. These regions are also the focus of global and national developmental initiatives such as healthcare. Poor health is a major impediment to economic and social development in developing countries and, not surprisingly, three out of the eight Millennium Development Goals (MDGs) are focused on tackling major health problems in these regions. Two or three other MDGs are also indirectly dependent on achieving good population health. In parallel with this global initiative is the global campaign to tackle the shortage of health workers in developing countries such as Africa. Africa is reported to have 10% of the world's population but bears 25% of the global disease burden, managed by only 3% of the global health workforce. A particular focus of this campaign is building health workers' capacity through ICT-enabled education and learning so as to empower them to effectively help reduce the level of disease. From the foregoing, it could be argued that m-learning has a great role to play toward this end.

What is health m-learning?

M-learning is defined simply as learning on the move and is thus referred to as nomadic learning (Kakihara and Sørensen, 2004). M-learning can also be seen as a marriage between e-learning and mobile computing (Han et al., 2004). It has been estimated that 80% of learning takes place in informal environments such as 'on the job' and 'on the move' (Kakihara and Sørensen, 2004). Health professionals are always 'on the job' or 'on the move' either in the hospital or clinic building or outside in community or peripatetic settings (Bergqvist and Dahlberg, 1999). The ability of health professionals to acquire skills and knowledge through m-learning across time and space has been described in the medical literature as 'distributed learning' (Parikh and Lazowska, 2006). This implies that learning can be provided to health professionals according to their mobility status. The mobility status of health professionals can be described and understood through the 'travelling', 'visiting', and 'wandering' constructs of mobile working (Gladwin et al., 2003). A health professional travelling from home to hospital can read on the bus or train to catch up on new medical developments through m-learning. 'Visiting' and 'wandering' could mean the same health professional during a ward round in the hospital and in home-based care respectively accessing health knowledge through mobile internet. In addition, the knowledge-intensive nature of health practice demands that information is available at the point of care and in emergency situations (Friedman, 2003). These situations can be used to argue for the importance of usability considerations in designing appropriate and user-friendly artefacts for different groups of health professionals having regard for their mobility status (Anand and Bärnighausen, 2007).

The use of m-learning to support the educational and clinical needs of health professionals could provide a means for maintaining and improving their health knowledge through repetition and reinforcement via ubiquitous and portable learning materials (Anand and Bärnighausen, 2007; WHO, 2006).

The context of the different health environments where working and learning by healthcare workers takes place is complex and varied and depends on the types of health professionals and their geographical location (Gladwin et al., 2003; Antrobus, 1997). The different contexts of the healthcare setting, together with the types and availability of mobile devices, affect the nature and content of m-learning applications that can be provided (Drucker, 1999; Pakenham-Walsh et al., 1997). Mobile devices that are used in healthcare include PDAs, mobile phones, smartphones, laptops, tablet PCs and MP3 players (Drury, 2005; Zachariah et al., 2006). The different contexts for the use of these devices range from clinic to hospital to community setting. In effect, the use of m-learning to support health professionals' education and practice is becoming embedded in the healthcare system.

Use of mobile computing devices by health professionals to access health information at the point of care is on the increase, especially in emergency health services (Castells, 2000). M-learning by health professionals could be taken to include the provision of health information and knowledge in their different working environments. Health information and knowledge could be provided through electronic health records (EHR), clinical decision-support software (CDSS), evidence-based medicine (EBM) guidelines, drug directories or formularies, journal articles, clinical handbooks and textbooks (Byrne, 2005; Lyytinen and Yoo, 2002; Wiredu, 2005).

Historically, m-learning has been about downloading software to hand-held computers in asynchronous mode; however, with the advent of mobile internet and wireless technologies, real-time updating of learning materials can be achieved (Nilsson and Hertzum, 2005). A notable example of this approach is the National Library of Health (NLM) initiative to make its vast PubMed database available through real-time and ad hoc mobile connections (Wiredu, 2005; Kuutti, 1996). Real-time access to health information through mobile computers has been presented as being relevant to critical healthcare (Nilsson and Hertzum, 2005).

The use of mobile technologies for communication, collaboration and co-ordination of activities is well developed in the domain of business and commerce, mostly in developed countries. These technologies have been used to support mobile workers in organizational processes and workflow even when away from their physical workplaces (Kakihara and Sørensen, 2004). The same trend has also been witnessed in the healthcare sectors of these countries, where highly mobile health workers are provided with mobile devices to facilitate access to evidence-based medical knowledge and enterprise databases (Han et al., 2004). This recent surge in the use of mobile technologies in healthcare is mostly in the developed world and there has been little use of mobile technologies such as Personal Digital Assistants (PDAs) or smartphones in less-developed countries (LDCs).

Information system (IS) studies on mobile work have focused mostly on technology usability and reliability and little work has been done on the mobile workers themselves, despite the fact that workers are social beings in regular interaction with their immediate and remote communities (Bergqvist and Dahlberg, 1999). This type of research should be considered as being more important in developing countries, where the itinerant and environmental conditions for mobile working are not comparable with those of the developed world (Parikh and Lazowska, 2006).

Hence, this chapter will present the case of community health workers in a developing country using PDAs networked with a GSM/GPRS Mobile Learning (m-learning) System (MLS) to give extra impetus to the processes of a decentralized health organization. Specifically, it will present how the ad hoc mobile health information system is enabling the co-ordination and co-operation of distributed, remote and peripheral health workers with the health organization.

CASE STUDY

The case study is based on a public health organization in a less-developed country (LDC) making use of mobile technology to build an m-learning system. The project involves providing access to health information and continuing medical education (CME) (medical e-learning materials), and uses hand-held computers, also known as PDAs, as end-user devices. These are connected via the GSM/GPRS cellular telephone network. The mobile health information system provides a two-way communication and data exchange network.

The supervising agents of the health organization recognize that access to accurate and timely information and the ability to collect, analyse, and use reliable data are vital to enable health workers to provide cost-efficient and effective healthcare to the population. The health organization's processes are enabled through a distributed health system. The health delivery model is a District Health System (DHS), a decentralized model of healthcare, comprising a hierarchical relationship between health sub-district, district and national levels.

Health information system

The system supports routine health data collection by community health workers (CHWs) at the lower level of the DHS through the use of PDAs, working either in the field or at health centres. The data are transmitted through the mobile network to a server located at the national level for data collation and analysis. In return, relevant local-content health information and CME are provided to the health workers. In future, it is hoped that the network will provide a personalized mobile e-mail system for communication between workers and with the administrators or managerial staff in the health system.

The end-user technologies used are Palm OS PDAs, 'Jacks', and a regional server located at the district health centre, which is in turn connected to a central server located in the capital city. The Jacks are wall-mounted portable, wireless, temporary servers that carry SIM cards and are located in the rural or community health centres (CHCs). The Jacks and the PDAs are powered by rechargeable batteries replenished by low-cost solar chargers. Data transmission through the network is made possible through File Transfer Protocol (FTP) and e-mails. The health workers distributed across the network use the connected PDAs to receive medical e-learning materials.

Typical use of the system by CHWs

A typical CHW working in a health centre has to move around a 5 km radius to see and attend to patients in their homes. Daily activity begins in the health centre with a CHW synchronizing his or her (mostly her) PDA with the wall-mounted Jack through a wireless infrared connection. The CHW will collect and enter patients' and epidemiological data on forms loaded on the PDA. On completion of daily activities or tasks, the CHW will return to the health centre to synchronize the PDA with the DHMIS (District Health Management Information System) via the Jack. The data collected will be uploaded to the Jack and transmitted through the wireless network to the servers. Medical e-learning materials that are customized to the CHWs' learning needs are downloaded to the PDAs during the synchronization. The health workers then read and study the materials at home after their daily tasks.

The rest of this chapter will define the status, roles and activities of CHWs and their relationship with the DHS and DHMIS. The relationship of the CHWs to the wireless or mobile information system will be explored through issues identified in the literature. The findings will then be used to identify the physical and social contexts that affect the activities of the CHWs as described above in the case study.

Community health workers and the health system in LDCs

CHWs are health workers who are selected and trained to work in the communities in which they live (Friedman, 2003). They carry out organizational tasks such as home-based patient care, communication within communities, improving the health environment, supporting health programmes such as large-scale immunizations, and diagnosis and/or treatment of diseases such as pneumonia, TB, HIV/AIDS, malaria, and maternal and childhood diseases. The importance of CHWs in health service delivery is underlined by the fact that they constitute about one-third of the health workforce (Anand and Bärnighausen, 2007), but this ratio may be higher in developing countries.

The World Health Organization (WHO) has recommended the use of mobile telecommunication technologies to support CHWs in order to improve health outcomes and to facilitate efficient logistical service delivery (WHO, 2006). In making the case for the strengthening of the health system in order to achieve the Millennium Development Goals (MDGs), the WHO has emphasized the importance of health information systems (HIS) in meeting the needs and requirements of all stakeholders (WHO, 2006). The improvement of HIS also requires the collaboration of the data users and producers (WHO, 2006). CHWs are both users and producers of data and hence are key stakeholders, deserving some attention.

Community health workers, m-learning and community health work

CHWs who provide nursing care in developing countries can be regarded as knowledge workers (Antrobus,1997). Knowledge workers are personnel who work in service- or technologically oriented roles, who spend a high percentage of their time communicating with colleagues or customers, and whose work involves accessing information, seeking expert opinions, generating data and information and performing tasks within a larger organization (Drucker, 1999). This definition has been applied to the growing number of mobile and distributed workers in business and commercial organizations in developed countries. The provision of current and reliable medical knowledge to health workers in the field in an appropriate and cost-effective way is necessary for the sustainable development of healthcare services in developing countries (Pakenham-Walsh et al., 1997), and mobile and wireless technologies provide an affordable platform for achieving this objective (Drury, 2005).

CHWs require tools for communication and collaboration with different cadres of health workers, patients and community members, and also need access to information for patient care. They also generate and collect health and epidemiological data and information for the organizational processes of the DHS. This special function of CHWs demands high mobility across time and space, as in the case of CHWs providing home-based healthcare services for HIV/AIDS and TB patients, and also working to reduce the social stigma associated with HIV/AIDS and TB through their interactions with household members and key community members. One country that illustrates the challenging roles of CHWs is Malawi (Zachariah et al., 2006), where the need to travel between different patients' residences and to relate to different community members as either educators or listeners represents the range of mobility and the distributed nature of healthcare services within the community. Castells (2000), in discussing globalization, stated emphatically that the empowerment of health workers at the local level reduces their risk of exclusion from societal participation and narrows the gap of the urban–rural dichotomy.

CHWs as 'health nomads' have extensive mobility needs and have adopted mobile technologies to provide access to personal e-mail systems for communication with peers, managers and administrators; to manage patient schedules and interventions; and to access the internet and organizational information systems to upload or download health information and data (Drucker, 1999; Lyytinen and Yoo, 2002). Wiredu (2005) stated that the perceived usefulness of mobile ICT depends on three factors: affordances of the system (human–computer interface (HCI)), modalities (range of human mobility), and motives (applications and intended use of the system). The next section focuses on exploring these affordances in relation to CHWs in less-developed countries.

CHWs, community health working and m-learning

Nilsson and Hertzum (2005) studied the effects of time and space on the work processes of community-based home care givers who used PDAs to co-ordinate their daily activities and to work in patients' homes with the health system. They reported that scheduled tasks (trajectories) and the repetition of the tasks (rhythms) provided a means of co-ordinating their activities and collaborating with the other workers in the health system. Wiredu (2005) described the implementation of networked PDAs to support the learning and training activities of lower-cadre clinical health workers in an NHS hospital in the UK. The health workers used the GPRS-enabled PDAs to access clinical information for clinical decision-making support and to collect and analyse data during their training both within and beyond the hospital building. Activity theory (Kuutti,1996) was used to analyse the health workers' interaction with their PDAs in their workplaces in the context of a large, distributed health organization. This multi-level theory fits the three factors of 'modality', 'environment' and 'application' described by Kristofersen and Ljungberg (1999) for analysing users' interaction with mobile ICTs. This framework will be used to shed light on how CHWs would carry out their daily activities using the mobile health information system.

'Application' refers to the design properties of the hardware, software, data and learning materials; 'modality' represents the degree of human mobility (travelling, visiting, and wandering); and 'environment' denotes the physical and social surroundings in which the work processes occur (Wirdeu, 2005). Modality as described here is similar to the micro, local and remote mobility proposed by Luff and Heath (1998). This signifies the amount of distance covered by the mobile ICT-mediated itinerary of CHWs with PDAs in developing countries. Hence, a CHW could be described as using m-learning and its applications to carry out daily health-related activities and tasks in the health centre and the community (environment). The 'modality' of the CHW could then be described as relating to the PDA (micro), working in the health centre with the PDA (local) and working in the community away from the health centre with the PDA (remote).

The 'environment' (Kristofersen and Ljungberg, 1999) influences the mobile working of the CHWs because of the particular physical and social characteristics of rural or community settings in developing countries. For example, the circumstance of relating to patients, their household members, other CHWs and different community members engendered by the nature of CHWs' duties (Friedman, 2002) can be defined as social environment. Physical environment could manifest as lack of adequate transportation (due to bad roads or non-availability of vehicles, a problem in many developing countries) to commute between patients' homes and health centres. This might have an interruptive effect on a CHW's ability to regularly interact with the wireless network (Jack) located in the health centre (Parikh and Lazowska, 2006). The erratic supply of or lack of electrical power prevalent in many LDCs might also have an impact on a CHWs' need to regularly recharge his or her PDA. These factors could have significant implications for the CHWs' ability to carry out their daily tasks and activities. Poor telecommunications infrastructures are also part of the environment.

Mobile workers' daily m-learning activities can be regarded as 'mobile service work', a process that is social and dynamic in nature, with reciprocal and consequent effects on workers' activities (Fagrell et al., 1999). Lyytinen and Yoo (2002) thus proposed a need to consider how individuals working in a team or in a dynamic social environment could be supported through appropriate services and infrastructure regardless of their 'physical or social mobility'. Of particular interest here is social mobility, defined 'as the ways in which and the ease with which individuals can move across different social context and social roles' (Lyytinen and Yoo, 2002). A social context in the case of CHWs in developing countries implies their different working environments, from the health centre to the homes of the patients in the community; and different social roles as health providers, counsellors, community advocates and even as community news providers. These dynamic and rather conflicting changes in position and status threaten to create discontinuities in CHWs' daily healthcare workflow and tasks. Further, CHWs in developing countries, whether 'visiting' homes to treat patients, 'wandering' in the field to collect health data or 'travelling' from one health post or home to another are modulated by their interaction with the physical entities (DHS, PDAs and learning content) and the social world (actors in the health centres and within the community) (Wiredu, 2005).

The limitation of Kristofersen and Ljungberg's (1999) model of mobile work is that it doesn't take into consideration actual work processes. Pica and Sørensen (2004) argued for consideration of the primary and secondary work processes of mobile workers supported with mobile devices.

Primary work is described as the original functions of a role, while secondary work is a function that is auxiliary to the original role. For example, primary work in the case of CHWs in developing countries is the provision of essential primary healthcare, while secondary work is the collection of health data and accessing of medical knowledge via the PDAs. The clash between these two functions could have either a positive or a negative effect on a 'mobile service work'. The CHW's socio-cultural experience, i.e. interaction with organization (DHS), patients and community members, is also to be considered. This conflict was observed in a study of hospital-based auxiliary health workers by Wiredu (2005). He observed that primary (physical) and secondary (virtual) work processes were not synchronized because the clash between two working paradigms resulted in the PDAs not being used for their intended functions. The eventual consequence was the abandonment of the devices by management (Wiredu, 2005). Physical work, in the context of CHWs, is the primary role of their job, while virtual work may involve a CHW using his or her PDA to help a community member or a local farmer to check out the latest news or prices of agricultural products on the internet, as an instance in the first case study. This observation is also reported in a study of mobile home carers using PDAs to support their health provision activities, where interaction with team members and patients affects their work processes (Nilsson and Hertzum, 2005). A typical example from the case study involved a CHW's use of her or his PDA to provide access to daily news to 'digitally excluded' and information-starved community members. This phenomenon is also supported in the literature (Pallot, 2005).

Pallot (2005), in developing a concept of a mobile community collaborative workplace, argued that mobile workers are required to transit from an individual workspace to a team-based one and eventually to a community workplace. Pallot (2005) further queried the effect of this dynamic working environment in introducing discontinuities into work processes and rationalized that workers in a team might be immune to this disruption because of institutional rules governing working relationships with team members. However, he stated that this type of rule is not readily applicable or available in community work settings, although this proposition was applied in the context of mobile online virtual working that involves communities of practice developed from a local or distributed team within an organization and a global social network outside the organization. In contrast to Pallot's vision (Pallot, 2005), CHWs are in a physical mobile working environment rather than a virtual one, whereby their working activities are modulated by team ethics within the health centre but are open to disruptions and distractions when they are working in the community because of the absence of rules of engagement. This institutional rule makes it unavoidable for a mobile CHW to interact and relate with patients or community members, thereby preventing the use of the PDA for its primary intended purpose of accessing medical m-learning content for patient care (virtual work processes). In another way, the institutional rule as explained above could also be counterproductive to the use of m-learning for virtual work processes. For example, if a CHW felt that using the m-learning could prevent her or him from obeying the institutional rule of proper attention to patients' care, s/he might regard virtual work processes as distractions, which might eventually lead to their abandonment (Wiredu, 2005). This potential 'impediment' to work processes should be considered when designing mobile ICTs to support CHWs in the community (Skattør et al., 2004). The interaction of CHWs with m-learning and its various applications can be understood by the principle of 'affordances', which is a measure of the usability (physical interface and system design properties) of a computer device (Wiredu, 2005; Gaver, 1996).

The absence of adequate human–computer interfaces has been identified as a major barrier to the routine use and acceptance of computing systems in healthcare (Kushniruk et al., 1997). Affordances in this context relate to the perceptions of the CHWs concerning the use of PDAs/m-learning within the health centres, patients' homes and the community. This behavioural response can be either overt or covert in its manifestation as a reciprocal relationship between the user (CHW) and the environment (Gaver, 1996). CHWs working in their environments require affordances to be appropriate. For example, the design of the user interface of the PDA should be such that access to information and data inputting should be quick, so as not to have any negative effect on the outcome of patient care.

Conclusion

This chapter has presented the various potential interruptions to the operation of highly mobile CHWs empowered with PDAs connected to an ad hoc wireless network for the achievement of organizationally set objectives in an LDC. The reality of working in the health centres and the community creates scenarios for discontinuities in their healthcare work-flow due to prevailing environmental and social circumstances. Koch et al. (2005), in a study of CHWs using PDAs for patient care and health data collection in home-based care, observed an improvement in their work performance. The observed changes were an increase in their confidence to request help and support to meet their technical needs; and greater access to medical information, enabling knowledge transfer and an improved understanding of their work processes and specifications. The implied organizational benefits of the use of PDAs by mobile health workers have been documented as including staff retention and recruitment. This supports the case for further exploration of this topic, on the basis of the potential advantages offered by this mode of working in resource-constrained and disease-ravaged less-developed countries.

This chapter has shed light on a previously unexplored research area of distributed and mobile collaboration, and on work that has previously focused on business organizations. It has also brought a new perspective to this research domain in the context of mobile health working by low-cadre health workers in the complex and socially active environment of a typical LDC.

References

Anand, S. and Bärnighausen, T. (2007) Human Resources for Health and Vaccination Coverage in Developing Countries: an econometric analysis, *Lancet*, 369/9569, 1277–85.

Antrobus, S. (1997) Developing the Nurse as a Knowledge Worker in Health Learning: the artistry of practice, *Journal of Advanced Nursing*, 25, 829–35.

Bergqvist, J. and Dahlberg, P. (1999) Considering the Social Aspects of IT Support for Mobile Meetings, *Proceedings of the Fifth Americas Conference on Information Systems*.

Byrne, E.(2005) Using Action Research in Information Systems Design to Address Change: a South African health information systems case study, *Proceedings of the 2005 Annual Research Conference of the South African Institute of Computer Scientists and Information Technologists on IT Research in Developing Countries*, 131–41.

Castells, M. (2000) *The Rise of the Network Society*, 2nd edn, California, Blackwell.

Drucker, P. F. (1999) Knowledge Worker Productivity, *California Management Review*, 41, 79–94.

Drury, P. (2005) eHealth: a model for developing countries, *eHealth International*, **2**, 19.

Fagrell, H., Ljungberg, F. and Kristoffersen, S. (1999) Exploring Support for Knowledge Management in Mobile Work, *Proceedings of the 6th European Conference on CSCW (Copenhagen, Denmark, 1999)*, Dordrecht, Kluwer, 259–76.

Friedman, I. (2003) *Community Based Health Workers in the South African Health Review 2002*, Health Systems Trust, Durban.

Gaver, W. W. (1996) Situating Action II: Affordances for Interaction: the social is material for design, *Ecological Psychology*, **8**, 111–29.

Gladwin, J. et al. (2003) Implementing a New Health Management Information System in Uganda, *Health Policy and Planning*, **18**, 214–24.

Han, S. et al. (2204) Physicians' Behaviour Intentions Regarding the Use of Mobile Technology: an exploratory study, *Proceedings of PACIS 2004*, 8–11.

Kakihara, M. and Sørensen, C. (2004) Practicing Mobile Professional Work: tales of locational, operational, and interactional mobility, *INFO: The Journal of Policy, Regulation and Strategy for Telecommunication, Information and Media*, **6**, 180–7.

Koch, S., Hägglund, M., Scandurra, I. and Mostrøm, D. (2005) *OLD@HOME. Technical Support for Mobile Close Care. Final report*, www.vinnova.se/In-English/Publications/Products-hidden/OLDHOME.

Kristofersen, S. and Ljungberg, F. (1999) Making Place to Make it Work: empirical explorations of HCI for mobile CSCW. In *Proceedings of the International ACM SIGGROUP Conference on Supporting Group Work*, 276–85.

Kushniruk, A. W., Patel, V. L. and Cimino, J. J. (1997) Usability Testing in Medical Informatics: cognitive approaches to evaluation of information systems and user interfaces, *Proceedings of the AMIA Annual Fall Symposium*, 218–22.

Kuutti, K. (1996) Activity Theory as a Potential Framework for Human–Computer Interaction Research. In Nardi, B. A. (ed.), *Context and Consciousness: activity theory and human–computer interaction*, MIT Press, 17–44.

Luff, P. and Heath, C. (1998) Mobility in Collaboration, *Proceedings of the 1998 ACM Conference on Computer Supported Cooperative Work*, 305–14.

Lyytinen, K. and Yoo, Y. (2002) The Next Wave of Nomadic Computing: a research agenda for information systems research, *Sprouts: Working Papers on Information Environments, Systems and Organizations*, **1**, 1–20.

Nilsson, M. and Hertzum, M. (2005) Negotiated Rhythms of Mobile Work: time, place, and work schedules, *Proceedings of the 2005 International ACM SIGGROUP Conference on Supporting group work*, 148–57.

Pakenham-Walsh, N., Priestley, C. and Smith, R. (1997) *Meeting the Information Needs of Health Workers in Developing Countries. A new programme to coordinate and advise*, British Medical Association.

Pallot, M. (2005) *Towards Community-based Collaborative Workplaces, 2005*, Twente, ESoCE-NET.

Parikh, T. S. and Lazowska, E. D. (2006) Designing an Architecture for Delivering Mobile Information Services to the Rural Developing World, *Proceedings of the 15th International Conference on World Wide Web*, 791–800.

Pica, D. and Sørensen, C. (2004) On Mobile Technology in Context: exploring police work, *CIT. Journal of Computing and Information Technology*, 12, 287–95.

Skattør, B. et al. (2004) Mobile Work – Mobile ICT Supporting Secondary Work Final Report, Oslo, 13 May.

WHO (2006) *Working Together for Health*, Geneva, The World Health Organization.

Wiredu, G. (2005) The Reconstruction of Portable Computers: on the flexibility of mobile computing in mobile activities. In *Designing Ubiquitous Information Environments: socio-technical issues and challenges*, International Federation for Information Processing, Boston, Springer, 2005, 197–212.

Zachariah, R. et al. (2006) How Can the Community Contribute in the Fight Against HIV/AIDS and Tuberculosis? An example from a rural district in Malawi, *Transactions of the Royal Society of Tropical Medicine and Hygiene*, 100, 167–75.

10

An effective mobile-friendly digital library to support mobile learners

Yang Cao, Mohamed Ally, Tony Tin, Steve Schafer and Maureen Hutchison

Introduction

As the demand for education grows and increasing numbers of adults return to university and college for continuing education and training, so grows the need for new technologies to facilitate learning. Online teaching and learning have provided great opportunities to increase the flexibility of time and location of study, in terms of availability of information and resources, synchronous and asynchronous communication, and various types of interaction via the world wide web (Cao and Greer, 2004). Today, there is a 'new buzz in the air along with a growing cacophony of beeps, ring tones, vibration' (Wagner, 2005), and distance education is about to shift once again to a new stage: mobile learning (m-learning) (Clyde, 2004; Wilson, 2005).

Mobile learning is enabled by the use of portable computing devices such as personal digital assistants (PDAs), ultra notebooks, smartphones and tablet PCs, which communicate over wireless networks. Hong, Thong, Wong, and Tam (2002) call for a shift in digital library research: more and more library and information science researchers believe that the future avenues of digital libraries' research must involve the interactions between the users and the systems (p. 99). Digital libraries are more versatile than simply exchanging e-mail or reading content from a personal computer. In other words, digital libraries delivered through mobile devices could offer increased flexibility in terms of access and forms of content; increased interaction between students, instructors and tutors; and increased hands-on learning opportunities. Various mobile learning research projects, such as WiTEC, have tested the usefulness of wireless devices in classroom environments (Wang et al., 2003; White, 2004) or in class field trips (Rieger and Gay, n.d.). A key benefit of m-learning is its potential for increasing productivity by making learning available anywhere, at any time. It has only been since 2005 that studies of digital libraries have moved outside the classroom. Waycott and Kukulska-Hulme (2003) focused exclusively on students' experiences reading course materials and taking notes using PDAs. However, the finding was not fruitful because of the limitations of the PDA technology at that time.

Dong and Agogino (2004) explored how downloading key information to a PDA would help to enrich the learning experience of students on a field trip. They concluded that m-learning is most useful when it links real-world situations to relevant information resources. In their study they explored the two approaches of (1) transforming and (2) transcoding to deliver digital content intended for full-sized personal computers to mobile devices. Transformation requires that all content be marked up in XML (extensible markup language) and that content is presented with style sheets appropriate to the capabilities of the remote device on which it will be displayed. Transcoding also takes into account the capabilities of the mobile device, as well as its network conditions, but it displays content without it being changed. Dong and Agogino did not use the approach of webclipping, such as AvantGO, in their study. Webclipping delivers only text content, by stripping out any multimedia content, an approach that does not exploit a digital library's versatility.

The technology of mobile devices has advanced dramatically since 2006. Screens are bigger and better, and systems have more memory, more multimedia capabilities and better methods for inputting data. The constant advancements in devices and the wide variety of systems and applications raise more questions about possible methods for delivering digital library content to mobile devices. According to Clyde (2004), the challenge 'is to identify the forms of education and training for which M-learning is particularly appropriate, the potential students who most need it and the best strategies for delivering mobile education' (p. 46). More research from a user perspective is needed to discover the best strategies for maximizing m-learning, including exploring which mobile technologies are the best to employ for accessing digital libraries, and what constitutes an effective m-library and how to use it to support m-learning and teaching.

For an open and distance education university, it is essential that its online resources be accessible to as wide a range of users and devices as possible. It is essential that both appropriate existing and emerging technologies be implemented for effective development, delivery and support for distance learners. In order for students to take advantage of what David Metcalf has called 'stolen moments for learning' (Metcalf, 2002) while riding the train or sitting in an airport waiting for a flight, there is an ongoing effort to make websites accessible to a wide range of mobile devices. For example, the m-library project at Athabasca University Library (http://library.athabascau.ca/) strives to build a platform on which an effective mobile-friendly digital library can be developed (Cao, Tin, McGreal, Ally and Coffey, 2006) for mobile and online learning. The m-library project and ongoing research on m-learning reflect the desire and motivation to provide a truly mobile learning environment at Athabasca University.

The objective of this project is to build a platform on which to develop an effective mobile-friendly library and to evaluate how well the library website works with popular mobile devices. The results of this study can be used to determine how libraries can make their websites useful to users with a wide range of choice in mobile devices. Some of the challenges in design and deployment of the m-library, along with possible solutions to the challenges, are presented in this chapter.

The m-library project

The m-library website provides a wide range of digital resources and library services, including the Digital Reading Room (DRR) or e-course reserve, the Digital Reference Centre (DRC), the Digital Thesis and Project Room (DTPR), a help centre, a search engine, a mobile portal for access to online journal databases, AirPAC (a mobile library catalogue application), and library services through the world wide web.

Exhaustive studies of the library website have been made to ensure that the format is 'fluid' to small screens, that is, that the format of the information changes in response to the device that accesses the website. The m-library system can auto-detect users' devices and direct them to the appropriate version (mobile or desktop) of the site that is being accessed. Additionally, the library catalogue is accessible and viewable with mobile devices through the use of AirPAC, a software module of Innovative Interfaces Inc. (III), which is an automated library system specifically designed for wireless mobile devices. Users can browse the library catalogue, check due dates, request materials and view their patron records using mobile devices.

System design

The existing Athabasca University (AU) Library website was developed with desktop computers in mind. The web pages have been traditionally designed with the assumption that the user accessing the website has a large, colour screen and adequate bandwidth for downloading multimedia-rich pages.

The mobile-friendly library website is designed to display content appropriately in the best format for either a desktop PC or a mobile device. It has been implemented in PHP programming language. In real time, the different browsers are detected by a server-side script. By parsing the HTTP_USER_AGENT, the server can identify the platform, whether it is Windows CE or Palm OS. The system chooses the correct style sheet and display model. As a result, digital information is reformatted on-the-fly for different browsers and screen resolutions (Figures 10.1 opposite and 10.2 on page 114).

CASE STUDY

This case study (Wasti, 2006) investigates the mobile-friendliness of the AU Library website and some external electronic resources and sites that are linked to from the AU Library website, specifically online journal databases. Features at those sites were tested to see whether they worked as expected. There were two key aspects of the test: (1) visual display and (2) functionality.

Some sites rendered well, with their layout intact on small screens, but some features became crippled because of the limitations of the underlying device and platform. Similarly, other sites appeared relatively distorted but had their features intact. The sites were evaluated for both of the above-mentioned factors.

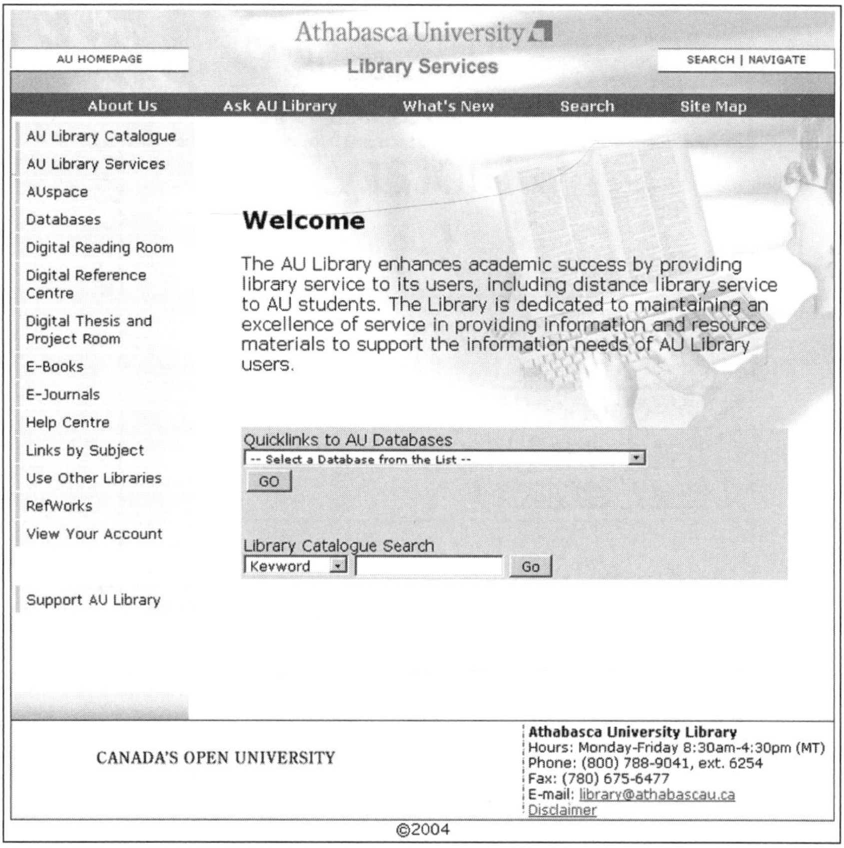

Figure 10.1 AU Library main page (desktop version)

Devices used

Numerous types of mobile devices capable of accessing the internet are available. Because of time and resource constraints, it was not possible to test each available device for compatibility with the websites. For the purposes of this study, three smartphone devices were chosen, each with a different screen size and slightly different browsing characteristics: (1) the HP iPAQ hw6500 (iPAQ®), (2) the BlackBerry® 8700r (BlackBerry®), and (3) the Audiovox SMT5600 (SMT).

Although the iPAQ hw6500 and SMT5600 both use the Windows Mobile 2003SE operating system, the feature sets supported by these devices are not identical. The Windows version in the SMT5600 is more streamlined for use by mobile phones, whereas the Windows system in the iPAQ is geared

Figure 10.2 AU Library main page (mobile version)

more towards personal digital assistants (PDAs). Historically, iPAQ hand-helds were used only as PDAs and the phone feature was a later addition. BlackBerry uses its own BlackBerry operating system and its own browser. The BlackBerry browser applies heavy optimization to web pages to allow them to fit and display on the screen with as much functionality as possi-ble. BlackBerry's optimization techniques include removing tables, resizing images, and changing the page layout. One of its remarkable features is that horizontal scrolling is completely eliminated. However, this feature comes with a price: forcefully eliminating horizontal scrolling can sometimes result in badly distorted pages.

The Microsoft Pocket IE browser (available for the iPAQ and SMT devices) is more flexible than the BlackBerry browsers, as it allows users to select different viewing modes: single-column mode, desktop mode, and default mode. Although some problematic web pages were viewed in different modes to find out whether the problem existed in all viewing modes, the test was primarily conducted in the default viewing mode. The default mode is the most likely choice for users and is the one that is likely to produce the best viewing experience for most websites.

Test result

The sites selected for testing were Library-related sites, including DRR, DTPR, DRC and Library help pages, journal databases, and hosted journal sites. Tests were performed on the devices by going to various AU Library websites and assessing them on a scale of 0 to 3, where 0 represents 'not very mobile friendly,' and 3 represents 'very mobile friendly.'

One major problem common to all devices is the inability to upload files. None of the tested mobile browsers allowed files to be uploaded because they could not recognize the file browsing buttons.

The usual limitations of devices applied to all sites were tested. For example, the SMT device could not install Flash player, and so any site using Macromedia Flash would not display properly on this device. It does not have a PDF reader, so trying to open a PDF file from any website would not work. Such limitations are considered to be restrictions inherent in the device itself and not shortcomings of the website. However, if a site relies primarily on the device being able to make use of those features, the mobile-friendliness grading of that site is reduced accordingly. These are the test results for some Library websites:

AU Library sites

Main site – http://library.athabascau.ca/
Digital Reading Room (DRR) – http://library.athabascau.ca/drr
Digital Thesis and Project Room (DTPR) – http://library.athabascau.ca/DTPR
Digital Reference Centre (DRC) – http://library.athabascau.ca/drc

All AU Library sites tested were found to be very mobile friendly. The DRR, DTPR and DRC use similar layouts that are fluid, allowing a smooth flow of text. As those sites do not use fixed-size tables, the display was consistent and predictable across all the devices. AU Library sites adapted to the client device for optimal mobile friendliness without sacrificing the richer web content. This is done by detecting what type of device is accessing the pages and then sending the appropriate version of the web page to the device (Figure 10.3).

Figure 10.3 AU Library main page (left) and Digital Reading Room (DRR) site (right)

The AU Library has recently integrated mobile conversion services, such as Google™ Mobile, Skweezer®, and IYHY into the reading resources in the DRR.[1] These third-party services work as proxy servers to provide suitable formatting of existing websites for mobile devices.

AU Library catalogue: AirPAC [2]

This site is a mobile-optimized version of the AU Library catalogue. AirPAC formats its response for the type of device that is used to access the site. It sends a smaller version of the page to the SMT and BlackBerry devices to accommodate the small screen area, while it sends a larger version to the iPAQ device, with more screen area available. The site displays very well in all three devices and in all view modes, and all links to this site work flawlessly.

Discussion

This study found that most of the AU Library websites (the main site, DRR and DTPR) were almost perfect visually and functionally when accessed from the smartphones that were tested. The sites were designed with specific attention to the requirements of mobile devices: the server sends responses that are customized to the device being used to access the sites. The benefit of this approach is that mobile device users can conveniently access the online resources without affecting the ability of desktop users, who can still make full use of their PC capabilities to receive multimedia-rich content and more advanced graphical displays. The downside is that there is a need to maintain different versions of the same web page for different device profiles.

Mobile learning requires new approaches for mobile-friendly website development. Some m-library design and development challenges and solutions are described here.

Defining content for the m-library

Current mobile devices are limited by the speed of their wireless internet connection, small screens, slow processing and limited storage capabilities. One of the most obvious obstacles is the limited memory of mobile devices, especially cell phones. Considering how technology or the medium affects the information displayed, defining what amount and what type of information is appropriate is an important factor for a successful m-library.

Format design of the m-library

The design and content suitable for a desktop computer may not be suitable for a mobile device because of the limitations of its small screen size. AU's library website was initially designed for the most common screen sizes, from 640 x 480 to 1280 x 1024 resolution, including header and footer images, a top horizontal navigation bar and a vertical navigation sidebar. However, this is too much information to be displayed on smaller, portable devices. Content for mobile display should be chunked into smaller segments for ease of use (Ally, 2005). In addition, the size of the text, images, graphics and tables, and the size and physical location of pop-up windows will need to be redefined, since some of them use absolute values. The absolute value is limited to certain machines, screen sizes, screen resolutions and the internet browser's default font size, which is not good for all.

Separate content from format

A good m-library solution should work for a broad range of devices; in other words, it should be device independent. This issue may be resolved through efforts to broaden the capabilities and flexibility of web browsers which separate the content from the format. A good solution is to use eXtensible Markup Language (XML), which allows the website developer to specify the content and how it appears on various devices, using XML Stylesheet Languages (XSL). However, this process would require some revisions to the content development process and associated tools.

Display models

There is no optimal or simple solution for an 'all in one' display model for various operating systems and web browsers. In addition to a generic cascading style sheet (CSS), we defined a mobile CSS that is suitable for portable mobile devices. We used a program to recognize whether the device is a portable PC or a mobile device. This then allows the system to choose the proper stylesheet and display model to specify the appearance of the page. Even though the two sets of stylesheets and display models result in difficulties in design and maintenance, it is nonetheless an interim solution until better, new applications become available.

Lack of mobile standard

Limitations inherent in existing technologies, current operating systems, and web browsers create a challenge for m-learning developers. Developers presently lack the capability or the flexibility for an application to be displayed properly on all devices. Some websites, for example, which link from our library website, may not display appropriately on mobile devices. Vertical scrolling is often necessary. Some pages or pictures seem to fit the screen of mobile devices, but then the images and the content inside the images are barely readable. Some web browsing services, such as Skweezer® (www.skweezer.net) and Thunderhawk® (www.bitstream.com/wireless), might be useful and helpful in reformatting and compressing web pages for optimal use on today's hand-held devices.

Handling of PDF documents

The m-library has links to learning resources in *Adobe* PDF format. Unfortunately, there is no native PDF support on BlackBerry devices. A BlackBerry user cannot view a PDF document using his or her web browser. The PDF document can only be viewed through an e-mail attachment or by subscribing to an online service such as DocHawk™. To resolve this issue, documents widely used in the m-Library site are reformatted into HTML for viewing with a BlackBerry.

Interoperability with library system

The m-library web pages are programmed in PHP. The Innovative library system (e.g., library proxy for user authentication) developed by Athabasca University does not support the PHP file format. The only type of web page that Innovative recognizes in its system is that which ends with .html. Also, in order to function with the system, these web pages must be on the Innopac server. This makes it difficult to incorporate the auto-detect device feature into the existing library system. To address this issue, the Athabasca University Library authentication page simply uses mobile-friendly HTML instead of PHP. The auto-detect device function is not present here. The library proxy server does not support cell phone access and proxy authentication. It would not accept a VeriSoft certificate (https) either.

Handling of multimedia file types

The m-library site has links to a wide variety of audio and video files. There is no audio or video support for the model being tested. This is a great challenge for the future development of the m-library, as large and complex learning objects require Flash, Shockwave™, Java applets and other plug-ins. All of these may not work in the BlackBerry and other PDA and smartphone environments. This issue may be adjusted in the future with the arrival of new smartphones such as the Apple iPhone®, which provides better multimedia support.

Conclusion

With the rapid evolution of technology, with increased educational opportunities, and with a techno-savvy generation emerging, the results of this research will be significant to the library and teaching community. The significance to Athabasca University, as a distance education and e-learning institution, is even greater. We have made significant progress in determining the mobile friendliness of our systems to accommodate various mobile devices, and continue to investigate mobile technologies and their use within our educational environments.

This project provides a general idea of how AU m-library sites work with the tested mobile devices and identifies the underlying reasons as to why they work that way. However, in the effort to make the sites as mobile friendly as possible, it is also important to consider what some possible solutions are. Redesigning all sites carefully, with due consideration to mobile devices, is one possibility, but it is a very impractical one. The cost of resources associated with this route could be enormous. Another possibility is creating a mobile-friendly version of each web page and serving those pages instead of the regular pages whenever mobile devices make page requests. This creates the huge burden of site maintenance, because of the need to maintain multiple versions of the same page for different devices. Another problem with this approach is that, as the capability of mobile devices changes, sites need to be updated accordingly to reflect the device's capability. However, this issue could be addressed to some extent by creating template-based dynamic pages, and, rather than redesigning the pages whenever the device capability changed, one could change the profile of the device, which in turn would be reflected in the dynamic page.

A totally different approach that is gaining some popularity is the use of an intermediary proxy-like adaptation layer for the web content. This approach means that there is no need to maintain multiple versions of the same website, and it also does not require the redesigning of existing websites. In effect, whenever a user makes a request to a web page, the request can be routed through an intermediary service that identifies the requesting device, gets the page from the web server on behalf of the device, and reformats the page – thus making it suitable for that particular device – and then passes it on to that device. The success of such an approach depends entirely on the capability of the intermediary service. One advantage of this approach is that the burden of making the web pages user friendly now shifts to the intermediary service from the web server or the web page administrator. Another advantage is that end-users do not need to make any special adjustments or install special software on their devices.

In summary, the AU Library is pioneering the development of m-learning resources and the m-library. This project has been designed to build a platform for Athabasca University to develop an effective m-library and evaluate how its use will support m-learning and teaching. As a result, the Library website has been recreated to ensure that it displays well on a variety of mobile devices. Now students can access a wide range of digital resources and library services and truly engage in learning activities using any mobile device, wherever and whenever they choose, and not just at their desktop PCs. Developments in MP3 format, podcasting and support for third-generation smartphones put AU Library at the leading edge of new and emerging trends in mobile learning and distance education. The mobile-friendly library and associated applications will continue AU's tradition of excellence and innovation in instructional design by maximizing accessibility and convenience for students.

References

Ally, M. (2005) Multimedia Information Design for Mobile Devices. In Pagani, M. (ed.), *Encyclopedia of Multimedia Technology and Networking*, Hershey, PA, Idea Group Inc.

Cao, Y. and Greer, J. (2004). Facilitating Web-based Education Using Intelligent Agent Technologies, *Proceeding of the 2nd International Workshop on Web-based Support Systems, in conjunction with the 2004 IEEE/WIC/ACM International Conference on Web Intelligence and International Conference on Intelligent Agent Technology, September 2004, Beijing, China*, 37–44.

Cao, Y., Tin, T., McGreal, M. R., Ally, M. and Coffey, S. (2006) The Athabasca University Mobile Library Project: increasing the boundaries of anytime, anywhere learning for students, *Proceedings of International Wireless Communications and Mobile Computing (IWCMC) conference, Vancouver, Canada*, 3–6 July 2006.

Clyde, L. A. (2004) Info Tech M-Learning, *Teacher Librarian,* 31 (1), (October), www.teacherlibrarian.com/tltoolkit/info_tech/info_tech_32_1.html [accessed 31 March 2005].

Dong, A. and Agogino, A. M. (2004) A Case Study of Policy Decisions for Federated Search Access Digital Libraries. In *International Conference on Digital Libraries,* Vol. 2, The Energy and Resources Institute, New Delhi, 892–8.

Hong, W., Thong, J. Y. L., Wong, W. M. and Tam, K. Y. (2002) Determinants of User Acceptance of Digital Libraries: an empirical examination of individual differences and system characteristics, *Journal of Management Information Systems*, 18, 97–124.

Metcalf, D. (2002) Stolen Moments for Learning, *eLearning Developers' Journal*, (March).

Mobile Google, www.google.com/gwt/n.

Rieger, R. and Gay, G. (n.d.) *Using Mobile Computing to Enhance Field Study*, www.oise.utoronto.ca/cscl/papers/rieger.pdf [accessed 23 November, 2004].

Wagner, E. D. (2005) Enabling Mobile Learning, *EDUCAUSE Review*, 40 (3), 40–53, www.educause.edu/er/erm05/erm0532.asp?bhcp=1.

Wang, H. Y., Liu, T. C., Chou, C. Y., Liang, J. K., Chan, T. W. and Yang, S. (2003)The Framework of Three Learning Activity Levels for Enhancing Usability and Feasibility of Wireless Learning Environment [*sic*], *Journal of Educational Computing Research*, 30, 331–51.

Wasti, R. (2006) *A Study of the Mobile-friendliness of Selected Athabasca University Websites*, research report.

Waycott, J. and Kukulska-Hulme, A. (2003) Students' Experiences with PDAs for Reading Course Materials, *Personal and Ubiquitous Computing*, 7 (1), 30–43.

White, N. (2004) M-Learning with Disadvantaged Kids, *Full Circle Associates Community Blog*, 2 November, www.fullcirc.com/weblog/2004/11/m-learning-with-disadvantaged-kids.htm [accessed 30 November, 2004].

Wilson, P. (2005) Where Macromedia Education is Headed, *Macromedia Higher Education Leadership Forum, San Francisco, California, 24 February, 2005*.

URLs

1   http://library.athabascau.ca/drr/mobile2.php?course=mba&id=441&sub=5.

2   http://aupac.lib.athabascau.ca/airpac.

Part 3

Initiatives, innovations and challenges

11

Accessing library resources while on placement: can mobile devices help students?

Lynne Callaghan, Susan J. Lea, Ruth Charlton and Emma Whittlesea

Introduction

This m-learning project brought together two core strands of development activity work within the Centre for Excellence in Professional Placement Learning (Ceppl): 'enhancing library access' and the 'm-learning project'. The joint work of these activities focused first on developing and assessing placement students' perceptions of an electronic library and resource guide that aimed to centralize resources for students enrolled on programmes within the Faculty of Health and Social Work (FHSW) at the University of Plymouth (UoP). Second, students were given the opportunity to test the use of mobile devices to access the guide and to reflect on their placement experiences in order to evaluate the usefulness of these devices.

The development of the guide was underpinned by the findings of a qualitative study undertaken in 2006 (Callaghan, Doherty et al., 2008). Focus groups carried out with health and social care students assessed their resource needs on placement and their requirements of a guide designed to meet those needs. Students on health and social care programmes typically spend up to 50% of their time engaging in placement learning, that is, learning that takes place in the work environment (Hills et al., 2003). Placement learning is seen by government and professional bodies as essential in providing students with direct contact with clients so as to understand the practical application of their theoretical understanding (ENB/DoH, 2001). The development activity included a stakeholder consultation with the UoP and National Health Service (NHS) librarians and social service knowledge managers. As a result, a draft of an electronic guide to library services for health and social care students at UoP was created. The guide provided centralized information regarding UoP, NHS and other useful libraries and resources including photographs, maps, borrowing rights and contact numbers. Further links to relevant catalogues and databases were included, with the aim of facilitating access to electronic resources while students were on placement.

The m-learning project within the Ceppl has highlighted the usefulness of mobile devices for students to access information while they are on placement. Previous work has shown that placement students tend to have a low level of understanding of mobile devices for information retrieval, but greatly value the ability to access information while out in the community (Walton et al., 2005). From conducting pilot tests with health placement students it was clear that certain steps are needed so as to facilitate the use of mobile devices to enhance students' learning experiences on placement (Callaghan, Newcombe et al., 2008). Consequently, it was considered vital that the development and evaluation of the guide take three issues into account. These were: first, the effects of the multiple contexts within which placement students learn; second, actively engaging students in the technology used to access and evaluate the guide; and third, focusing the evaluation and development of the guide around student needs rather than on the capabilities and functionality of the technology.

Method

Qualitative methodology was used to examine student perceptions and generate a rich source of data. Students were invited to participate in uni-professional focus groups or single participant interviews. These gave them the opportunity to navigate the guide using a variety of mobile devices and to discuss their experiences and perceptions of how the useful the guide would be on placement. Ethical permission was obtained from the UoP Faculty of Health and Social Work Human Ethics sub-committee.

Recruitment

The researchers spoke to students during lecture time about the study and invited interested individuals to participate. Students were asked to return completed consent forms to the researchers if they wished to take part. On receiving completed consent forms, the researchers arranged either focus group sessions or individual interviews as appropriate.

Procedure

A variation of the Nominal Group Technique (NGT) was used in the focus groups to explore student perceptions of the library guide and the usefulness of mobile devices for access to it. This technique was chosen because it encourages input from all participants, thus avoiding more vocal individuals monopolizing the discussion (MacPhail, 2001). The groups were organized according to the first four stages of Lloyd-Jones et al.'s (1999) version of NGT, as described here.

Introduction and presentation of questions

Students were presented with the guide on Apple Mac laptops, which were shared between two or three students. The researchers encouraged students to acquaint themselves with the guide. Students were then provided with mobile telephones and personal digital assistants (PDAs) with which to access the guide. They were encouraged to explore the guide and the devices themselves. Support was provided by the researchers as appropriate. Two questions were then presented for the participants to consider: first, 'How can the electronic guide be improved to support placement students in health and social care?' and second, 'What issues would there be regarding use of mobile devices to access the guide while on placement?'

Silent phase

Participants were asked to write down as many responses to the above questions as they could without conferring with their peers. This phase continued until all participants had completed the task.

Round-robin phase

The researchers asked each participant in turn to provide a response. This stage was continued for both questions until no new responses were forthcoming. Responses were recorded on a flip chart by a researcher.

Item clarification and discussion

During this phase participants discussed each of the issues generated by the silent phase in order to understand their meaning and to further examine the students' perspectives of these issues. These discussions were digitally recorded with the participants' permission.

Lloyd-Jones et al. (1999) present a fifth phase that involves participants ranking the issues raised and yields quantitative data. However, as the aim of the study was to understand the students' perspectives through the generation of rich qualitative data, this phase was not considered appropriate.

Two students took part in single participant interviews, as no other students from their professions had volunteered to take part in the study. In both cases, participants were provided with the same information and the guide, as in stage one above, and were then asked to talk about the issues related to each of the questions regarding the guide and the usefulness of the mobile devices. The interviews were digitally recorded.

Analysis

On completion of data collection three focus groups (two with podiatry students, one with learning disability nursing students) and two interviews (with dietetics and physiotherapy students) had been conducted. All data compiled on flip charts and digital recorders were transcribed to aid analysis. Transcribed data were then coded and analysed using Thematic Content Analysis (Smith, 1992).

Findings

Three themes emerged from the analysis of both the written and oral data. These were: 'enhancing the placement learning experience', 'support' and 'equalizing opportunities?' Each of these themes is discussed below, illustrated with students' observations from the transcribed discussions and interviews.

Enhancing the placement learning experience

Participants spoke at length about the potential of the guide to enhance their placement experience in terms of both preparation for the placement and accessing resources while on placement. All groups and individual participants were positive about the guide and saw it as a future fundamental support while on placement:

> I was just wondering where we access this because I think it's really helpful and also for . . . there's a lot of nursing sites on there that you can link straight through. I think it's fantastic.

It was clear that the students believed that preparation for placement was of great importance to their placement learning experience. They made several suggestions regarding the guide so as to further enhance their preparation. These included:

- information on computer, internet and wireless facilities in each placement area/library
- a map showing mobile network coverage
- maps of clinics within each of the placement areas
- links to public transport services
- information regarding accommodation close to the placement area for those required to live away during their placement.

Although the majority of the above additions were not directly related to access to academic resources, it was clear from participants' discussions that this information was considered important for successfully planning their placement. The dialogue of the podiatry students below is illustrative:

> they sent me maps and everything. If that was all downloaded on there it would be so much easier wouldn't it? . . . They gave me maps for each clinic, they really were good. (P1)

> I went to Bournemouth and they were the same. I had a little map you know, showing me sort of the sites of the clinic within a few streets, but they also had like links to the local bus service and to, um, one of the map search engines. They were very organized, they made it very easy for me. (P2)

However, the availability of such information appeared to be limited for the majority of students pre-placement, thus confirming the need to provide this information in the guide:

> I think I was pretty much left on my own with regard to finding different clinics and
> different hospitals when I actually arrived at my placement, but would there be a
> facility or is it under the scope of something like this to give a map of all the differ-
> ent clinics that are within your placement area?

In terms of accessing resources while on placement, students made a number of suggestions regarding links to sites that would be useful to them.
These included links to professional society sites, local health promotion
centres, NHS catalogues and partner college libraries and systems.
Although it would be straightforward to add links to websites within the
guide it was acknowledged by students that links to NHS catalogues, for
example, would be problematic due to difficulties in accessing passwords
to enter these systems. Students also saw the provision of mobile devices
with which to access these resources as enhancing their experience by facilitating their learning:

> . . . the clinical guidelines. So you might just want to do a search online quickly, which
> isn't always possible if you've got one or two people on the wards who feel like they've
> got priority over a machine, so that you as a student are kind of, well you might, you
> might say that it's, um, we're second priority really, because the patients come first,
> so, so that's understandable. But having some mobile service where you could, you
> could use to get access to the resources would be good.

Support

Although it was clear that the availability of a guide and the provision
of mobile devices to access it could be immensely valuable in participants'
placement experiences, it was also apparent that students would require
support in terms of both accessing resources and using the devices. A need
for two forms of support emerged from the data – user support and peer
support. First, students expressed the need for responsive support for both
technical and library resource issues that they might have while on placement. Although they would appreciate online tutorials to help them to
access and use electronic resources successfully and appropriately, a more
personal approach to support was preferred.

Second, the guide included an area for discussion forums, for which students offered ideas that they felt would benefit their placement learning experience. Suggestions mirrored those for additions to the guide, discussed above, in support of non-academic preparation and logistical arrangements while on placement, as well as support for academic resource access. Students felt that they could support each other in preparing for placements by sharing reflections on experiences of placement, providing directions to placement areas, and offering comments about and ratings of placement accommodation. An area where general questions could be asked and answered was thought to be useful. With regard to peer support specific to learning, suggestions included sharing useful references for coursework; providing book reviews with star ratings; and sharing knowledge of working with different professions. Students were generally enthusiastic about the benefits that this type of support could offer, suggesting inclusion of an interactive element within the guide. Although some participants felt that they would benefit from profession-specific support for some learning issues (e.g. profession-based clinical skills), students generally perceived that sharing knowledge across professional boundaries would be more beneficial, thus highlighting the need for a generic guide.

> Yeah, that sounds good with the essays and things, or things that people have found on placement and people's experiences and things to put on there, and then to ask questions. And I think it would be nice if it was open to all the cross branches, um, so everyone was able to look at it, cause there might be people come across work in mental health or learning disability, or there might be something medical that we might need to know . . . I think that would be quite bonding and actually would bring cross branches together.

Equalizing opportunities?

When considering the potential advantages of using mobile devices to access resources while on placement, students tended to provide examples that illustrated how mobile devices could facilitate the achievement of parity across learning contexts. This was particularly evident when students discussed the use of mobile telephones that offer access to the internet using the GPRS (General Packet Radio Service) system. The primary concern of students in relation to accessing resources on placement in both this and the previous stage of evaluation (Callaghan, Doherty et al., 2008) was the inequality of access to PCs and the internet across placement areas. Students discussed lack of resources, staff and student hierarchies, and mentor attitude to resource access during the working day as common barriers to internet access on placement. Students perceived that using mobile telephones would equalize learning opportunities by providing personal, discreet and portable access to the internet that would impact positively on the placement experience:

> . . . and even if you get one terminal, you might be sharing it with three or four other students so having the flexibility to log on and look at blood results on your own and then go off gives you more autonomy and just saves time, I think.

Access to resources in the placement context could be challenging, as many students experienced difficulties obtaining passwords to enter the placement area IT system. For students on programmes with short placements, passwords may only be provided two weeks prior to the end of a five-week placement. For these students in particular, provision of mobile telephone access to the internet would ensure parity with other students in terms of access to resources during placement.

Information on the guide itself was also seen as enabling an equivalent level of knowledge across students, who often had different understandings of the provision of resources. For example, a discussion regarding the inclusion of SWIMS (South West Information Management System) uncovered differences in student knowledge of this resource and how it is accessed. These could be easily resolved by the guide.

Although discussion of the use of mobile devices generally generated positive comments in terms of the potential for attaining equivalence of access, students also noted that relying on mobile devices to access the guide could in itself aggravate perceived existing inequalities. One of their main concerns was the cost of the devices if students were required to buy the equipment themselves, as well as running costs (e.g. paying for downloads). Further, even if devices could be loaned (as they can for trials in Ceppl's m-learning project), students were anxious about security and insurance in placement areas where they were not provided with secure storage. In terms of learning, however, participants expressed concerns about inequality between students who were familiar and comfortable with technology and those who were less so, in that those who lacked the necessary skills might feel at a disadvantage and/or that engaging in mobile learning, although ultimately beneficial, would create more work during an already busy placement. Thus, the introduction of the guide and the use of mobile devices would need careful management and support to facilitate their success and information would still need to be available in multiple forms so as to avoid this perceived potential inequality:

> It might worry students, you know, if it's thought of as making more work. It makes you a bit negative. (P1)

> Yeah, I mean some of us are good with technology but there are certain people who, you know, are gonna cause real problems for, and they'll struggle with it . . . but if we rely so much in these mobile devices and they don't end up using them and the other resources have been stopped, then they'll be really stuck. (P2)

> That goes back to support and proper support. (P1)

Summary

Overall, students who took part in this study considered the provision of the library guide to have the potential for a positive impact on their placement learning experience in three ways. These were: first, by assisting preparation for placement; second, by centralizing resources within one guide and thereby facilitating access; and third, by helping to create a supportive environment for knowledge sharing and discussion. In terms of using mobile devices to access the guide, students could see their potential for enhancing both their learning and their overall placement experience. Finally, while Walton et al. (2005, 58) argue that 'mobile technologies are not yet in a position to be significant in allowing nursing students remote access to learning resources', it would appear that in 2008 mobile technologies offer students an exciting and effective method for accessing resources and enhancing learning. However, it is only with appropriate management and support that these devices have the potential to achieve parity across professions and placement contexts.

References

Callaghan, L., Doherty, A., Lea, S. J. and Webster, D. (2008) Understanding the Resource Needs of UK Health and Social Care Placement Students. *Health Information and Libraries Journal*, forthcoming.

Callaghan, L., Newcombe, M., Abey, S., Gore, O. and Lea, S. J. (2008) Trials and Tribulations: three key elements to running a successful mobile learning trial in a health care setting, *Learning and Teaching in Higher Education*, forthcoming.

ENB/DoH (English National Board for Nursing, Midwifery and Health Visiting/Department of Health) (2001) *Placements in Focus: guidance for education in practice for health care professions*, Report dated January 2001.

Hills, J. M., Robertson, G., Walker, R., Adley, M. and Nixon, I. (2003) Bridging the Gap Between Degree Programme Curricula and Employability Through the Implementation of Work-related Learning, *Teaching in Higher Education*, 8 (2), 211–31.

Lloyd-Jones, G., Fowell, S. and Bligh, J. G. (1999) The Use of Nominal Group Technique as an Evaluative Tool in Medical Undergraduate Education, *Medical Education*, 33, 8–13.

MacPhail, A. (2001) Nominal Group Technique: a useful method for working with young people, *British Educational Research Journal*, 27 (2), 161–70.

Smith, C. P. (ed.) (1992) *Motivation and Personality: handbook of thematic content analysis*, Cambridge University Press.

Walton, G., Childs, S. and Blenkinsopp, E. (2005) Using Mobile Technologies to Give Health Students Access to Learning Resources in the UK Community Setting, *Health Information and Libraries Journal*, 22 (suppl. 2), 51–65.

12

Public libraries, mobile learning and the creative citizen

Geoff Butters, Margaret Markland and Robert Davies

Introduction

One of the major goals agreed by European ministers of education is to open up education and training to the wider world, as part of Europe's i2010 (European Commission, 2006) initiative, which calls for 'inclusion, better services for citizens and quality of life', and emphasizes the enhanced use of information and communication technologies (ICT) for lifelong learning and social inclusion. A key initiative under this programme encourages a focusing of research and deployment efforts in the field of 'digital libraries', specifically to use high-tech tools to make Europe's rich heritage available to as many people as possible in order to combine individual creativity with ICT.

It is believed that in a knowledge economy 'digital literacy' should be one of the basic skills of all Europeans, alongside the contribution of ICT to learning in general, especially for those who, due to their geographical location, socio-economic situation or special needs, do not have easy access to traditional education and training. 'Digital literacy' is deemed to encompass (1) positive attitudes toward ICT use personally and in society; (2) knowledge about ICT components, operations, capabilities and limitations; and (3) skills in using ICT to perform relevant tasks and to retrieve and make use of digital content.

Further, it is perceived that in a knowledge economy lifelong learning takes place in a range of sites and over sustained periods of time. Learning increasingly is seen to occur through the leisure activities that now often involve digital technologies as part of people's (especially young people's) social and cultural lives, but which are often viewed by formal educationalists as being outside the realm of valued educational experience – such as children's playing of computer games; use of chat rooms and social networking sites; exploitation of digital media; digital television; etc. This perception also focuses attention on what can be learned from these activities that may help in designing approaches to formal education and on how this kind of learning may come to be valued by teachers, schools and the curriculum.

Thus, interest in informal learning has now become much more of a mainstream concern at European level. This attention to informal learning is also inclined to make more evident the experiential nature of learning, involving notions of wonder, surprise, feelings, peer and personal responses, fun and pleasure. It is clear that learning is not confined to formal institutions such as schools, colleges and universities – supporting the concept of a wide 'ecology' of learning where educational institutions, home, families and friends, the workplace, consulting with people in all walks of life and leisure activities, as well as interaction with libraries and other community cultural organizations – all play their part.

Learning and libraries

The role to be played by non-formal/informal learning institutions, such as public libraries, is a matter at the heart of the strategic issues described above. Europe's extensive network of public libraries, with a total membership of some 180 million people, should increasingly be able to extend learning experiences to visitors from all age groups and sectors of society. In order to fulfil their potential to contribute to the goals of the Lisbon Agenda (European Council in Lisbon, 2000) and i2010, public libraries need to consider what new and innovative services and activities could be offered that empower citizens to successfully pursue lifelong learning, including those enrolled in recognized courses and those simply wanting to improve their skills. Libraries have a vital job to do in supporting individual learners' needs, providing them with choices and flexibility, helping people to continue and return to learning, enabling adults to get a job or qualification, signposting and inspiring people to take up other courses, helping children to learn, and supporting schools in diversifying children's experiences. There have been many calls for greater collaboration between libraries, schools and the adult education sector in the context of lifelong learning.

Accordingly, a significant amount of effort has been devoted at national and European levels to developing the learning role of public libraries in the digital era. Public libraries have already made significant investment in training and equipment for services to support lifelong learning. Several statements have come out from EU programme-driven initiatives: the Copenhagen Declaration (1999) from PubliCA;[1] the Oeiras Manifesto (2003) from PULMAN (www.pulmanweb.org); and from CALIMERA (www.calimera.org), under successive Information Society Technology (IST) Framework programmes. Projects in programmes now grouped together under the European Commission's Lifelong Learning Programme (LLP), such as PuLLS (Public Libraries in the Learning Society) (www.pulls.dk/); DILMULLI (Dissemination of Lifelong Learning Activities in Museums and Libraries projects);[2] PULIMA (Public Library Management and New Information Technologies);[3] SLAM (School Libraries As Multimedia centres);[4] ISTRA (Improving Student's Reading Abilities) (www.istranet.org/) particularly by using school/public libraries, are beginning to create awareness, while projects such as eMapps.com (www.emapps.com/) under IST Framework Programme 6 (IST FP6), and AITMES (Applying IT Mobile Education in Schools) (www.aitmes.org/) and Il Greco (http://ilgreco.europole.org/) (Implementing Learning Game Resources based on Educational Content) under LLP have contributed innovative environments for the use of new technologies such as games-based learning, involving public libraries to some degree. At national and regional level, networks of agencies such as the UK's Museums Libraries and Archives agency (MLA) have devoted substantial resources to work in this area.

Learning and ICT

Significant levels of ICT integration are reported across European countries, especially within formal education and those institutions providing e-learning, whether as a specific subject, integrated within specific subject disciplines or as an enabling skill. Increasingly, higher education institutions and other training providers use ICT to make resources available to their students and for distance learning purposes. However, specific data and impact studies for the adult education sector in this area are not widely available, although a number of countries are examining the role of ICT in adult education curricula at a strategic level.

It is becoming clear that many of the transactions with ICT that allow people to experience activities which support learning do not take place in traditional educational settings: all sorts of learning go on in a range of different settings. It is becoming normal for people, especially children and young adults, to be immersed in ICT-related activities in their homes and with their friends, supporting the concept of a wider 'ecology' of education involving parents, families, friends and homes; clubs and community centres; libraries, museums, galleries, science centres and archives; and generally consulting with people in all walks of life. This learning contributes to the capacity to learn the formal knowledge that is conventionally valued in society. In other words, it is possible to have both formal and informal learning occurring in both formal and non-formal spaces. The home environment alone may offer a range of digital experiences for young people, including watching DVDs, playing computer games, using revision CD-ROMs, interactive voting with digital television, editing digital photographs and participating in social networking environments. Equally, some activities encourage informal engagement with socially valued information resources, but through non-curriculum-linked approaches. The experiences of public visitors to libraries, science centres and museums fit into this category.

So, a new set of relationships is emerging between objects, learners and digital technology, in which cultural institutions are places of exploration, discovery, interpretation and learning. Libraries (in the very broadest sense), archives and especially museums uniquely provide access to 'objects' in digital and physical formats. By various means they seek to build learner participation, interactivity and a collaboration between institution and learner. Standards are emerging that allow 'chunks' of content to be cost-effectively used, adapted, shared, reused and developed by both teachers and learners.

In all, the ICT context for learning is evolving rapidly. Broadband connectivity is spreading rapidly into all parts of Europe and is being extended to public education institutions of many kinds by a variety of means, including extension of access to academic 'backbone' networks and through radio, wireless and satellite technologies. While cost and coverage in some regions remain significant issues, it is becoming increasingly feasible to think in everyday terms about the practical applications of learning that rely on internet and mobile communications for human and machine interaction and for the use of distributed digital content. Libraries have the potential to greatly enhance their role as centres of creativity and learning, by deploying new technologies. Indeed, it is possible that institutions such as libraries and museums have embraced the new-technologies approach to learning more readily than schools.

Some of the key technical developments that are likely to influence this context and to which libraries need to adapt in developing service provision are:

- personalization, enabling individual learners to use technologies to exercise choice and to take responsibility for their own learning and provide a channel for the recording and sharing of personal experience
- new 'Web 2.0' delivery modalities such as mobile devices, blogging, podcasting, videocasting, collaborative 'web spaces', multimedia content creation (e.g. mashups), location-based technologies (GPS and digital maps) and games technology – all of which are beginning to be used in e-learning
- the enabling of ever more readily available user technologies for creation of animations, music, videos, graphic and web designs.

Learning and games

Games have always been used in education. Video games have been around for nearly 30 years. But for ICT-based games to take on a meaningful role in formal or informal education, the education sector and the wider public and media need to better understand the potential and diversity of such tools.

In most European countries, although the availability of ICT facilities and networks such as computer laboratories, high-speed internet connections and interactive whiteboards and networks is clearly growing, relatively few examples of sustained uses of ICT-based games in either formal or informal education are available. There has, though, been considerable interest in the pedagogical potential of computer games for some years and there is a huge literature on the subject. Kirriemuir and Mcfarlane (2004) have provided an excellent, if now slightly dated, overview and bibliography, and one of their conclusions is:

Use of mainstream games in schools remains rare and is unlikely to be integrated into the curriculum. Reasons for this include:

- it is difficult for teachers to identify quickly how a particular game is relevant to some component of the statutory curriculum, as well as the accuracy and appropriateness of the content within the game
- the difficulty in persuading other school stakeholders as to the potential/actual educational benefits of computer games
- the lack of time available to teachers to familiarize themselves with the game, and methods of producing best results from its use
- the amount of irrelevant content and functionality in a game which could not be removed or ignored, thus wasting valuable lesson time.

None the less, teachers and parents recognize that games play can support valuable skill development, such as:

- strategic thinking
- planning
- communication
- negotiating skills
- group decision-making
- data-handling.

Significantly, the experience of game play seems to be affecting learners' expectations of learning activities. Preferred tasks are fast, active and exploratory, with information supplied in multiple forms in parallel. Traditional school-based learning may not meet these demands.

Prensky (2001) suggested that games engage learners in at least twelve different, though related, ways. They

1 Are fun to play giving enjoyment and pleasure;
2 Are a form of play, giving passionate involvement;

3 Have rules, and thus provide structured activities;
4 Have goals and thus motivate;
5 Are interactive, so that players are active, doing rather than just receiving;
6 Have outcomes and associated feedback, and thus provide learning;
7 Are adaptive, providing flow;
8 Have win states, providing gratification;
9 Have conflicts, competitions, challenges and opposition, thus raising levels of adrenaline (in the 'fight or flee' response);
10 Require problem solving, thus creating creativity;
11 May be interactive, so requiring social skills;
12 Have a storyline and character representation, thus promoting emotional involvement.

Not all games will necessarily display all of these characteristics, but to be successful it is likely that they will produce a majority of them.

The integration of computer graphics with real-world environments, called Augmented Reality (AR), blurs the line between what is real and what is computer generated. Video games that incorporate this technology are known as Augmented Reality Games (ARG), and can transform interaction so that it is no longer simply a face-to-screen exchange but involves players in the 'real' environment. The term 'mixed reality' is also sometimes used in relation to these games; see, for example, The Harbour Game: A Mixed Reality Game for Urban Planning.[5] While Prensky's 12 ways of engagement above relate primarily to software-based games, there is no reason to think that different characteristics apply to mixed-reality games. On a completely Virtual Reality (VR) plane, the success of Second Life (http://secondlife.com/), a 3-D virtual world entirely built and owned by its residents, should be noted. Since opening to the public in 2003, it has grown explosively and today is inhabited by nearly 7 million people from around the world. Second Life is a digital continent teeming with people, entertainment, experiences and opportunity in which residents retain the rights to their digital creations; they can buy, sell and trade with other residents.

However, AR technology is still too complicated and expensive for many learning environments and may involve, for example, the use of 'wearable kit'. This is likely to change as computer hardware becomes smaller and less expensive. In the mean time, a partial solution is available in the form of augmented reality via mobile devices – hand-held computers, also called Personal Digital Assistants (PDAs), or Smartphones (combined mobile phone and hand-held computer) – which provides a viable strategy, being used with some success in learning, especially when combined with a game-based approach.

A number of initiatives around Europe are investigating the value and potential of games in education in conjunction with use of the ICTs described above. The activities of several projects have set out to demonstrate on an experimental basis how, in practical terms, the role of libraries and other cultural institutions in this area may unfold and become explicit. These include The VeriaGrid (www.theveriagrid.org/) and the games-based approaches of eMapps.com (which is described in more detail below), AITMES (www.aitmes.org/), and Il Greco.

Established by Veria Public Library in Greece, The VeriaGrid is an innovative platform based on digital cartography linked to multimedia content which can be created using mobile devices and used by different audiences, for example in education and tourism promotion.

eMapps.com: games and mobile technology in learning

Funded under the European Commission's Information Society Technologies (IST) 6th Framework research programme, eMapps.com is a project whose focus is on demonstrating that games and mobile technologies can be combined for use in education. New and enriching experiences can be provided for children in the school curriculum, supporting creativity in the classroom and outside which will contribute to practice for developing new approaches to teaching. The eMapps.com games application is being piloted and tested in 16 schools across eight countries of Europe's new member states with children in the age group 9–12.

The main outcomes of the project will include a web-based game learning platform for implementation with schools, libraries and other informal settings, using games that can be played 'live' on the new generation of mobile, hand-held devices, together with supporting handbooks, evaluation tools, training courses and two international conferences. Key target audiences for eMapps.com include policy makers in school education, teachers, parents and children.

Learning, games and mobile technology

Many of the skills valuable for successful game play, and recognized by both teachers and parents, are as yet only implicitly valued within a school context. There seems to be an obvious natural alliance between games, learning and personal mobile technology, so that it is becoming feasible to equip learners with powerful tools to support their learning in many contexts over long periods of time. A major potential barrier to integrating games use in learning and the school curriculum, or at any level, is the perceived mismatch between the skills and knowledge developed in games, and those recognized explicitly within education systems. Teachers need to be engaged and to recognize and map the relationships between activities in games and the associated learning before they can embed the use of games within the wider learning context and be enabled to frame tasks, within the game or leading up to or following on from a lesson.

The approach of eMapps.com is closely related to constructivist concepts of learning, which hold that, by reflecting on their own experiences, all learners actively construct their own understanding of the world based on both their previous and current knowledge. Research shows that people learn best when they are entertained, when they can use creativity to work toward complex goals, when lesson plans incorporate both thinking and emotion, and when the consequences of actions can be observed. However, this enthusiasm is tempered by the recognition that the majority of commercial 'edutainment' products have been largely unsuccessful in harnessing this potential to effective educational use.

The eMapps.com games platform is based on 'mixed reality', which is closely aligned to Alternate Reality Games (ARG). Unlike other game genres, ARGs have no defined playing field or game space but involve immersive, real-world encounters which transcend the limitations of the 'game' and reach into the everyday world of the player. They can utilize pre-set scenarios, which represent reality graphically, and fragmented narratives which the players are required to reassemble. Groups of players are brought together into communities to work together to solve the 'mysteries of the game'. They allow interactive authoring, whereby the 'creators' are players able to observe other players virtually, in real time, and react to what they are doing and feeling; players can be motivated by being able to affect what happens in the game. Multiple levels are built into the games; players cannot move to a higher level until competence is demonstrated at the current level. Although ARGs originate and take place predominantly online, they employ mobile and other digital devices and allow simultaneous, multichannel communication.

The eMapps.com platform

The eMapps.com games platform runs on digital devices such as mobile phones, PDAs, smartphones, tablet PCs, etc. operating over the mobile phone networks, and includes game control mechanisms, chat forum and pre-set map-based local scenarios. The games are played on an open platform through multiple networks and devices. Weblogs, podcasts and videocasts are key components. 'Pins' located in a map-based pre-set scenario are linked to information held in folders in the control console: objects (photo, audio, video or text) can be placed in the folders directly from the console PC or from remote devices, including mobile hand-held devices. Any mobile device that supports a browser can be used for uploading the content to any folder. The map also supports links to external objects accessible over the internet, such as files held on a website. The map is a Graphical User Interface (GUI) that interacts with the objects and can be used for mapping existing objects in a given territory, based on GPS co-ordinates. It also has a route editor and comes with a series of tools to allow zoom-in and -out and to move the focus up, down, right, left.

The GUI supports any language and is independent of the network or software used for uploading. The map supports unlimited numbers of layers and can be produced from satellite images, aerial photographs and maps created ad hoc; these layers are geo-referenced over the original map.

Overall, eMapps.com will provide a means of designing a new learning game where teachers set the theme – the world-space where the game takes place – and the player can then explore and experience whatever permutations of that theme he or she desires. This approach will also require the participants to draw upon a wide range of contextual content and to use new mobile devices in the creation and use of that content, while developing and playing games. It is hoped that the results will have a significant impact in validating new learning paradigms in both school and informal settings and will contribute to strategic thinking about the school and curriculum reform process in the new EU member states and more widely across Europe.

Conclusion

Libraries play a vital role in delivering learning and skills agendas for both children and adults. They have the potential to greatly enhance their role as centres of creativity and learning by deploying new technologies utilizing mobile devices, multimedia content creation, Web 2.0 technology, games technology and location-based technologies (GPS and digital maps). They can provide a channel for the recording and sharing of personal experiences, and to promote informal learning and social inclusion in a way which has not previously been achieved.

References

European Commission (2006) *i2010 – A European Information Society for Growth and Employment*,
   http://ec.europa.eu/information_society/eeurope/i2010/index_en.htm.
European Council in Lisbon (2000)
   http://europa.eu/scadplus/glossary/lisbon_strategy_en.htm.
Kirriemuir, J. and Mcfarlane, A. (2004) *Games and Learning*, Futurelab,
   www.futurelab.org.uk/resources/publications_reports_articles/literature_reviews/
   Literature_Review378/#wrapper.
Prensky, M. (2001) *Why Games Engage Us*,
   www.marcprensky.com/writing/Prensky%20-%20Why%20Games
   %20Engage%20Us.pdf. From *Digital Games-based Learning*, McGraw-Hill.

URLs

1   http://cordis.europa.eu/libraries/en/projects/publica.html
2   www.dillmuli.feek.pte.hu/tool-kit.htm
3   www.elearningeuropa.info/directory/index.php?page=doc&doc_
    id=427&doclng=6
4   www.karmoyped.no/slam/
5   www.havnespil.dk/graphics/havnebilleder/artikler/wbi_presentation.pdf

13

Mobile support for distance learners: an investigation

Jane Lunsford

Introduction

This chapter describes an action research project that was ongoing in the Student Services Unit of the Open University (OU) in the UK, and illustrated some of the materials that tutors had developed for their individual student groups.

The purpose of the work was to investigate the use of mobile technologies, in the form of devices and techniques, by tutors with their students for both course-related and general support.

Context

The OU is a distance-learning organization with some 200,000 students. Associate lecturers (ALs) are part-time tutors who are responsible for a group of around 25 students for each course they teach. They may have one or more groups of students for one course, and they may teach several different courses. A course presentation may begin one or more times during a year, depending on its length and other factors. The particular issues involved in being an OU student include the fact that there is an open access policy, the time commitments of mature learners, and the challenges of studying at a distance.

Extensive research literature has been published since the mid-2000s concerning the use of mobile technologies for learning (Attewell, 2005; Kukulska-Hulme and Traxler, 2005; Sharples et al., 2005), but little of the focus is on the potential of m-learning for student support, which would be of particular interest in our area of work. The project was set up through a unit that develops online information, advice and guidance (IAG) for students and also for their tutors. Our web-based IAG for students has been designed and built to be accessible by mobile devices, but we wanted to explore further the potential benefits of mobile learning in our area of practice. As a consequence, the work was designed to investigate whether hand-held technologies would provide effective and alternative ways of supporting and enabling students by giving course-related and learning support. It was an opportunity to gather ideas about the materials and techniques that would be successful, and to discover the reactions of students. How easy or difficult would it be for this material to be developed by tutors and what resources could be provided to help them?

There are about 8000 ALs employed on a part-time basis, and while a small unit can not offer one-to-one support on the educational aspects of new technologies, we can develop online or printed material. The results of this research would inform the production of materials and advice that could be used by the wider OU community, particularly to assist tutors in using alternative, tested ways to communicate with and support their students, by including the provision of guidance and examples. This would result in offering students 'mobile' access to learning objects, using audio, video and interactive features that might help them adapt more successfully to the higher education environment.

The purpose of the project was to discover the following:

- To what extent are mobile technologies and devices useful for communicating with students and developing student learning?
- What materials are appropriate for, and harness the capabilities of, access by mobile devices?
- Is it feasible for tutors to create these alternative materials?
- What support and resources do tutors need in order to do this successfully?

Beginning the project

The plan was to work with five tutors, but because there was a great amount of interest from over one-third of the 300 people initially contacted, the number of tutors involved was extended to 16. There was an introductory workshop in February 2007, shortly before most of them began their course teaching. The workshop explained the project and the tutors' role within it, showed and discussed some possible ideas, and gave the tutors a chance to meet each other and the four members of the project team who would support them. Fourteen tutors were able to take part.

Tutors would develop alternative media that could be accessed through mobile devices – material had to be accessible to all students and not involve them in extra work, as it was to provide alternative methods of access rather than additional material. It was important that students were introduced to the project in a way that explained that it was an alternative option for them to use, which would not take more of their study time than other materials that the tutors offered. We did not want students to feel like 'guinea pigs', nor that they were getting anything special over and above other students taking the course with other tutors. Students could use the materials whether or not they consented to take part in the project evaluation.

The tutors' main role in this work was to plan and develop the alternative materials. It was up to them to create their own resources, based on their knowledge of the course content and addressing students' learning needs (Laurillard, 2002), knowing where students commonly have misconceptions or need encouragement. They also chose to use software or techniques that they judged would fit that purpose. Their secondary role was to liaise between the project team and their own students. This included giving an introduction to the project, collecting consent forms and surveys, and providing information about the materials as they became available. This approach was used to ensure that students and tutors developed their normal working relationship, while lessening any feeling that could develop of being 'researched'. Although students were only in contact with their own tutors, they had access to a member of the central team of four who managed the project, organized administration and supported tutor and student queries. A forum was provided where tutors could share and discuss whatever they needed.

Resources and software

The OU is currently developing its new virtual learning environment (VLE), but at the start of the work in February 2007 it was not yet available, so other tools had to be found. There was a small amount of money available for costs such as microphones, but we were unable to provide technical equipment; indeed one aspect of the study was to see what could be achieved with what was freely available. Not all OU courses make use of a forum as part of the course, so for some tutors sharing the files for their alternative materials would be difficult. Open and freely available software and services were investigated, including web space provision and software for audio editing, video capture and quiz development. A trial was arranged with a text service provider to allow some tutors to use text messaging.

Some of the options used were:

- blog with WordPress[1]
- audio editing with Audacity[2]
- video editing with Wink[3]
- file transfer through the OU document publishing system
- text messaging
- crosswords with Eclipse[4]
- quizzes with Quia.[5]

Here are some examples of how the various options were used by individual tutors:

- English language – recorded tutorial discussions to MP3 to share with those unable to attend
- law – audio explanations of concepts and recorded presentations made at tutorials
- pure mathematics – visuals of the tutor working through problems, with audio commentary
- science and health – review and revision crosswords, personal audio messages and reminders
- child development – involvement of students in developing blog structure and content, recording audio material
- social science – video of student discussions to review their achievements, especially in key skills development
- biology – audio reminders and comments about assignment feedback, commentated video about using a digital microscope

■ openings (access) courses – wiki or blog to gather student examples, notices and audio files; contact using text messaging.

The short introductory audios that some tutors offered sounded very welcoming. Using the human voice in an audio file seems to be a simple but powerful tool for those tutors who often find students difficult to reach by telephone, because all humans make judgements from people's voices about their character and approachability. Tutorial discussions allowed those who were unable to attend not only to hear the content of the discussion and comments from the tutor, which could help with their own progress, but also to hear how the queries and comments from other students were similar to their own. It is common for students to think that everyone else knows more than they do and that others always make well-considered points in tutorials, whereas the reality of tutorial work is that it is a place to question, work through and come to understand the course material. The provision of media-rich materials allowed greater engagement with students' different senses, which could suit those with audio or visual preferences, while quizzes and crosswords engaged students with the topic.

There were various reasons why tutors developed their materials. One was to assist students who were unable to attend tutorials, because they miss the discussion around the subject and the knowledge that other students are often in a similar position to themselves, feeling confused about course material or getting behind in their work. Some tutors wanted to provide, in addition to personalized feedback on an assignment, general feedback on each assessment that often applies to many students in a group. They also wanted to share advice and information and to review ideas such as quizzes or crosswords to help with unit or exam revision, and guidance for end-of-course assessment. These different reasons for use formed part of the evaluation of the tutors' work and its effectiveness by the tutors and their students.

Project evaluation

The findings of the project would inform the resources to be developed centrally, as well as what might be expected of tutors in terms of developing materials themselves, and would gauge students' reactions to this type of material or contact, so evaluation of the progress of the work was important. The evaluation plan included initial surveys of students to find out what they were using, whether they had any problems and what they thought of the tutorials, and a later survey to find out what they thought of the materials as a whole, what they had preferred and any comments on what they found most and least useful. A first survey of tutors asked them to judge their competence with technologies at the beginning of the course, what they had decided to use, their reasons for developing the material, any problems they had encountered and how those had been solved. The second survey asked whether they thought this type of work was feasible for tutors to undertake in their teaching, what resources were needed to support tutors, whether students had used and appreciated the material, and whether the tutors planned to continue with this type of work in future courses.

Apart from the surveys, tutors each produced a final evaluation report and collected student comments about the work. An analysis of the queries and discussions in the forum was also planned. Follow-up interviews with tutors or students were arranged as necessary to clarify any responses received. This was qualitative rather than quantitative evaluation, as the perceptions of those involved have a great effect on the acceptance, development and use of the materials.

Participants

The selection of tutors covered a wide range of tutoring experience, with all of them being new to the technical aspects of the project. The tutors (and thus their students) came from ten out of the 13 regional/national centres, at all levels from introductory Openings courses through to postgraduate, and their subjects covered science, law, social science, health, business, education, technology and mathematics. This wide range of contexts allowed us to see whether the alternative materials were suitable and useful in a wide variety of situations. Tutors liked the idea that this was a proactive way of offering support, and that providing well-planned materials allowed them to cover known areas of difficulty and could save time that would otherwise be taken up in answering individual questions. Many said that they could see the benefits to the students, which was echoed in student comments, and that they planned to continue to develop and use such materials. Some will be able to reuse the materials they made for their last group.

The following comments came from one tutorial group of students.

They support the view that such materials could offer students a way to address typical issues that arise and that the materials could be used for mobile access. However, for some students there were technical difficulties, and some actually preferred written material.

> As I was unable to attend any of the tutorials I felt more 'connected' with the tutor/group.
>
> I would love to have longer resources to conveniently download onto my iPod that I could listen to when commuting.
>
> Computer wouldn't play podcasts to start with (never worked out the reason) so had to get help from a friend.
>
> Helped me cover areas in my course-work I may have missed otherwise.
>
> Although I have found the podcasts helpful I would find it much better having a transcript. I could skip over any parts I didn't need to find the nuggets I do need!
>
> Used the podcasts for advice on assignments.
>
> Extra info is used as helpful background as I can't make it to class.

What we have learned so far

For the students, there were occasional difficulties in accessing the materials, in some cases because of the sizes of files, and for a few who did their studying at work and had firewall problems. Some students were not interested in using them, apparently because they thought it would take extra time, although materials were specifically designed to provide alternatives rather than additions and this had been explained at the start of the project.

As tutors were completely new to the technical aspects they had a number of difficulties in developing the material. Many described the 'steep learning curve' that they went through, as development that involved unfamiliar hardware or software took them a long time and could be quite complex, depending on what they had planned. For example, there were occasional computer crashes, and problems in transferring from a PC to a Mac. In some cases it was quite difficult to find suitable available software for tutors to use because the VLE and its tools were not yet available. Some tutors needed lots of time to talk through their development of materials, and it was fortunate that two members on the project team had considerable expertise: one in video and audio, and one in online skills and training.

Phase 1 findings

The following sections describe some preliminary findings from the study.

To what extent are mobile technologies and devices useful for communicating with students and developing student learning?

We know from the surveys and unprompted comments that for some students these alternative materials provided a good option that they enjoyed and used. In reality, many of the students actually used the materials from their computers, but the option for mobility was there and certainly used by some.

What materials are appropriate for, and harness the capabilities of, access by mobile devices?

Tutors were able to choose from a variety of options that suited the course and the level, knowledge and needs of the students. They are now keen to disseminate what they have learned, and will be able to share their experiences with other tutors when we develop further online tutor resources.

Is it feasible for tutors to create these alternative materials?

This is certainly the case and they have the professional background and ideas to help their students with any difficulties. However, it took considerable time for them to deal with the technicalities of production, and perseverance in the face of difficulties and setbacks.

What support and resources do tutors need in order to do this successfully?

They need practical information about possible techniques, and simple tools with simple instructions, plus web space, helpdesk support and time to practise, as well as ideas and examples, templates or frameworks. Some needed hardware, such as a microphone or digital recorder. Importantly, at the beginning it took more time than they imagined it would, so motivation is key.

Developments since the beginning of the project

Within our own online IAG materials we have this year added several audio downloads for the use of students, including advice on managing stress and various study skills. We are planning to incorporate RSS feeds for such material. We have also added information about making use of mobile devices in various ways and about using and recording audio.[6,7] Tutors from the project will be disseminating their expertise by developing case studies, which will be provided in the main online tutor area so as to provide other tutors with ideas about what was done, the pedagogical rationale and methods. Advice on using these techniques will be included, together with instructional materials on how to use the new VLE tools, thus providing a centralized resource that not only explains how to use a tool such as a blog, but also the reasons why it is an effective way of supporting students for certain types of work and tips on how to make the most of what the tool can offer.

Elsewhere in the OU the new VLE is being introduced across courses, and new tools are becoming available that include forums, wikis, audio recording tools, a portfolio tool and blogs. Because these will all be gathered within one area for users, this will make it much easier for tutors to produce these alternative materials and for students to access them. Some OU courses involve the use of such materials as part of their learning design, and in other courses there are tutors who have chosen to use such alternative technologies and materials with their tutor groups. New audio recording studios have been provided to support those wanting to produce podcast material for courses. A project on using texting for student contact is ongoing, which includes finding out what students are willing to receive in terms of content type and frequency. More staff are becoming involved in researching the uses of technologies such as podcasting.

Conclusion

For some students, access to these alternative materials was perceived (by themselves and by their tutors) to be of benefit to their learning and understanding. The tutors' work clarified topics, discussed assignment issues, involved students in tutor-group work or prompted them in new ways to review what they had learned. One development was that students felt a stronger relationship with the tutor and other students, a factor which can be of great importance in the distance learning field.

Other students were not persuaded that it was worth their efforts to access and use the material. Part of this reluctance could have been because the project work had to be set up as research for which students had to give permission, which implies a very different situation from the usual student's learning with their tutor and fellow students. Whatever the reasons, in any similar work by tutors or course teams it will be important that such resources are introduced as integral parts of the teaching blend, so that students simply accept them as such. This will be easier in future, as the OU's VLE will offer an integrated platform from which materials can be accessed, avoiding any need for students to find different sources of information, as they did during the project.

There are training implications for staff using the new tools, but of immediate benefit would be a practical awareness of the different ways in which they can be used, and some help in how to go about the work. The tutors involved in the project will produce short case studies as a means of presenting this information to their colleagues.

The findings from this particular practical action research will help to illustrate to tutors the benefits of the different options among the new tools that they can use with their students, and also ensure that tutors have the resources they need to make their work as simple as possible.

References

Attewell, J. (2005) *Mobile Technologies and Learning: a technology update and m-learning project summary*, Learning and Skills Development Agency.

Kukulska-Hulme, A. and Traxler, J. (eds) (2005) *Mobile Learning: a handbook for educators and trainers*, Routledge.

Laurillard, D. (2002) *Rethinking University Teaching: a framework for the effective use of learning technologies*, 2nd edn, RoutledgeFalmer.

Sharples, M., Taylor, J. and Vavoula, G. (2005) Towards a Theory of Mobile Learning, *Proceedings of the mLearn 2005 Conference*, Cape Town.

URLs

1   http://wordpress.org/
2   http://audacity.sourceforge.net/

3   www.debugmode.com/wink/

4   www.eclipsecrossword.com/

5   www.quia.com/

6   www.open.ac.uk/pc4study/toptips/using-gadgets.php

7   www.open.ac.uk/pc4study/ou-computer-use/using-audio.php

14

M-learning and m-teaching architectures and the integration of evolving multi-campus educational support e-services

Ivan Ganchev, Máirtín O'Droma, Damien Meere,
Mícheál Ó hAodha and Stanimir Stojanov

Introduction

Modern mobile communications devices exhibit major potential for integration into the spheres of learning, campus-wide communication and the social inclusion/cohesion of society as a whole. It is likely that the dominant mode of access to the internet will soon be in the form of wireless technologies, whereby what has commonly been known as e-learning will be enhanced by the new communicative potential that is m-learning. New insights provided by a range of specialists in the areas of social science, cognitive research and computer science research have led to greater developments and advances in the architectures for interactive and mobile learning environments. The most exciting results indicate that mobile technologies can be used to revolutionize learning and provide discontinuous rather than incremental learning opportunities in libraries and campuses worldwide. Teachers, lecturers, librarians and information workers are increasingly collaborating as pathfinders in the fast-growing learning environment of mobile technology and online learning. Since 2000 the internet has spawned many innovations and services that stem from its interactive character. There are many indications that the ongoing process of adding mobility to interactivity will transform the role of the internet and pave the way for yet another wave of innovations and services.

The convergence of computing and communication is a process which turns mobile phones and PDAs into powerful multimedia computing units. The combination of voice, data and video (triple play) corroborates the view of educational philosophers such as Dewey and

McLuhan that there is an intrinsic connection between communication, information provision and the learner community. Although most students nowadays use mobile phones, there has, to date, been little activity in integrating them into the realm of mobile learning and library/information environments. Therefore the idea that new m-learning technologies will transform learning practices has yet to achieve its collaborative ideal. This chapter describes the establishment of an innovative collaborative project between the University of Limerick and the University of Plovdiv – the Distributed e-Learning Center (DeLC) (Stojanov et al., 2003a; Stojanov et al., 2003b; Stojanov et al., 2003c; Ganchev et al., 2004). This centre aims to provide a distance e-learning and e-teaching facility available at any place and at any time to individuals and groups of students/lecturers both in online (synchronous mode) and offline (asynchronous mode). The DeLC provides intelligent mobile services needed for better organization and functioning of the entire e-learning/e-teaching process in a university environment. An initial outline proposal for this was given in Ganchev et al., 2003 and Ganchev et al., 2004. The new version of the centre (Ganchev et al., 2006; Ganchev et al., 2007) focuses on providing m-learning and m-teaching facilities by allowing electronic access from virtually any device (stationary and/or mobile) in the user's possession. Overall, to reflect the structure of the e-learning architectural reference model elaborated in the comparative study by O'Droma et al. (2003) on e-learning systems is an underlying objective.

For the project we proposed to extend the DeLC network model to a three-tier structure by introducing InfoStations and additional components needed for the provision of intelligent mobile services (e.g. intelligent redirectors, profile managers, intelligent agents acting as personal assistants for users, etc.). This chapter describes the main elements of the DeLC service architecture necessary for the support of m-learning and m-teaching. It is organized as follows. In the next (second) section we present the DeLC network model and its enhancement. Section 3 introduces the wireless access network types needed for the support of DeLC mobile services in the university information/library environment. Section 4 highlights some pilot DeLC mobile services, detailing the interactions that occur between the different network entities during service provision. Section 5 is dedicated to the implementation issues and the proposed re-engineering approach. Finally, section 6 concludes the chapter by describing future work.

DeLC network model

The DeLC network model proposed by Stojanov et al. (2003a, 2003b, 2003c) consists of DeLC nodes (DeLCNs) established and supported by real administrative units offering a complete educational cycle (e.g. laboratories, libraries, departments, faculties, colleges, universities). In the first DeLC version users get access to DeLCNs directly through the participating university intranets (or the internet) by using networked PCs. In Ganchev et al. (2004) we discuss the development of a second DeLC version with improved access possibilities for mobile users. To achieve this, the DeLC model has to be expanded to a three-tier structure (Figure 14.1 on the next page) consisting of:

1 *Mobile devices* (with intelligent agents acting as personal assistants for mobile users) such as cellular phones (e.g. GSM, GPRS, UMTS); Personal Digital Assistants (PDAs); laptops/notebooks; vehicle communication terminal systems (VCTS).

2 *Information stations (InfoStations)* deployed in the participating university libraries and at other key information points and providing network access/connectivity for mobile users with wireless devices. The InfoStations accept requests from mobile devices and forward them to an InfoStations centre for further processing. The InfoStations are used for downloading urgent messages, internet caching, synchronization of offline e-learning processes with the online m-learning system (e.g. tracking of a learner's progress, sending questions asked offline to lecturers/librarians, receiving answers, sending of other relevant offline information such as test scores, time spent on tasks etc.). The InfoStations obtain all updating information from the InfoStations centre.

3 *InfoStations centre* implemented as a server module in one of the DeLCNs. This centre controls all InfoStations and provides updating and synchronizing information. It also contains intelligent redirectors (e.g. needed to redirect a message or incoming phone call to the current user location and most appropriate current user terminal as specified in the user profile) and corresponding profile managers.

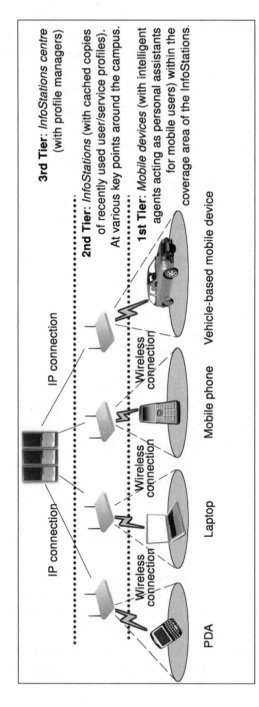

Figure 14.1 The three-tier DeLC network model and communication infrastructure supporting m-learning and m-teaching

DeLC wireless access networks

The following wireless access network types are considered to provide m-learning and m-teaching in the DeLC:

1 *WPAN (Wireless Personal Area Network)* – based on the Bluetooth/IEEE802.15 standard with a coverage of 100 m (and even up to 1 km with the new EZURiO Bluetooth class approved in 2007). The supported data rate is up to 3 Mbps.
2 *WLAN (Wireless Local Area Network)* – cheap costs and various standards (e.g. IEEE 802.11a/b/g/n). WLANs provide higher data rates than WPANs (i.e. 11 Mbps with IEEE 802.11b, 54 Mbps with IEEE 802.11a/g, and >100 Mbps with IEEE 802.11n). WLANs are increasingly popular, especially in hot spots (e.g. airports, restaurants, hotels, university campuses, libraries, office buildings, other public places) but have lower coverage than WMANs (<300 m).
3 *WMAN (Wireless Metropolitan Area Network)* – based on the IEEE 802.16e standard, capable of providing high-speed (up to 15 Mbps) wireless networking over great distances (up to 3.2 km), and supporting greater numbers of mobile users than WLANs and WPANs.

DeLC mobile services

These are services provided for users with mobile devices. This group requires development of a new subgroup of context-aware services that understand the users' context (Sadeh, 2002; Sadeh et al., 2002), e.g. user location, information environment, mobility attributes required/requested, courses/modules users are engaged in, issues of time criticality, serialization, goal-driven sequencing of tasks engaged in by the user; environmental context issues such as classmates and/or librarian/lecturer interactions.

Two examples of pilot mobile services are described in the following subsections.

Intelligent message notification

This service is needed to broadcast MMS/SMS messages to a group of users, e.g. message notification sent by a lecturer to a class of students about cancelling/postponing the lecture, or message sent by a librarian announcing a library demonstration. The lecturer/librarian types the message and sends it on his/her mobile device via available Bluetooth, WLAN or WMAN connection to the nearest InfoStation. The InfoStation then forwards this message to the university's message gateway, which is deployed as a module in the InfoStations centre and functions as an *intelligent message redirector*, deciding what is the most appropriate, quickest and cheapest way of delivering this message to each student in the class according to his/her current individual location (and device in possession) specified in the student profile. All registered DeLC users (lecturers, librarians and students) have dynamically updated profiles (user driven) in the DeLC containing (among other things) information about the best way of forwarding urgent messages to them at any particular moment, e.g. by MMS/SMS, e-mail, fax, voice-mail or otherwise.

Figure 14.2 illustrates sample interactions between entities involved in the facilitation of this service. A mobile user (e.g. lecturer, librarian or student) entering within the range of an InfoStation goes through an AAA (authentication, authorization and accounting) procedure and selects a service for use, in this case the *Intelligent Message Notification (IMN) service*. The intelligent agent (personal assistant) on the mobile device forwards this user service request to the InfoStation, which instantiates the service. The InfoStation updates the mobile device's virtual address book, which lists all currently available registered users. This is constantly updated and maintained by the system. From the virtual address book, the user selects the desired destination for the message and creates it in the form of SMS, MMS, e-mail etc., which is then forwarded by the personal assistant to the nearest InfoStation. The InfoStation analyses the recipients' profiles and makes an intelligent decision on the most reliable, appropriate, quickest and cheapest way of delivering the message to each of the recipients. This decision takes into account factors such as the recipient's current location, mobile device, and other most recent information contained within his/her profile.

If the recipient is within range of a (participating) InfoStation, the InfoStation forwards the message directly to him/her (and optionally reformats the message beforehand if necessary, e.g. when an SMS/MMS is to be delivered to an e-mail address and vice versa). If, however, the message recipient is outside the range, the InfoStation forwards the message to the InfoStations centre, which in turn delivers the message

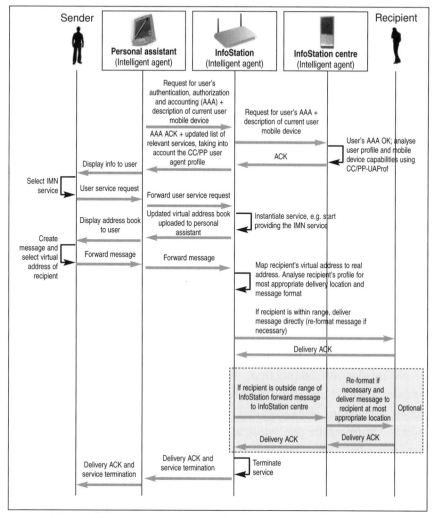

Figure 14.2 Intelligent message notification service provision

to its destination (i.e. most appropriate recipient's location). Once the message has been delivered to the relevant user(s), the InfoStations centre forwards a delivery acknowledgment to the InfoStation, which then forwards it to the PA installed on the sender's mobile device and terminates the service. The personal assistant in turn displays this confirmation to the user.

Intelligent m-test

This service is crucial to a complete e-learning process. The m-test provides a means of evaluating the students' acquired knowledge and
provides valuable feedback to students concerning their progress. This service also allows lecturers to analyse, shape to optimize and enhance the
learning experience of the students according to the subject matter and
desired learning outcomes. However, for this service to be successful, synchronization of the offline e-learning process with the online m-learning
process is imperative. This is a challenge in InfoStation scenarios, due to
this paradigm's geographically intermittent connection.

Figure 14.3 illustrates a sample interaction between the entities
involved in this service. As outlined previously, when a mobile user
enters within the range of an InfoStation, s/he goes through the normal
AAA procedure and selects the relevant service, in this case the *m-test*
service. Once the student is allowed access to the service, s/he may
begin the test. As the student progresses through the test, the service
profile is maintained to reflect this progress. Further, we consider the
possibility of the student doing the test while on the move and out of
range of an InfoStation. Due to the geographically intermittent nature
of an InfoStation connection, the student's mobile device may lose
contact with the initial InfoStation (InfoStation 1). However, the
personal assistant (PA) installed on the user's mobile device allows the
user to continue the test while at the same time maintaining the user's
service profile. Thus, the student may complete the test while outside
the contact range of any InfoStation, with the user service profile
reflecting the student's progression.

Once the PA comes within range of another InfoStation (InfoStation
2), this InfoStation will authenticate and authorize the user (AA
procedure). The PA analyses the user *m-test* service profile and sends the
updates to the InfoStation (this is basically the delivery of the
completed test for grading purposes). The InfoStation forwards this
updated user service profile to the InfoStations centre in order for the
student's assessment to be graded and the *m-test* service profile to be
updated. The control information included in this profile update allows
the lecturer to monitor the student's test scores and progress through
the assignments (i.e. time spent for each question + total time), thus
providing lecturers with an invaluable statistical resource.

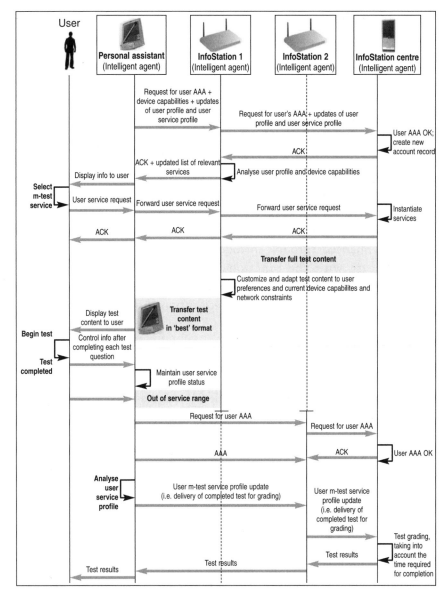

Figure 14.3 Intelligent m-test service provison

Assessment results are returned to the PA and user/student via the InfoStation in accordance with individual lecturer/course rules set for such feedback, together with directions for undertaking other assessments, next course stage and so on.

Implementation issues

For the realization of the mobile services described above, a significant enhancement of the flexibility of the existing DeLC architecture is required, along with introduction of possibilities for intelligent interaction and interpretation of the exchanged data and contents between the three parties involved in the execution process of mobile services, namely the InfoStations centre, InfoStations, and users' mobile devices. To achieve this goal, we developed the second version of the DeLC system architecture on the basis of the first one (in which services are implemented as web services) by using a *re-engineering approach*. This led to a more open information environment, supporting context-based discovery and access to user's personal information. The flexibility and intelligence of the system was enhanced through introduction of intelligent agents, which communicate with the functional modules, implemented as web services/library modules. For the interaction between the agents and the web services we used the OWL-S specification (Ankolekar et al., 2004; Coalition, 2002).

Our re-engineering process included the following steps:

1 Expanding the set of services (deployed on DeLC nodes) with additional services needed to provide interfaces respectively to:
— the existing server parts of services, e.g. central academic time schedule, intelligent diaries, library catalogue etc.
— the Infostations
— the users' mobile devices/library workstations.
2 Development of InfoStation software related to intermediate processing of information needed for identification of users and services. The software is agent-oriented or service-oriented according to the model chosen in the server part.
3 Creation of the client part of the mobile services, i.e. development of personal assistants (for users) implemented as intelligent agents.
4 Setting up communication between the client part (personal assistants) and the server part (web services) by the means of the OWL-S protocol. The use of the OWL-S as a protocol for interaction between the software components (deployed on different DeLC nodes) provided a good opportunity for the realization of a software architecture with sufficient flexibility and suitable environment for the support of a variety of mobile services.

The use of OWL-S within this system has been dealt with by Ganchev et al. (2007).

Following these steps led us to a DeLC system architecture similar to those proposed in Fabien and Sadeh (2003); Kuno and Sahai (2002); Hendler (2001); Singh, Sycara et al. (2002).

Conclusion and future work

The main elements of the DeLC service architecture providing better support for m-learning and m-teaching have been described in this chapter. This architecture (part of the second version of DeLC) has been developed on the basis of the re-engineering process, which has been described here. The existing DeLC node architecture is implemented by means of the JetSpeed framework (Apache), which uses XML-based meta-structures (e.g. users' profiles and services' profiles). This is similar to the OWL-S specification. A kernel consisting of tools and appropriate interpreters (similar to those described by Paolucci et al. (2003) were developed as a first step. All requirements of the JetSpeed and OWL-S specifications in respect of shared structures were satisfied. This was then followed by implementation of the steps proposed for finalizing the enhanced version of DeLC. The new m-learning architectures we have proposed and analysed are emerging as one of the most promising technologies for supporting learning and information acquisition in a university or library/information context. The collaborative potential of emerging wireless communications technologies can support lecturers/librarians with new possibilities for information acquisition that can be used by their customer base as follows: it can provide learners/library users with new mobile computational tools for exploring and sharing their knowledge with peers; provide teachers/librarians with new communications channels so as to visualize students' ideas and suggestions; foster collaboration among students, students and teachers, and students and librarians/other information providers. Our aim is not simply to provide new m-learning or wireless e-services but rather to explore new and varied learning architectures that become available through the design and application of innovative educational technologies.

Acknowledgements

The authors wish to acknowledge the support of Ireland's HEA Strategic Initiatives Funding Programme 'Technology in Education' and of the Bulgarian Ministry of Education and Science for Research Project 'Consumer-Oriented Model and Architecture for Mobile E-learning Services (COMMERCE)' Ref. No. ВУ-МИ-101/2005.

References

Ankolekar, A., Burstein, M. et al. (2004) *OWL-S: semantic markup for web services*, DAML Program.

Apache, http://jakarta.apache.org/jetspeed.

Coalition, D. S. (2002) DAML-S Web Services Description for the Semantic Web, *1st International Semantic Web Conference, ISWC '02, Sardinia, Italy*.

O'Droma, M., Ganchev, I. and McDonnell, F. (2003) Architectural and Functional Design and Evaluation of eLearning VUIS based IEEE's LTSA proposal, *The Internet and Higher Education*, 6, (September), 263–76.

Fabien, G. and Sadeh, N. (2003) *Semantic Web Technologies to Reconcile Privacy and Context Awareness*, School of Computer Science, Carnegie Mellon University, Pittsburgh, USA.

Ganchev, I., O'Droma, M. et al. (2003) Provision of Mobile Services in a Distributed eLearning Center, *International Conference on Automatics and Informatics, Sofia, Bulgaria*.

Ganchev, I., Stojanov, S. et al. (2004). Enhancement of DeLC for the Provision of Intelligent Mobile Services, *2nd International IEEE Conference on Intelligent Systems (IS 2004), Varna, Bulgaria*.

Ganchev, I., Stojanov, S. et al. (2006) An InfoStation-Based University Campus System for the Provision of mLearning Services, *IEEE-ICALT 2006, Kerkrade, The Netherlands*.

Ganchev, I., Stojanov, S. et al. (2007). An InfoStation-Based Multi-Agent System Supporting Intelligent Mobile Services Across a University Campus, *Journal Of Computers*, 2 (3), 21–33.

Hendler, J. (2001) Agents and the Semantic Web, *IEEE Intelligent Systems '01*.

Kuno, H. and Sahai, A. (2002) *My Agent Wants to Talk to Your Service: personalizing web services through agents*, Hewlett-Packard Laboratories.

Paolucci, M., Sycara, K. et al. (2003) *Towards a Semantic Web E-commerce*, Carnegie Mellon University, Pittsburgh, USA.

Sadeh, N. (2002) *Mobile Commerce: new technologies, services and business models*, Wiley.

Sadeh, N., Chan, E. et al. (2002) MyCampus: an agent-based environment for context-aware mobile services, *AAMAS02 Workshop on Ubiquitous Agents on Embedded, Wearable, and Mobile Devices, Bologna*.

Singh, R., Sycara, J. and Payne, T. (2002) Distributed AI, schedules and the semantic web, *XML Journal*, 3 (11), (November), 40–5.

Stojanov, S., Ganchev, I. et al. (2003a) DeLC – Distributed eLearning Center, *1st Balkan Conference on Informatics BCI 2003, Thessaloniki, Greece*.

Stojanov, S., Ganchev, I. et al. (2003b. A Model for Integration of Electronic Services into a Distributed e-Learning Environment, *14th EAEEIE International Conference, Gdansk, Poland*.

Stojanov, S., Popchev, I. et al. (2003c). A Concept for Building of the DeLC, *Scientific and Practical Conference on the New Education Technology, Sofia, Bulgaria*.

15

Designing and developing e-learning content for mobile platforms: a collaboration between Athabasca University and the Open University

Tony Tin, Hassan Sheikh and Colin Elliott

Introduction

The use of mobile devices continues to expand, with a growing number of these devices also having access to the internet. The number of mobile users in the UK is 43 million (or 82% of the total population) (Dickey, 2006) and the total number of mobile users in North America is 171 million. Along with this growth in devices and internet access, the interest in mobile learning (often called ubiquitous learning) and performance support capabilities grows. These mobile devices can take the form of hand-held computers or personal digital assistants, mobile phones including the new smartphones, audio players (such as the Apple iPod), video players, UMPCs, tablet PCs, and even wearable devices. They can be connected through a desktop, a laptop, or a network, either wired or wireless. They can be stand-alone and possibly synchronized periodically, intermittently connected to a network, or always connected.

As the demand for access to education grows and increasing numbers of adults return to university/college for continuing education and training, so grows the need for new technologies to facilitate learning. Online teaching and learning is well established, providing great opportunities to increase flexibility in time and location of study, and in terms of availability of information and resources, synchronous and asynchronous communication and various types of interaction via the world wide web. A key benefit of m-learning is its potential for increasing productivity by making learning available anywhere, any time. However, it is a resource that is currently untapped, as it seems that few academic libraries, if any, are taking significant strides to accommodate access and display for mobile devices. Further, little research from a student's perspective has explored which mobile technologies are the best to employ, or what constitutes an effective m-library and how to use it to support m-learning and teaching.

The Athabasca/Open University collaboration

In 2007, Athabasca University (AU) and the Open University UK (OUUK) Library development teams started collaboration on content delivery systems for mobile and hand-held devices. The project was initiated during a visit by Dr Mohamad Ally (Professor at Athabasca University in Canada) to the OUUK in November 2006 to deliver two seminars on his work at Athabasca University around mobile content delivery systems. At the seminars, Dr Ally demonstrated the ADR (Auto Detect and Reformat) system developed inhouse by his team. The ADR system automatically detects the type of mobile device used to connect to the website and both renders and optimizes the contents to fit appropriately on the mobile screen. The idea was of particular interest to the team developing the OU's new library website and led to discussions about reusing the source code of ADR and building a partnership between AU and the OU to further enhance the functionality of ADR software. This partnership brings a number of benefits to both parties. It will save the OU development time and resources and will offer both partners the opportunity to work together to develop some innovative services.

AU Library and its mobile projects

Athabasca University (AU) is a pioneer in distance education and is Canada's leading distance education and e-learning institution. AU serves over 32,000 students and offers over 700 courses. AU's mission statement is:

> Athabasca University, Canada's Open University, is dedicated to the removal of barriers that restrict access to, and success in, university-level studies and to increasing equality of educational opportunity for adult learners worldwide.
>
> Athabasca University, 2007

AU is committed to excellence in teaching, research and scholarship, and to being of service to the general public.

Mobile learning helps AU to fulfil its mission statement by removing barriers to learning and allowing students to study 'anytime and anywhere.' The AU Library has pioneered a number of projects with the aim of allowing students flexibility and accessibility, and meeting the needs of diverse learners, including those in remote areas.

Three of the mobile projects that the AU Library has worked on are: the mobile library website, the mobile Digital Reading Room (DRR) and the mobile ESL (English as a second language) project. These projects have been successful and address the growing mobile needs of our students.

The mobile library at Athabasca University enables students and staff to access library services and materials through the world wide web using mobile devices. The materials the students can access include:

- mobile device-ready learning objects, including MP3 versions (text to speech) of journal articles, video clips and e-books
- existing AU Library electronic resources organized for m-learning
- a comprehensive list of m-learning application tools
- a best-practice document for m-learning instructional design (http://library.athabascau.ca).

The AU mobile ESL project provides English grammar lessons and inter-active exercises to anyone with a mobile device (cellphone, PDA, smartphone) which has access to the internet. Students can brush up on their English language skills while waiting for a bus, over their lunch break, or whenever they have the time to review grammar. The digital ESL content is based on Penguin's bestselling introductory English grammar lessons and exercises, released by the author as 'open source' material (O'Driscoll, 1988, 1990). Students have access to the basic tools of English grammar in an interactive modular format, accessible on mobile and fixed computing devices (http://eslau.ca).

The DRR is an interactive online reading room, offering digital files for course readings and supplementary materials. It is used for almost half of the courses at Athabasca University and it houses 25,000 different objects. The mobile ESL project has been extremely popular and has had over 7000 unique visitors during the year (2006). The most popular devices for both of these websites are the Palm Treo, HP iPAQ, BlackBerry, 2G phones, and selected models of 1G phones. The iPhone is now gaining in popularity as well and is being used more often to access content (http://library.athabascau.ca/drr).

The OU Library and its mobile projects

The Open University is the largest UK university. Over 2 million people have studied with the OU since its inception. In 2004–5, the OU had 203,000 registered students, equating to 74,000 full-time students. The OU also has 21,000 students studying in Europe and worldwide. There are currently 1100 academic staff, 7500 tutorial staff and 3500 support staff working at the OU.

For an open university such as OUUK, it is very important for its online resources to be made accessible to as wide a range of users and devices as possible. It is essential that both appropriate existing and emerging technologies be implemented for effective development, delivery and support to and for remote students. In order to keep up to speed with mobile learners' needs, several project initiatives have taken place within the Open University, including:

1 *The Mobile Learner support project*[1] aims to ensure that support is provided for OU students and learners while they are on the move, working away from their normal environment, and who may be using mobile devices to engage with content and delivery.
2 *StudentHome mobile* is a cut-down version of the OU students' home page initiated within the Computing Unit. Its aim is to offer key student administrative services on mobile devices.
3 *OUTexts* is a pilot project to send text messages to students containing useful information such as exam dates, assignment submission dates or reminders to sign up for their next course. The project is currently being piloted with one course but, depending on the feedback, there are plans to roll it out with further courses. The OUTexts project has been initiated by the OU's Student Services Unit.
4 *Mobile Open Library 2.0* has been developed within the OU Library (in partnership with Athabasca University) and is a mobile version of the new Library website (www.open.ac.uk). The project is based on ADR (Auto Detect and Reformat) software to automatically detect

whether the user is connecting from a mobile or hand-held device and reformat the page contents accordingly to fit nicely on a small screen. The mobile Open Library 2.0 system is in pilot phase and has been available to users since November 2007. It received over 1800 page hits between November 2007 and January 2008 and user comments have been very positive. The areas with most hits from mobile users include the home page, search engine, collections, 'library info' and the research page. We have tested the system on various mobile and hand-held devices including BlackBerry, HP iPAQ, Nokia N95, iPhone, Qtek and Toshiba Portege. There are plans to add more devices for testing the website in phase 2 of the development.

5 *Mobile Safari* is another AU/OU joint initiative developed at the ILU (Information Literacy Unit) within the OU Library. Safari (Skills in Accessing, Finding & Reviewing Information) is the OU's online information skills tutorial.The mobile Safari is based on AU's mobile ESL system (http://eslau.ca) and takes bespoke learning objects (specifically written for mobiles) and renders them to a plain HTML-based learning activity. The project is being piloted initially with a learning object on evaluating information.

Designing for mobiles

What is the future?

Based on the experiences of AU's mobile projects and of their users, there are a number of possible improvements and new directions for the future. For users of the AU Library mobile website, DRR and the mobile ESL website, the following are some of the features suggested:

1 Users and developers have both expressed the need for more multimedia content. This will make the lessons and learning objects more practical and relevant for users.
2 The structure and design of web pages will be further developed for mobile use. This will include pages being device specific and separately navigable; the number of pages needs to be kept to a minimum, to avoid excessive charges, and the navigation has to be kept as simple as possible so that users can find parts of the course easily and start again from where they left off.
3 Support for learning management systems (LMSs) such as Moodle

is another important future development. Students will be able to access their complete course and do much of their course work on a mobile device.

As well as these suggested features, there are several indications and trends that point to promising developments for mobile technologies. According to McGreal, the two types of distance education technologies (type I – information media; and type C – communication media) are converging through mobile technology to allow for type S (social) applications. These applications 'allow learners to become acquainted, work collaboratively, schedule learning and in other ways enhance learning' (McGreal, 2005). These applications will spawn further demand for mobile content and mobile-accessible websites. This growth will also be intense, because of the relative immaturity of mobile devices.

Locational learning will also be facilitated by mobile technology. Learning partners, for collaborative work, and customized learning experiences will be available through mobile connections to content. Users will be able to access the resources and people they need seamlessly and quickly from anywhere.

The future will see a great demand for mobile multimedia content and applications and a flexible web structure that adapts to each device while keeping the navigation and pages as simple as possible. Locational learning through mobile devices will guarantee that each user receives a learning or browsing experience designed to meet his/her needs.

Tips and tricks

Making web content mobile friendly involves a variety of adjustments in order to ensure that the end user has appropriate functionality when accessing the web pages. Many mobile devices have small screen size, small input devices, low bandwidth, and challenges when navigating through the information (Ahonen et al., 2003). To compensate for these limitations, appropriate material must be selected and presented efficiently. For larger graphics, a general outline of the graphic should be used and navigation tools provided to allow the user to see the complete detail on another screen. To compensate for low bandwidth and low memory problems, the content must be chunked into smaller segments for faster access and to avoid exceeding memory limitations.

Some other methods for ensuring that a page is viewable on a mobile device are:

- avoid using width-specific markups for HTML blocks
- ensure the layout is fluid/liquid and reflowable for viewing on different screen sizes
- eliminate the use of tables for layout purposes
- eliminate the use of images for textual content and link buttons
- avoid the use of frames.

As well, third-party integrated proxies such as Skweezer (www.skweezer.net) process content into smaller parts and make it mobile friendly. This service, and others like it, can format external content as well as making linking to other resources better for mobile users.

These methods help to ensure that pages are viewable on any mobile devices and that the page changes easily to fit each different screen size. The other important feature is to incorporate auto-detection so that, as a page is accessed by a device, that device is detected and the content that fits that device is then delivered. Figure 15.1 (overleaf) outlines this process.

Challenges and issues

There are numerous challenges that have to be overcome in order to make mobile browsing more seamless.

Bandwidth

Many mobile devices are limited to slower wireless connections. Multimedia requires faster connections and delivering multimedia content to mobile devices is not always possible.

Content

Content must be properly formatted for each mobile device. If it has not been formatted, the content will be difficult to read and navigate. In the future XML and style sheets should help to resolve this problem.

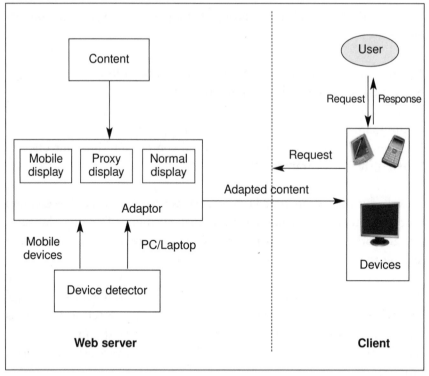

Figure 15.1 Auto Detect and Reformat process

Printing

Mobile devices do not support mobile or wireless printing. If users want to print, they have to use a third-party program, but not all devices are supported.

Operating system

Mobile devices come with many different and proprietary operating systems. This interferes with making pages that are readable by any device, since each operating system may treat them differently.

Screen size

Mobile devices have small screens which limit how much information can be displayed. They also limit the type of information and both of these limitations can cause navigation issues for users.

Memory

Mobile devices have limited and unstable memory. The amount of content and the length of time it can be stored both create problems for web browsing. The unstable memory of mobile devices means that if a device is left uncharged it could lose anything stored in its memory.

Recommendations for embarking on mobile content design
User interface and usability

▤ the screen size is small, so avoid putting too much on one page; keep it simple and focus on the key content required by the users
▤ do not write lengthy text – bullet points work well
▤ provide navigational links to enable users to navigate around the website
▤ avoid images unless there is a real need; use jpeg or gif format
▤ minimize the levels of navigation hierarchy.

Markup languages

▤ WML (Wireless Markup Language) – is delivered via a WAP gateway. WAP-enabled devices run micro-browsers (with low memory and low bandwidth constraints). WML was the former language choice for WAP 1.0.
▤ xHTML Mobile Profile (MP) – xHTML is the extension of HTML that enforces strict syntax checking of XML. The Mobile Profile variant is a subset of xHTML that addresses some of the constraints of mobile browsers. With the introduction of WAP 2.0, xHTML-MP became the official markup language. Nearly all devices sold today support xHTML and are WAP 2.0 enabled and they can access not only WML and xHTML-MP based sites but the ordinary websites too, which are designed for PCs.

Some mobile emulators on which to test the websites

A number of online resources provide mobile phone simulations, which enable you to view your website as it appears on standard mobile phone screens. Some of these are:

- Google Mobile Proxy[2]
- Palm OS Emulator[3]
- Windows 2003-based Pocket PC Emulator[4]
- Windows 2003 SE Smartphone Emulator.[5]

Conclusion

Athabasca University and the Open University UK both deliver courses to students via distance education. One of the greatest challenges that both face is how best to design and deliver content to students, especially those in more remote locations. The growing use and capabilities of mobile devices have created interest in mobile learning. One of the key strengths of m-learning is that it can deliver content to students – anytime, anywhere. This helps to solve the challenge of meeting increased demand from students to study when and where they want. M-learning supports just-in-time and ubiquitous learning so that students can receive up-to-date material instantly – no matter where they are located.

M-learning has great potential to allow students to become more productive and to meet their needs for studying when and where they want. For libraries, relatively little has been done to explore how to exploit this technology to help students. Athabasca University and the Open University UK have collaborated to develop m-libraries and have been able to deliver content to students via mobile devices. Many challenges remain before this becomes a completely seamless experience for students, but as the capabilities of mobile devices increase, these problems will be resolved.

References

Ahonen, M., Joyce, B., Leino, M. and Turunen, H. (2003) Mobile Learning: a different viewpoint. In H. Kynaslahti and Seppala, P. (eds), *Mobile Learning*, 29–39.

Athabasca University (2007) *Athabasca University Calendar* (1 September), www.athabascau.ca/calendar/ [accessed 3 November 2007].

Dickey, Tony (2006) UK Mobile User Numbers Show Market Growth in Data, *Mobile Magazine* (16 January), www.mobilemag.com/content/100/353/C6015/ [accessed 10 October 2007].

McGreal, R. (2005) Mobile Devices and the Future of Free Education, *ICDE World Conference 2005*, 24–28 October, New Delhi, International Council for Distance Education.

O'Driscoll, J. (1988) *Basic English Grammar*, Penguin.

O'Driscoll, J. (1990) *English Grammar Exercises*, Penguin.

URLs

1   http://conclave.open.ac.uk/dev-ouvle/?page_id=142

2   http://www.google.com/gwt/n

3   www.palmos.com/dev/tools/emulator

4   www.microsoft.com/downloads/details.aspx?FamilyID=57265402-47a8-4ce4-9aa7-5fe85b95de72&displaylang=en

5   www.microsoft.com/downloads/details.aspx?FamilyID=791bae52-b057-4d72-b263-105534825ca5&displaylang=en

16

Open Library in your pocket – services to meet the needs of on- and off-campus users

Hassan Sheikh, Susan Eales and Mariano Rico

Introduction

The Open University is the largest UK university. Over 2 million people have studied with the OU since its inception and currently 35% of UK part-time undergraduates are OU students. More than half of OU students do not have the level of formal qualifications required by campus universities, so have not come through a traditional route, and 16% are under 25, with the median age of new undergraduates being 32.

The Open University Library and its services

The OU Library has 93 staff based in a purpose-built building at the main Walton Hall campus in Milton Keynes, which is 50 miles north of London. It is open to anyone who is able to come to the building, including members of the local community. Events are held regularly in the Library, including a programme of Library seminars on topics of interest to libraries and the wider e-learning community. However, students can only register with the physical Library service if they can come to the building and, because of the size of the student body, the Library is unable to provide postal loan or document delivery services to students. Therefore, the website is *the* Library for our students and must perform all the functions of a digital library, including those which would normally be confined to the library catalogue. As network bandwidth increases, nationally and internationally, library information 'on the move' for time-poor students is also becoming increasingly important, and there are also opportunities for information skills training to be offered in bite-sized chunks for anytime, anywhere access.

Library projects

The Library's Strategic and Services Development (SSDG) team, with its experienced project managers, is responsible for managing all library projects. The portfolio of projects ranges from small Library developments, to larger projects such as Digilab (http://digilab.open.ac.uk) – a physical, non-threatening space for on-campus staff to try out the latest technologies for effective learning.

The Library is proud of its collaboration with other OU units and is also leading on aspects of university-wide projects such as a new Enterprise Content Management system and the OU Virtual Learning Environment (VLE) Programme. As part of the VLE Programme, the Library is leading on the development of a new, federated search service for OU resources, including library resources. It is also looking at how use of library services can be made more seamless and better integrated, using the suite of tools being developed as part of the VLE Programme.

The Library is also currently involved in a number of externally funded projects, and is planning to continue to actively seek opportunities to further staff skills and expertise in key areas such as multimedia repositories management, preservation, metadata and web-based services provision through taking part in national projects.

Open Library 2.0

In 2004 and 2005, five years after the launch of the original Open Library website, a review was undertaken. This involved extensive user consultation through a survey, interviews and focus groups with students. It was clear that the current website was becoming out of date and the complexity of the site was making it difficult for users to make full use of the online resources that the Library subscribes to. The review produced a clear set of requirements and recommendations for improvement. These were:

- easier navigation
- easier access to online journals

- task-orientated approach
- jargon-free language
- subject-based search option
- personalization
- database driven for easier updating by library staff.

In 2006, a project team was set up and a further literature review and benchmarking exercise was carried out, particularly exploring potential for inclusion of some of the emerging Web 2.0 innovations. During this process, a posting on the Free Range Librarian site was discovered.[1] This contained sound bites from 'a passionate young librarian who cares' on dissatisfaction with library systems and services and was used to form the basis of a brainstorming workshop with Library staff. Content of a presentation by Lorcan Dempsey at the 'Edina is 10' event at the University of Edinburgh[2] was also extremely useful in forming the vision for the new Library website.

Building on the recognition achieved by the Library's efforts to be corporate and integrated more fully within the wider OU, a stakeholder workshop was held at the beginning of the project, involving key people and departments across the University who could be influencers, helping us to achieve our goals, or whose work might be affected by our plans. This included the VLE Programme Director and the Central Computing Services Projects Manager and enabled the Library to articulate clearly its vision and discuss with others where there might be overlap with other developments, where further communication would be needed and opportunities for fruitful collaboration.

Open Library 2.0 Phase 1

Phase 1 of the project was launched in October 2007 (http://library.open. ac.uk). This featured a new database-driven site with a content management system which can be used by all Library staff. The content has been completely rewritten and the number of pages reduced by around 90%, in a collaborative activity involving around 40 Library staff, coordinated by the Web Manager. New dynamic pages were created wherever possible, making use of the database-driven site and reducing the need for duplication and manual updating.

Considerable attention was paid to the look and feel of the site. It was modelled on commercial websites, rather than other library sites, to enable us to focus on the requirement to be task orientated and jargon free. Images have been used extensively and new images were purchased, involving families and young people, to give the site a fresh appeal.

New services that have been implemented in Phase 1 of the project include:

- a new 'browse by subject' service which brings together resources from all the Library databases under standard subject headings, mapped to the Joint Access Coding System (JACS) national standard
- a new OpenUrl Resolver and online journals management system (SFX from Ex Libris)
- a 'Find it at OU' button in Google Scholar search results where the title is available in the OU Library
- 'Ask an OU Expert', developed as a web service for the Library from an award-winning project in another OU unit
- RSS feeds for news and some Library services on the home page
- a Library 2.0 'Toolbox' page to provide our more technically minded users the opportunity to try new externally and internally developed prototypes which are Library related and to feed back on which they find most useful
- the Library catalogue search box can be added to web browser tool bars and *iGoogle* personalized pages
- a prototype version of the site for mobiles, developed in collaboration with Athabasca University.

An Editorial Group has been set up to maintain the site's integrity and to ensure that it is updated on a regular basis and that it remains jargon free and task orientated.

Qualitative feedback has been very positive and there is growing evidence that the number of directional helpdesk enquiries is reducing as a result of the new site.

Open Library 2.0 Phase 2

Work continues now exploring further enhancements to the website. These have been grouped into four main areas:

- Personalization
- Rich Media
- New Web Services
- Services for Mobiles.

The Personalization project includes:

- customization of home page and services page
- search
    — implementing Lucene to search dynamic web pages
    — benchmarking with other Library websites
- improvements to the 'Libraries Near You' service – a key value-added service provided for our distance learners
- workshops for requirements gathering for a 'My Research Library' service
- work towards personalization using SAMS, the University's single sign-on system, in collaboration with the central computing service.

The Rich Media project includes:

- 'meet the librarian' regular feature
- 'resource of the month' feature
- adding podcasts and videos of Library seminars to the website for the benefit of all our users
- report on future infrastructure requirements
- report on user requirements
- recommendations for future sustainable activity.

The New Web Services Project includes:

- find OU Library books from Amazon
- adding reviews and tags to Library Seminars podcasts and videos
- literature review, scoping and feasibility study on
    — web services from the website
    — web services from the Library catalogue
- LibraryThing – explore using this web service with researchers to share favourite resources.

Mobile Open Library 2.0 (http://library.open.ac.uk)
Background

Dr Mohamed Ally of Athabasca University visited the Open University, UK in November 2006. One of the presentations he made during his visit focused on the work of his team at Athabasca University Library to develop library services and content for delivery via mobile devices (Ally, 2006).

Aims and objective

Online teaching and learning has provided great opportunities to increase flexibility of time and location of study, in terms of availability of information and resources, synchronous and asynchronous communication and various types of interaction via the world wide web. Today, mobile learning is enabled by the use of portable computing devices, such as personal digital assistants (PDAs), ultra notebooks, smartphones, and tablet PCs, communicating over wireless networks. A key benefit of mobile library is its potential for increasing productivity by making learning available anywhere, at any time. However, little research from a student's perspective has explored which mobile technologies are the best to employ, or what constitutes an effective m-library and how to use it to support m-learning and teaching.

For an open university such as the OU, it is very important for its online resources to be made accessible to as wide a range of users and devices as possible. It is essential that appropriate existing and emerging technologies be implemented for effective development, delivery and support for remote students. The key objective of the Mobile Open Library 2.0 project is to build a platform for the OU to develop an effective mobile-friendly library and to evaluate how well the OU Library web site works with popular smartphone devices. The results of this project can then be used to determine how the University can make its websites useful for users with a diverse range of mobile devices.

Phase 1 developments

In the first phase of the project, we have optimized the Library website to render on hand-held devices. The key services developed so far for the mobile version of Open Library 2.0 include:

- implementation of ADR (Auto Detect and Reformat) software in partnership with the Athabasca University team to present an optimized Library website to mobile devices;
- redesign of layout and structure of the Library website for mobile devices;
- customized search engine.

Tools and technologies

We have used a range of mobile devices to test the website, including:

- Nokia N95
- iPhone
- Qtek 9100
- Toshiba Portege G900
- BlackBerry 8800.

We have also tested the website on different mobile platforms and browsers, including:

- Symbian OS (Nokia web browser)
- OS X (Safari web browser)
- Windows CE (IE for mobiles)
- Windows mobile 6.0
- BlackBerry OS 4.x.

Figures 16.1 and 16.2 (pages 192 and 193) show a couple of the mobile Open Library 2.0 screens.

Usage statistics

The number of Open Library 2.0 page hits from mobile/hand-held devices between October 2007 and February 2008 was 1847, with the average number of page hits per month being 462.

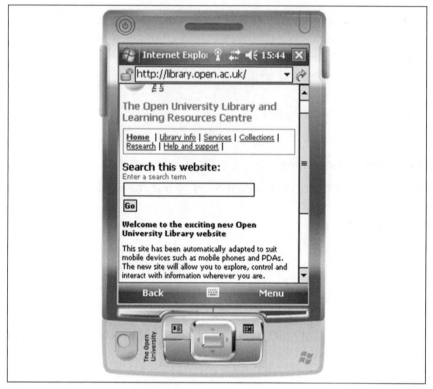

Figure 16.1 Mobile Open Library 2.0 – home page

What mobile users are doing with the website
Most viewed pages (number of page hits in parentheses)

1 Home page (580)
2 Search (309)
3 Collections (126)
4 Library info (98)
5 Research (77).

Top search terms

1 Routes (the OU Library's database of quality-assured websites)
2 Athens (some resources require a separate Athens password)
3 Resource
4 Business
5 Research.

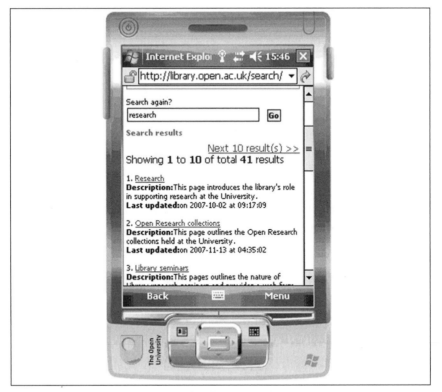

Figure 16.2 Search page on Mobile Open 2.0 Library

Most common mobile devices used to connect to Library website

1 BlackBerry
2 HP iPaq
3 Nokia N95
4 Sony Ericsson K810i
5 Motorola V3.

Top OS and mobile browsers

1 Windows CE (IE mobile 6.12)
2 SymbianOS
3 Opera mini 3.1
4 RISC OS (NetSurf)
5 Linux (Opera 9.02).

Phase 2 – current development plans

We are currently working on enhancing the mobile Open Library 2.0 system and planning to develop further mobile-driven services including:

- improvement of contents – one version fits all
- user requirements analysis
- implementation of personalization – users choose what services they want
- Web 2.0-oriented services – users interact with the systems by adding reviews, tags and comments
- SMS-based facilities – e.g. users text an ISBN to find whether a book is held in the OU Library.

Designing and developing for mobiles

Tips and tricks

Here are some suggestions for developing website content for mobiles:

1 Strip out image tags for faster content download (hiding them in CSS does not always work).
2 Auto-detect the mobile device and offer the trimmed-down version of the website – users like it! But provide an option to switch between the mobile and full-size versions of the website.
3 Detect the mobile user once, rather than each time the user accesses a page, and set a session (or URL) variable.
4 Include the maximum number of device models in your detection, but the ideal solution would be to detect the device screen size and classify the templates accordingly.
5 Define smaller-size text for the form elements or create different versions of forms for mobiles and PCs (e.g. feedback forms).
6 Enable users to resize text.
7 Show relevant navigational links rather than the links of all sections.

Challenges and issues

Mobile content development is a relatively new area and despite emerging/improved smartphones and a faster WAP gateway (WAP 2.0) which supports advanced functions, developing and designing mobile websites poses many challenges and issues such as:

- mobile users prefer short and to-the-point content – be precise when writing content (even for PC versions)
- large pictures take too long to download – hide pictures or strip out the img. tag altogether
- users will want specific mobile services – consult them and ask about their preferences rather than trying to reproduce the whole site
- there are thousands of models of hand-held devices and it is not possible to develop content that is optimized for every device – if there is a way to identify the screen size of the device a handful of templates will need to be designed for the screen-size classes
- multimedia applications are currently too big and clunky – don't use large-size audio/video files for mobile delivery
- Flash is not supported by all mobile devices – keep the content simple (plain HTML is highly recommended)
- advanced HTML features are not supported by many smartphones – use basic HTML tags for mobile content delivery.

Conclusion

The use of mobile devices is growing and so is the demand for online services for mobiles and hand-held devices. The latest models of smartphones and PDAs offer WiFi functionality which makes it cheaper for users to stay online, and mobile web browsing is becoming increasingly popular. With the increasing number of online mobile users, the pressure is on universities and libraries to respond by fine-tuning their internet-based systems and optimizing their websites for mobiles. However, it is important to understand that users may not be interested in having simply the bare-bones functionality of the website on their mobile devices, and the mobile version of the site should offer specialized services and contents which are optimized to render on smaller devices. There are several good examples of websites offering cut-down versions for mobiles. TypeAd, for example, is a blogging system that offers just four key functions – comment, create a new blog post, manage posts and manage mobile settings – when connected through an iPod touch or iPhone. BBC and Google offer customized versions of their websites which are easy to use and navigate from a mobile phone.

Someone browsing from a site mobile has very different needs and expectations from a desktop user. Mobile users are limited by their devices and are not, for example, accessing a site in order to download large documents or browse high-quality podcasts. It is therefore important to consult users and identify their requirements and the functions they would want of the website.

URLs

1   http://freerangeelibrarian.com/2006/06/03/the-user-is-not-broken-a-meme-masquerading-as-a-manifesto.
2   http://edina.ac.uk/events/edina10th.

17

On metadata for the operationalization of m-libraries

Jim Hahn

Introduction

Exploring the possibilities for the operationalization of bibliographic objectives in a mobile digital library is a useful inquiry for m-library practitioners. Evidence to show the congruence between the bibliographic system paradigm and the emerging m-library concept will serve to inform the approach to m-library solutions in a philosophically grounded and intellectual manner. The lessons to be learned and adapted from the bibliographic paradigm will benefit users of the mobile system.

Librarians descend from an intellectual foundation evidenced in the canon of library and information science literature. This thesis is promulgated by Elaine Svenonius (2000). She articulates the idea that librarianship embraces conventions of information organization that are well researched and are useful to library practitioners. Underscoring the foundations of library and information science helps practitioners to understand information organization as the librarian's raison d'être. The services that librarians provide are their concomitant subspecializations; I think here of the reference librarian, the instructional librarian, the cataloguer involved in metadata creation, annotation and management, the systems librarian who helps make our disparate software pieces interoperable. These professional service-oriented skills have a common intellectual foundation.

A mobile digital library is an example or sub-type of a digital library, and that digital library is a type of bibliographic system. The objectives of a full-featured bibliographic system as promulgated by Svenonius

(2000, 20) include those of finding, collocation, choice, acquisition and navigation. These objectives are refined from the work of the International Federation of Library Associations and Institutions (IFLA) Committee on Functional Requirements for Bibliographic Records (IFLA, 1998) – the collective intellectual output of many library and information science practitioners – and descend from earlier international library co-operative committee work on bibliographic standards, such as the Paris Principles (IFLA, 1962).

The objectives of a bibliographic system can be realized by creating and managing metadata. The metadata attached to an entity both describe content and bring like content together; this is the collocating function of a bibliographic system. Metadata are instrumental in the development and usefulness of digital libraries, and in realizing the success of m-libraries. This chapter is not a comprehensive review of mobile metadata, but an inquiry into how the bibliographic model, as conceived in the canon of library and information science, contributes to the access, organization and preservation of digital learning objects for mobile learning.

This chapter examines metadata for learning objects: the Learning Object Metadata (LOM) standard, and the IMS Access for All specification. It also investigates cell phone picture data annotation as a means for presenting and making accessible user-generated content, and examines context-aware services enabled via Bluetooth transmission and theoretical physical library applications for the Serendipity architecture, developed and patented by researchers at the MIT media lab. The chapter concludes with an examination of the possibilities of ontology for defining m-libraries and library service development for ubiquitous computing.

Traditional metadata for learning objects and additional specifications

Digital content developed for mobile-specific hardware is not systematically accessible without metadata. Metadata is a crucial component in the discovery of digital resources. A question librarians need to ask as they develop content for mobile service is: will users discover this resource through their mobile devices or is discovery of this content a desktop-based activity? The solutions employed for discovery and access must be guided by user-centred principles.

Learning Object Metadata (LOM) is one metadata standard developed for describing entities for educational use. One critique of metadata creation for digital objects is that it is a time-consuming and resource-intensive task. Not all libraries are so fortunate as to have dedicated metadata specialists on their staff. Software to assist in the process of LOM creation is one possible solution (McGreal, 2006). M-learning researchers have identified a need for enhancing current learning object metadata to better meet the needs of mobile learners. Proposed additional metadata fields fall under rights management and include 'sharing rights, validation, mobility, and use' (Chan et al., 2004).

Within the IMS *Access for All Metadata Specification* (IMS, 2004) is the metadata field <AccessForAll>, which allows learning objects to be tailored to the user environment. Halm (2003) proposes the use of this field to 'benefit all users in a learning situation which requires alternative modes of use, such as an extremely noisy environment where captions are needed for a video'. It may be wise to take this possibility further and suggest automating the metadata input drawing it in from context-aware sensors available within the device. There has been research into the theoretical applications of intelligent agent systems that could be adapted for such an application (Wang and Gasser, 2002). Librarians will want to pay attention to the multiple data elements that mobile devices collect and emit which, when collected, collocated and made actionable, can result in new services, greater access to library and information resources and new tools for discovery of information.

Mobile media metadata

At the University of California at Berkeley School of Information Management Systems, researchers have investigated multiple metadata sources to facilitate media sharing (Davis et al., 2005). The research project addresses the problem of making user-created camera data from a cell phone accessible to other users in an intuitive manner. The Mobile Media Metadata for Media Sharing (MMM2) is a context-aware application using Bluetooth ID metadata, as well as metadata about previously sent pictures, to better infer and promote data sharing. Interesting attributes of this system are context-aware Bluetooth metadata (spatial, temporal and social) and metadata that users assign to pictures they have taken (Davis et al., 2005). The MMM2 software solution also includes a web-based desktop PC component for media management.

Having users define their pictures is akin to what may be referred to in the bibliographic model as annotation. Further extrapolating this idea, one can view a user's cell phone as a digital library in which the objectives of finding and choice may not be fully operationalized. Anecdotal evidence of unused and inaccessible picture data will support this assertion. Sharing media objects by way of multiple metadata sources paired with a context-aware solution does indicate improved data access.

Librarians will be interested in ongoing research on search by picture (Jia et al., 2006). Though still in the emerging phase of development, search by media will be an important development for m-libraries. The opportunity already exists for the physical and virtual library to use picture-search query to search the image databases.

Roma personal metadata

A substantial portion of the chapter you are reading was lost in the revision stage. By mistake, I downloaded an earlier version and overwrote the needed file. This is the peril of being a mobile individual: having copies of similar, nearly identical files in multiple locations. Had I been a user of the Roma Personal Metadata Service (Swierk, et al., 2002) then maybe my cell phone would have carried metadata about which document version I had been working with and my attempt to access the document I needed would have been less disastrous.

The Roma service does not store document data in its entirety; rather it stores document metadata. Roma allows the user to carry with them their personal metadata, supported by a centralized server-side application. This is considered a credible solution, in view of the fact that metadata is traditionally smaller than the data that it describes.

A different implementation of personal devices for information access is the PDLib system (Alvarez-Cavazos et al., 2005). This architecture facilitates access to content that has been uploaded to a server and can then be accessed via a user's cellular device. The architecture employs middleware solutions for managing access on demand.

Research into strategies for maintaining electronic evidence has investigated approaches for marking data records with metadata hashes in order to better understand the provenance of a record (Bearman,

1996). The tactic Bearman investigates for management of electronic records is that metadata hashes should be mutually identifiable; if a hash in the record points to the metadata, then the metadata should point back to the corresponding hash (1996). These techniques are applicable when the metadata does not exist within the entity being described. This is a departure from the traditional data package model of the Open Archival Information System (CCSD, 2002) and networked computing in general, which can be understood in a 'data package'-like paradigm.

Socializing the mobile digital library

Serendipitous discovery of sources with similar 'about-ness' on a library bookshelf is due to classification. A user is able to find like information because like information is classed together. Building on context-aware architecture, the creative research approach at Berkeley and MIT, using modified open source ContextPhone software developed by Ratento (Ratento et al., 2005) and Bluetooth technology, reflects the same thematic conceptualization. This is an aptly named Serendipity application developed and trademarked by researchers at MIT, relying on Bluetooth IDs and the paired user profile to allow cell phone users to make serendipitous connections based on like interests (Eagle and Pentland, 2005).

The architecture is dependent on users enabling their mobile devices for Bluetooth discovery and configuring a user profile. In the Serendipity system, users who have similar profile interests have threshold benchmarks whereby they are sent introductory messages asking each user to agree either to meet or not to meet.

A library application of this service architecture would include student profiles and Bluetooth IDs whereby students studying the same course material would be able to connect with each other to form ad hoc study groups. The nature of large research universities and lecture classes of hundreds of students underscores the need for social serendipitous encounters.

A librarian might configure a Bluetooth ID and profile so as to advertise library services. Using context-aware architecture in a library setting might be one way for students to realize the benefits of just-in-time services. Serendipity services might help to alleviate the struggle of the digital resources librarian in the quest to deliver resources in a just-in-time manner.

Consider the following scenario as a librarian-centred application of Serendipity architecture: a student is engrossed and perplexed in research at a computer and does not want to leave and visit a reference desk for fear of losing her seat at the desktop computer. She uses her cell phone, which is loaded with the Serendipity application, the infrastructure of the library picks up both the student's and the librarian's IDs and the student sees that a librarian is available for research assistance.

One might further realize context-aware solutions building on Bluetooth by advertising other library programming. A student may not want to connect at the person level but perhaps would like to use his cell phone to locate other services, such as library events and lectures. These services could be advertised to the student through a Serendipity profile where the system would only notify him of an event if he had configured his profile to send notification if he is within a certain distance of the library and if it is directly applicable to his major field of study.

The e-science initiative for data management is applicable to m-libraries research and development. The application of Bluetooth ID data and profile data management for reuse during their life cycle is a librarian's skill and is in line with the goals of cyberinfrastructure, which are to enable the sharing and reuse of data so as to give it value throughout its life cycle for the purposes of research, scholarship and study. Though conceptualizations of grid computing generally imagine high-speed super-computing applications, the management of mobile device data is a non-traditional research possibility.

Friend of a Friend (FOAF) is a metadata specification deployable through RDF/OWL in which it is possible to identify people as resources (Graves et al., 2007). The specification notes[1] regarding discovery of FOAF files indicate the uncontrolled nature of this vocabulary. A controlled vocabulary (possible in closed systems) is an important aspect of subject languages. The application of the mobile service will inform the need for subject languages. For a server which the library will create and maintain, the collocation of information, and hence greater retrieval, can be realized through controlled vocabulary. For any large-scale application, beyond the infrastructure of the library, FOAF web-based, auto-discovery tools will play an important part.

M-library ontology

Communities can be fostered and articulated through ontologies (in the technical rather than philosophical sense). The VIVO digital library (http://vivo.cornell.edu/; Devare et al., 2007) at Cornell Health Science Library is built using the ontology of Cornell research as its ontological commitment. The VIVO project provides us with another useful example of bibliographic collocating, which is too precious a bibliographic standard to abandon in the digital library (Svenonius, 2000).

Ontology can make clear the tasks of the m-library. Ontology as applied by the artificial intelligence community uses task-based logic. Librarians can use task-based ontology constructs to aid our understanding of information-seeking behaviour and better help library users to search for information. The bibliographic ontology as conceptualized in the IFLA statement on *Functional Requirements for Bibliographic Records* is one starting place for the development of ontology on information search. Ontology for service definition may prove worthwhile in ubiquitous computing.

Ontology can define a conceptualization of a field of study (Gruber, 1993). As the field of mobile digital librarianship evolves, it will be a worthwhile study to examine what it means to be an m-library. This conceptualization will change over time as the field is experienced by users and explored by future generations of librarians. It may be worthwhile to research the shifting conceptualizations of what the study and practice of m-librarianship entails. The addition and discussion of terminology and conceptualizations of m-libraries can be a shared global endeavour.

Mobile digital libraries are a type of system that can be operationalized by fulfilling the objectives of the bibliographic model. For such fulfilment ample attention to both traditional metadata and non-traditional metadata is important. Bibliographic ontology is a useful thematic construction; multiple ontologies can be used for conceptualizing and for task and service deployment of m-libraries. It may also be useful to adopt ontologies that have been defined for different purposes.

The possibilities for m-libraries are within the grasp of practitioners. To best represent digital content, the metadata created and used will be crucial. The m-library will not replace the profession or practice of librarianship. Technology is but a new tool to be integrated into the practice of the profession. The new datasets and data sources which personal computing hardware emits and collects are a target for considerable creative application. These strategies will enable the operationalization of the m-library.

Acknowledgements

The author gratefully acknowledges the help of Kathleen Kern at University of Illinois at Urbana-Champaign and Lara Whitelaw at the Open University for their comments on drafts of this chapter.

References

Alvarez-Cavazos, F., Garza-Salazar, D. and Lavariega-Jarquin, J. (2005) Pdlib: personal digital libraries with universal access, *JCDL '05. Proceedings of the 5th ACM/IEEE-CS Joint Conference on Digital Libraries, 2005* (p. 365), DOI (digital object identifier) 10.1145/1065385.1065468.

Bearman, D. (1996) Item Level Control and Electronic Recordkeeping, *Archives and Museum Informatics*, **10** (3), 195–245.

CCSDS (Consultative Committee for Space Data Systems) (2002) *Reference Model for an Open Archival Information System (OAIS)*, CCSDS 650.0 0-B-1.

Chan, T., Sharples, M., Vavoula, G. and Lonsdale, P. (2004) Educational Metadata for Mobile Learning, *Proceedings of the 2nd IEEE International Workshop on Wireless and Mobile Technologies in Education, 2004*, 197–8.

Davis, M., House, N. V., Towle, J., King, S., Ahern, S., Burgener, C., et al. (2005) MMM2: mobile media metadata for media sharing, *CHI '05 extended abstracts on Human Factors in Computing Systems*, 1335–8.

Devare, M., Corson-Rikert, J., Caruso, B., Lowe, B., Chiang, K. and McCue, J. (2007) Connecting People, Creating a Virtual Life Sciences Community, *D-Lib Magazine*, www.dlib.org/dlib/july07/devare/07devare.html.

Eagle, N. and Pentland, A. (2005) Social Serendipity: mobilizing social software, *Pervasive Computing, IEEE*, **4** (2), 28–34.

Graves, M., Constabaris, A. and Brickley, D. (2007) FOAF: connecting people on the semantic web, *Cataloging & Classification Quarterly*, **43** (3/4), 191–202.

Gruber, T. (1993) A Translation Approach to Portable Ontologies, *Knowledge Acquisition*, **5** (2), 199–220.

Halm, M. (2003) Beyond the LOM: a new generation of specifications. In Glynn, Catherine M. and Acker, Stephen R. (eds), *Learning Objects Contexts and Connections*, Columbus, Ohio, Ohio State University.

IMS (2004) *Access for All Metadata Specification*, www.imsglobal.org/accessibility/accmdv1p0/imsaccmd_oviewv1p0.html.

IFLA (International Federation of Library Associations and Institutions) (1962) *Report: Proceedings of the International Conference on Cataloging Principles, Paris, 9–18 October, 1961*, International Federation of Library Associations.

IFLA (International Federation of Library Associations and Institutions) (1998) *Functional Requirements for Bibliographic Records: Final Report. Recommended by the IFLA Study Group on the Functional Requirements for Bibliographic Records*, UBCIM Publications, New Series Vol. 19, Munich: K. G. Saur.

Jia, M., Fan, X., Xie, X., Li, M. and Ma, W. (2006) Photo-to-Search: using camera phones to inquire of the surrounding world, *7th International Conference on Mobile Data Management, 2006. MDM 2006.*

McGreal, R. (2006) Implementing Learning Object Metadata for Mobile Devices Using CanCore, *Telecommunications, 2006: AICT-ICIW '06, (Advanced) International Conference on Internet and Web Applications and Services*, 5.

Ratento, M., Oulasvirta, A., Petit, R. and Toivonen, H. (2005) ContextPhone: a prototyping platform for context-aware mobile applications, *Pervasive Computing IEEE*, 4 (2), 51–9.

Svenonius, E. (2000) *The Intellectual Foundation of Information Organization*, MIT Press.

Swierk, E., Kiciman, E., Williams, N. Fukushima, T., Yoshida, H., Laviano, V. et al. (2002) The Roma Personal Metadata Service, *Mobile Networks and Applications*, 7 (5), 407–18.

Wang, J. and Gasser, L. (2002) Mutual Online Ontology Alignment. In Cranefield, Stephen, Finin, Tim and Willmott Steve (eds), *Proceedings of the Workshop on Ontologies in Agent Systems*, www.isrl.uiuc.edu/%7Egasser/papers/oas-aamas2002-wang-gasser.pdf.

Sources consulted

Bearman, D. (1994) *Electronic Evidence: strategies for managing records in contemporary organizations*, Pittsburgh: Archives and Museum Informatics.

Chan, L. and Zeng, M. (2006) Metadata Interoperability and Standardization. A Study of Methodology, Part I: achieving interoperability at the schema level, *D-Lib Magazine*, www.dlib.org/dlib/june06/chan/06chan.html.

Zeng, M. and Chan, L. (2006) Metadata Interoperability and Standardization. A Study of Methodology, Part II: achieving interoperability at the record and repository levels, *D-Lib Magazine,* www.dlib.org/dlib/june06/zeng/06zeng.html.

URL

1   http://rdfweb.org/mt/foaflog/archives/000041.html.

18

Designing mobile digital libraries in a clinical domain

Anne Adams

Introduction

Social contexts and work practices can have a significant impact on a community's engagement with new technology systems (Duncker, 2002; Kling, 1999; Theng, 2002; Cunningham, 2002). Lave and Wenger (1991) argue that social practices shape how we learn and, in turn, who we become. Digital libraries (DLs) are used in a wide variety of ways and to support a multitude of needs across different domains (e.g. academic, clinical, business). The social contexts and needs of these various domains are different, yet DL design varies very little to support those differences. Adams et al. (2005) and Adams and Blandford (2006) detailed comparative research into digital libraries in academic and clinical contexts that provides insight into the use of this technology within contrasting social structures, task and knowledge goals and communities of practice. In academia, the importance of DLs as a learning resource is highlighted, while in the clinical domain their role in decision support is paramount. In the UK the latter has been driven by a governmental push for healthcare professionals to use current best evidence in everyday clinical decision making, often termed 'evidence-based medicine'. However, in clinical settings the mobile nature of the professions and the location of the technology and support systems (e.g. librarians) can lead to digital libraries either empowering or excluding clinicians (Adams et al., 2005).

Background

Since 2004, in various domains and organizations, there have been increased drives to digitize and computerize information and work practices. However, the legal and health services have retained many of their paper-based approaches and associated practices. Legal proceedings still rely on paper resources passed between legal representatives. Similarly, patient records are often still kept in paper format, even if also replicated digitally. Many of the reasons behind slow technology take-up lie in security and legal issues such as accessibility, privacy, trust and legal accountability. One report (Fairey, 2004) highlights how the investment in IT per employee in the US health service is less than half that of private industry and one-third of that in banking. In the UK a 'National Progamme for IT' (Fairey, 2004) has been set in motion to bring computing into the National Health Service (NHS) over a 10-year period. The 'NPfIT' is described by the NHS as a means of:

> transforming the way the NHS works. Information will move around more quickly with health care records, appointment details, prescription information, and up-to-date research into illnesses and treatment accessible to patients and health professionals whenever they need it. (Department of Health, UK, 2005)

A less extensive programme in the US seeks to provide a national 'always-current, always-available' electronic healthcare record system on all US citizens (Fairey, 2004). However, Hendy et al. (2005) reviewed senior management and clinicians' perceptions and identified that local circumstances were not understood or were ignored in the programme's development. This was then identified as creating increased perceptions of disempowerment and uncertainty, resulting in organizations' poor implementation of the programme.

An organization's culture has a direct impact on the informal practices that can develop into social and organizational norms (Schein, 1990). When hospital information systems were first introduced, it was found that the greatest difficulties in their deployment lay not with technical issues but with the users, on whom new demands were being placed (Harrison, 1991). Health informatics research has continued to detail the social and organizational factors that determine the success or failure of healthcare IT developments (Gremy and Bonnin, 1995; Heathfield, 1999; Heathfield et al., 1998).

Digital libraries in healthcare

Covi and Kling (1997) argue that understanding the wider context of technology is essential to understanding digital library use and its implementation in different social worlds. Reddy and Dourish (2002) reviewed information-seeking behaviours in a clinical setting, and identified two important points:

- colleagues are the first information reference point for clinicians
- clinical and organizational issues are intertwined.

They found that clinical staff provide the contextual information that cannot usually be provided in a hard-copy format. They also identified the importance of mobile interactions with information, noting a sense of temporal and situational relevance noted. Schneider and Wagner (1993) also highlight the importance, in a clinical setting, of local knowledge, informal collaboration and technology to support the sharing of information within different contexts. Similarly, Cicourel (1990) notes that team members on medical ward rounds provide contextualizing information to each other.

Technological developments, specifically those involving digital libraries, are increasingly focusing on the importance of directing design towards the work practices and communities they support (Covi and Kling, 1997; Marchionini et al., 1997). Todd et al. (2003) highlight the fact that nurses' current work practices (e.g. shift patterns, ward-bound duties) restrict their access to libraries and the internet. The difficulty some professionals experience in accessing the physical library and the push for evidence-based medicine have resulted in different approaches to implementing digital library technology – such as remote DL access, mobile DL access, computers on the wards and outreach information intermediaries. However, as discussed below, these different approaches, when interacting with work practices and social structures, can produce both perceived exclusion and empowerment for different communities of practice within the organization.

Mobile devices have been used in healthcare and in hospitals for decades. The use of the pager as an alerting mechanism for clinicians is inbuilt into the practices of many clinical professions. The computerized development of these devices, however, has been very slow. It could be argued that the change incorporated in many developments requires far more practice changes, without clear benefits. A pager acts as a simple alerting mechanism with information on who is alerting you and for what purpose. PDAs and smartphones provide rapid information support for decision making, producing a perceived threat to current practices and notions of expertise. For example, a student nurse accessing medical digital libraries could identify flaws in a consultant's diagnosis or the treatment practices, and the consultant could perceive this as a threat to their status. This chapter reviews several projects conducted on clinical digital library use in clinical settings to study the impact of clinicians' perceptions of the changing modes of mobile information access.

Method

The findings detailed here present a specific focus on the data from a large-scale study that covered three different contexts of use, over a four-year period, in the domain of healthcare. Here the findings are reviewed in relation to clinical mobile issues around digital libraries. Results from 119 users (Table 18.1) – end-users, librarians, designers and management – were gathered, compared and contrasted to identify socially relevant issues, both specific to each domain and generic. Current work practices were identified and the impact of digital resources on those practices was assessed. A pre-defined concept of a 'digital library' was not used, so that users could explore what they perceived as comprising a digital library.

Table 18.1 Study participants and current clinical digital library usage

Group	Ref	Status & Role	No.	Major DLs used
Inner London hospital	St1a	Pre-registration to registered nurses	36	
	St1b	Doctors, consultants, surgeons, allied health professionals, managers and IT	37	Medline, the Cochrane Library and the UK National electronic Library of Health (NeLH).
Provincial hospital	St2	Nurses, consultants, managers, library and IT	20	
Outer London hospital	St3	Nurses, doctors, consultants, psychologists, social workers	26	

Inner London hospital study (St1)

The first clinical setting studied was a London teaching hospital. In this hospital there were computers on the wards, with web access to digital libraries. Focus groups and in-depth interviews were used to gather data from 73 hospital clinicians (see Table 18.1). Of the respondents 50% were nurses while the other 50% were junior doctors, consultants, surgeons, and allied health professionals (AHPs), e.g. occupational therapists, managers and IT department members. In this and in the other two hospital-based studies (2 and 3), there was a wide range of computer abilities and digital library experience among those interviewed. In all three cases, although a wide variety of digital resources were mentioned, the three main DLs discussed were Medline, the Cochrane Library and the UK National electronic Library of Health (NeLH).

Provincial hospital study (St2)

A further study in the clinical domain was conducted in a provincial teaching hospital. In this hospital, although all computers allowed access to web-accessible digital libraries, they were not placed on the wards, but in specific offices and in the library. Twenty in-depth interviews were used to gather data from management, library, IT, consultant and nursing employees (see Table 18.1).

Outer London hospital study (St3)

Finally, an evaluation of an information intermediary's role within clinical communities of practice was undertaken. Twenty-six in-depth interviews were conducted across eight different clinical teams (see Table 18.1) over a six-month period, as well as an observational study of one team and information intermediary collaborating during a drop-in session.

Issues

Four issues guided the focus of questions analysed in each of the studies:

- perceptions of the participant's role within the organization, and their information requirements

■ perceptions of current information practices, social structures and organizational norms

■ the impact of current practices, structures and norms on information resource awareness, acceptance and use

■ technology perceptions (specifically of DLs) and how these affected other issues already identified.

An in-depth analysis of respondents' perceptions was conducted using the Grounded Theory method. Grounded Theory (Strauss and Corbin, 1990) is a social science approach to data collection and analysis that combines systematic levels of abstraction into a framework around a phenomenon which is verified and expanded throughout the study. Once the data is collected, it is analysed in a standard Grounded Theory format (i.e. open, axial and selective coding and identification of process effects). Compared to other social science methodologies, Grounded Theory provides a more focused, structured approach to qualitative research. The methodology's flexibility can cope with complex data, and its continual cross-referencing allows for grounding of theory in the data, thus uncovering previously unknown issues.

Results and discussion

Within the clinical domain, although management and junior clinicians recognize the potential of technology, it is still far from being an everyday resource with practical applications:

> I've seen the advantages as technology has grown but we are still growing with it aren't we?
> (St2: Specialist nurse)

Technology was sometimes referred to as distracting from and obstructing current working practices:

> I think it's driving it from the top, it's a whole concept of how we integrate as people, how we interrelate as human beings and they're [the technology] not allowing that normal process.
> (St2: Nurse)

It was found that, within the traditional clinical model, information dissemination is predominantly either via hard copy or oral.

> They reach for a book . . . or they go and ask somebody, they don't reach for a dig-
> ital resource at the moment, it's not yet a natural part of their everyday clinical lives.
> And that's one of the main hurdles to be got across, I think.   (St3: Consultant)

Senior clinicians characterized clinical evidence knowledge as something that slowly increases and, for them, requires intermittent updating. Daily decision making, in contrast, is perceived to be based on their own and colleagues' similar experiences. This is because they see experiential knowledge as being more pertinent to localized daily problem-solving tasks while published research, being more generic, requires more extrapolation. However, junior clinicians and management often misinterpreted these approaches as being due to clinical arrogance.

> Some clinicians, I know, feel it's perhaps below them to look for evidence. You
> know, the view is 'I know this, I've been a consultant for a long time and I've got a
> lot of experience'.   (St1b: Clinical governance)

As previously noted, the slow acquisition of experiential knowledge was also related to social structures. It was noted by senior clinicians that junior clinicians required the practical experience to interpret theory-based evidence. The implementation of technology increasing accessibility to theoretical knowledge was therefore perceived by some senior staff as a benefit of status:

> People lower down. Well they would resort to the actual standard text.
>   (St1a: Nursing manager)

The location of technology increased social structure tensions. Although computers were, theoretically, accessible by all, nurses' and AHPs' access in the hospital was often limited by either physical or social restrictions (e.g. passwords, computer locks, location of computers), and computers on the wards increased friction between different user groups (e.g. doctors and nurses, senior and junior staff) trying to access them.

> I know there is some friction between the junior doctors and the nurses about who
> the computers are there for . . . sometimes the computer has been put in a place where
> it is very obviously in one territory.   (St1b: Doctor)

It could be argued that mobile technologies allocated to or owned by individuals would alleviate the problems of technology location. The use of a digital pen or a PDA would enable use of mobile resources and accessibility for all clinicians. However, there is an issue of security with these resources, such as risk of theft on the wards. Also the use of mobile devices does not alleviate the underlying problems of social norms in relation to information accessibility. Mobile designers need to understand the contextual importance of who has access to what information within clinical social structures and work practices. These systems must understand and support the complex social collaborations that clinicians require in their daily decision-making activities. The clinician is repeatedly driven to acquire tacit knowledge through colleagues and communities of practice, with interaction patterns governed by local social structures and norms. Latour (2005) talks about the complexity of this process as being tied to the negotiation and production of knowledge. It is within this complex, changing social interaction that these technologies are implemented. Designing systems applicable to these complex clinical roles and contextual needs is of paramount importance to their successful uptake, implementation and efficient use. It should come as no surprise, then, that the intricate mobile devices providing access to complex, time-consuming and dense clinical digital resources are not used in daily decision making. Similarly, the simplistic mobile devices alerting clinicians as to when they should wash their hands have received negative uptake responses.

What needs to be understood is the potential benefit of temporal and situational information that mobile devices can provide, which, combined with the knowledge available through digital libraries, would make clinical mobile digital libraries invaluable resources. How invaluable it would be for a clinician to have the digital library clinical evidence available wherever their whereabouts, merged with location-specific knowledge that was regularly updated with current changes, and to be able to identify local experts on hand to support decision making. Mobile sensors, RfID tags, merging digital libraries and local repositories with situational knowledge could provide these advances. Previous research (Hinze et al., 2006) looking at temporally merging digital resources (e.g. press releases on current health scares merged with current best evidence in the field to support patient consultations) has proved to be of interest to the health professions. We are on the verge of transforming clinical work practices for the better, through mobile digital libraries. However, implementing them in a way that is perceived as supporting, rather than alienating and devaluing, clinicians is a major hurdle that cannot be overestimated.

References

Adams, A. and Blandford, A. (2006) Implementing Digital Resources for Clinicians' and Patients' Varying Needs, *International Journal of Medical Informatics and the Internet in Medicine*, **30** (2), 107–22.

Adams, A., Blandford, A. and Lunt, P. (2005) Social Empowerment and Exclusion: a case study on digital libraries, *ACM Transactions on Computer–Human Interaction*, **12** (2), 174–200.

Cicourel, A. V. (1990) The Integration of Distributed Knowledge in Collaborative Medical Diagnosis. In Galegher, J., Draut, R. E. and Egido, C. (eds), *Intellectual Teamwork*, Hillsdale, NJ, Lawrence Erlbaum Associates, 221–42.

Covi, L. and Kling, R. (1997) Organisational Dimensions of Effective Digital Library Use: closed rational and open natural systems model. In Kiesler, S. (ed.), *Culture of the Internet*, Hillsdale, NJ, Lawrence Erlbaum Associates, 343–60.

Cunningham, S. J. (2002) Building a Digital Library From the Ground Up: an examination of emergent information resources in the machine learning community, *Proceedings of ICADL '02, Digital Libraries: People, Knowledge and Technology*. Heidelberg, Springer, 301–2.

Department of Health (2005) www.dh.gov.uk/en/index.htm.

Dunker, E. (2002) Cross-cultural Usability of the Library Metaphor, *Proceedings of JCDL '02*, ACM Press, 223–30.

Fairey, M. (2004) US Government Follows NPfIT Lead, *British Journal of Healthcare Computing and Information Management*, **21** (9), 7, www.bjhc.co.uk/news/1/2004/n41118.htm.

Gremy, F. and Bonnin, M. (1995) Evaluation of Automatic Health Information Systems: what and how? Assessment and evaluation of information technologies. In Gennip, E. and Talmon, J. L. (eds), *Medicine Van*, Amsterdam, IOS Press, 9–20.

Harrison, G. S. (1991) The Winchester Experience with the TDS Hospital Information System, *British Journal of Urology*, **67** (5), 532–5.

Heathfield, H. (1999) The Rise and Fall of Expert Systems in Medicine, *Expert Systems*, **16** (3), 183–8.

Heathfield, H., Pitty, D. and Hanka, R. (1998) Evaluating Information Technology in Health Care: barriers and challenges, *BMJ*, 316, 1959–61.

Hendy, J., Reeves, B., Fulop, N., Hutchings, A. and Masseria, C. (2005) Challenges to Implementing the National Programme for Information Technology (NPfIT): a qualitative study, *BMJ*, 331 (7512), 331–6.

Hinze, A., Buchanan, G., Jung, D. and Adams, A. (2006) HDL Alert – A Healthcare DL Alerting System: from users needs to implementation. In Adams, A. and Kostokova, P. (eds), *Health Digital Library*, special issue of *Health Informatics Journal*, 12, 121–35.

Kling, R. (1999) What is Social Informatics and Why Does It Matter? *D-Lib Magazine*, 5 (1), www.dliborg/dlib/january99/k/ing/01/<lmg.hgml.

Latour, B. (ed.) (2005) *Reassembling the Social: an introduction to actor-network-theory*, Oxford University Press.

Lave, J. and Wenger, E. (1991) *Situated Learning: legitimate peripheral participation*, Cambridge University Press.

Reddy, M. and Dourish, P. (2002) A Finger on the Pulse: temporal rhythms and information seeking in medical work, *Proceedings of ACM CSCW '02*, ACM Press, 344–53.

Schein, E. (1990) Organizational Culture, *American Psychologist*, 45, 109–19.

Schneider, K. and Wagner, I. (1993) Constructing the 'Dossier Representatif': computer-based information sharing in French hospitals, *Computer Supported Cooperative Work*, 1, 229–53

Strauss, A. and Corbin, J. (1990) *Basics of Qualitative Research: grounded theory procedures and techniques*, Sage.

Theng, Y. L. (2002) Information Therapy in Digital Libraries, *Proceedings of ICADL '02, Digital Libraries: people, knowledge and technology*, Heidelberg, Springer, 452–64.

Todd, A. M. et al. (2003) Access to the Internet in an Acute Care Area: experiences of nurses, *British Journal of Nursing*, 12 (7), 425–34.

19

Use of a mobile digital library for mobile learning

Mohamed Ally, Rory McGreal, Steve Schafer, Tony Tin and Billy Cheung

Introduction

As information and training materials are digitized, the role of libraries will change dramatically. In addition to being providers of information, libraries will be responsible for the design, development and storage of learning materials in electronic repositories for access by anyone. The project described in this chapter illustrates the importance of libraries playing specific roles in learning and training. The learning material for the project was designed in the form of digital learning objects and was stored in the Athabasca University Library's electronic repository. Libraries will also have to keep up with emerging delivery requirements, as the use of wireless mobile technology such as PDAs, cellular phones or iPods in education and training is making learning more flexible, such that students can learn anywhere and at any time. Mobile learning is novel in that it facilitates delivery of learning materials to the right person, at the right time, in the right place using portable electronic devices. In the near future, mobile learning will become a normal part of lifelong education and self-directed learning. Libraries will play a major role in this.

The project described in this chapter developed and evaluated innovative approaches to learning English as a second language (ESL) using mobile devices in a variety of learning contexts. The digital ESL content is based on the best-selling Penguin introductory English grammar and exercise books which have been released by their author as 'open source' (O'Driscoll, 1988, 1990). This project supports research into the adaptation and delivery of learning objects using mobile devices. It attempts to advance the use of information technologies for learning and to foster a culture of innovation by providing new, evidence-based research into the activities of independent adult learners, including post-secondary students and adults in community organizations. Adults learn the basic grammatical tools of English in an interactive modular format, accessible from electronic repositories on mobile devices. Adult learners are invariably busy with numerous work and family obligations; enabling them to learn anywhere and any time using mobile devices will provide valuable flexibility in learning. This project evaluated the experience and performance of adults using mobile phones to learn English grammar.

Use of mobile devices in learning

Research on mobile learning is a recent development and limited research has been conducted in this area (Attewell, 2005; BECTA, 2004; Keegan, 2002; Savill-Smith and Kent, 2003). Preliminary investigations report on the limitations of mobile devices, especially the limitations of the small screen size, but also limited processing power, battery life and memory capacity. Other problems have been encountered because of the wide range of operating systems (Palm OS, Windows CE, Linux) and the differing input devices (Holzinger et al., 2005). Overall, research on the educational use of mobile devices is very limited and at an early stage.

Research shows that mobile devices can be more easily integrated across the curriculum than desktops (Moseley and Higgins, 1999). This is possible because many students already have mobile devices and wireless mobile devices do not need so extensive an infrastructure as desktop computers. The mobility enabled by these devices can also foster a greater feeling of work ownership on the part of students. The pedagogical approaches and goals must be clear as in traditional teaching (BECTA, 2004). Teachers find they have greater confidence in supporting students and greater access to data from anywhere, combined with increased efficiency and accuracy (Perry, 2000). Brown (2004) at the University of Pretoria is already proving the value of using mobile phones in the management of distance learning. Taylor (2005) is researching the use of mobile devices in teacher education in Kenya. White (2004) has conducted research using mobile devices in disadvantaged communities in a developed country. ESL and other languages are also being taught using mobile devices. Song and Fox (2005) found significant improvements in learners' performance of language tasks. Others have successfully used mobile devices for teaching pronunciation and listening skills (Uther et al., 2005). Tense ITS is an adaptive system used for teaching English tenses to ESL learners, with significant positive outcomes (Bull et al., 2005).

Research has also looked at the adaptation of content for mobile learning using learning objects and creating appropriate metadata (Ally, 2004a, 2004c; Friesen et al., 2005). Learning object metadata for mobile devices is also the subject of research in Europe and Asia (Davis et al., 2004; Kawarasaki et al., 2004; Yang et al., 2005). In addition, library systems are implementing international standards-based content for use in mobile environments (Magusin et al., 2003; McGreal, Anderson et al., 2005; McGreal, Cheung et al., 2005; McGreal et al., 2005). Research is also looking at the use of intelligent agents for online learning (Ally, 2004b; Esmahi and Lin, 2004; Lin, 2004; Lin and Esmahi, 2004). Baggaley (2004) has conducted research in the field of mobile teaching and its relationship to mobile learning.

Student experience with mobile learning

The research project involved a 'before–after' design, following the achievements of target groups, using pre- and post-tests on three different student groups (n=46). Subjects were given a pre-test to determine their current level of expertise in English grammar. After completing the grammar lessons, subjects were given a post-test and a retention test. The project was implemented in three different institutions where students study ESL. All students completed the same lessons and also filled out a questionnaire to give their opinions on the mobile technology and m-learning.

The course content consists of 86 lessons and related exercises teaching the basics of the English language, ranging from the difference between 'is' and 'are' to verb tenses, countable nouns and other aspects of basic grammar in the English language. The content is interactive, where students are given constant practice using a variety of question types. Four different types of question were used to make the grammar exercises more interactive, easy to access in the mobile device and to test the students' ability. The question types were true/false, multiple-choice drop-downs, changing the order of sentences, and matching. The content is available in Adobe PDF and Microsoft Word formats and can be downloaded to the desktop and to mobile devices.

Students completed three grammar tests during the study. The pre-test was written before the students attempted the lessons on the mobile phones. The average score on the pre-test was 15/20 (Figure 19.1). The post-test was given immediately following completion of the ten assigned grammar units. The post-test average was 17.7/20. A retention test, in the same format, was given to the students one week later. The average score was 18/20. A slight improvement was shown after the students accessed and studied the grammar units on the mobile phone. There was further improvement on the retention test, administered one week after the post-test.

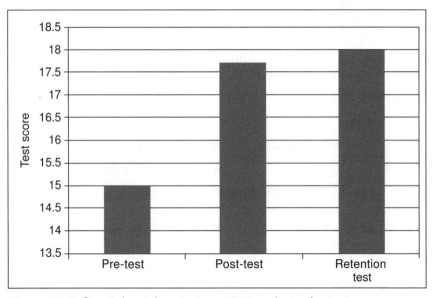

Figure 19.1 Comparison of pre-test, post-test, and retention test scores

Subjects' experience using mobile technology

After subjects had completed the ESL lessons on the mobile phone they were asked to complete a questionnaire to provide feedback on their experience of using the mobile technology to learn English grammar. Table 19.1 shows the response distribution for each question.

Table 19.1 Subject feedback on use of the mobile technology (n=46)					
Question	**Strongly agree (%)**	**Agree (%)**	**Neutral (%)**	**Disagree (%)**	**Strongly disagree (%)**
Information on screen was properly formatted for reading	11	60	29	0	0
This technology provides flexibility for me to learn anywhere and at any time	36	58	2	4	0
Information on screen was easy to read	22	49	20	7	0
Amount of information presented on screen was acceptable	11	53	24	9	0
Input device to enter information was adequate	13	49	27	9	0
The interface to course materials was easy to use	16	62	20	2	0
Learning with mobile technology increases the quality of my learning experience	18	49	27	4	2
The technology was easy to use to access the course materials	20	58	18	4	0
The use of this type of technology could increase access to learning materials	20	58	18	2	0
Navigation (moving) through the lessons was easy	16	53	22	7	2
The graphics on the screen were clear and easy to read	22	56	16	6	0
I would like to take other lessons using mobile technology	16	47	22	13	0
I would recommend that other students complete their courses using mobile technology	16	42	31	7	0

Most participants expressed a positive experience using the mobile phone to learn English grammar. In the descriptive responses, they indicated that the use of mobile technology for ESL would be a good supplementary medium for learning at such times as waiting for a bus or travelling on a train, or whenever there was some spare time available. However, participants believed that the mobile devices could not be a substitute for classrooms and more traditional ways of learning through interaction with other students and with a teacher. But the flexibility of anytime availability of the mobile ESL materials was certainly appreciated by the students. One major concern expressed over the use of cell phones to access the internet and the lessons was the cost of internet access. Availability of WiFi-capable phones should address the concern about the cost of access. Additional issues raised by the participants relating to the mobile lessons and exercises are listed here:

- use of audio would improve the learning experience
- the screen of the phone is too small, which causes eye-strain
- clearer examples would aid better understanding of the questions
- the mobile technology could be used to help the student find a teacher and to allow him/her to interact directly with the teacher.

A suggestion was to make the course more sophisticated. For example, a student should be able to ask whether a given sentence was grammatically correct and to receive feedback.

Some of the concerns raised by the students can be addressed by incorporating more sophisticated modules and focusing on improving the course site. On the other hand, some concerns, such as the size of the screen, are inherent limitations of the devices used to access the site and are highly dependent on what devices the students are using. However, recent developments in mobile technology, such as the virtual keyboard and screen, could solve the problems of input device and screen size.

Testing methods on mobile technology

Subjects were asked to provide feedback on which type of questions they found suitable for mobile devices. The majority of participants reported that true/false and multiple choice questions are suitable for mobile technology. Ninety-three percent thought that true/false questions were suitable and 75% thought multiple choice questions were suitable (Figure 19.2). Almost half (47%) of the participants found word-ordering questions suitable for mobile devices. Only 18% of participants thought that matching-type questions were suited to mobile technology. The main reason given for the least preference for matching questions was inconvenience. Matching questions posed a need for frequent scrolling back and forth, as the screen was too small for everything to fit on one screen.

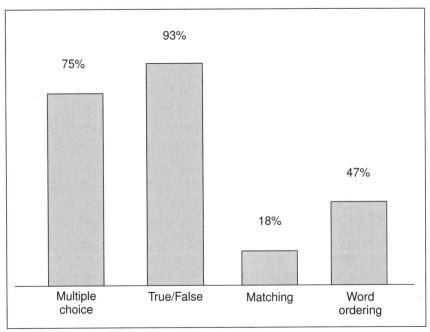

Figure 19.2 Student opinions about different question types (n=46)

Conclusion

As seen in this project, which was managed and administered by a library, the role of libraries is changing in the digital age. Libraries will be more involved in mobile learning and learning materials will be digitized. As learning materials become digitized, there will be more access via mobile technology. There are many benefits in using mobile technology for learning. One of the most important is the facility to learn anytime and anywhere and to receive immediate feedback. As students work through exercises one by one, they can receive instantaneous feedback on how they are performing (after clicking 'Submit' they can find out which questions they got wrong, etc.); and even if they get questions wrong, they can try again and learn from their mistakes. Students can cross-reference to other sites and resources. Mobile devices with constant online access (wireless etc.) enable users to surf the world wide web and view related websites that may assist them in their learning.

Using mobile devices to access the online course content increases motivation and opportunity for learning. Having the content online and right at students' fingertips, just one click away, means they can learn wherever they are, despite the constraints of busy work schedules, commuting, etc. Moreover, as students achieve success and progress through the exercises, they may be motivated to learn more of the English language. A benefit of learning a language is the learning that happens between individuals or in a group. Language learning should provide an opportunity for interaction between students. Mobile delivery of language learning should include opportunities for students to talk to other students and to the instructor to practise their language skills. Mobile devices are becoming an integral part of teaching languages. More and more people are using internet-capable mobile devices such as cell phones and PDAs. Using these already widespread devices for teaching/learning activities can be an attractive option for busy people. They can use their spare time in productive ways, such as for learning grammar, when they are away from school and home. Providing opportunities for students to use mobile devices for learning in their private time allows the learning to be individualized to some degree; if students are having trouble with a lesson, they can re-read it and do the exercises again without fear of delaying their fellow students or of asking questions in public. If they feel confident in a lesson, they can skip it and not have to sit through a redundant lecture from the teacher.

As mobile learning continues to grow, libraries will be responsible for digitizing learning materials for delivery on mobile devices. The learning materials will be stored in electronic repositories for access anywhere and at any time. Libraries will be responsible for maintaining and delivering the learning materials via a variety of computing technologies.

References

Ally, M. (2004a) Designing Effective Learning Objects for Distance Education. In McGreal, R. (ed.), *Online Education Using Learning Objects*, RoutledgeFalmer, 87–97.

Ally, M. (2004b) Intelligent Tutoring Systems for Distributed Learning. In Lin, F. O. (ed.), *Designing Distributed Learning Environments with Intelligent Software Agents*, Hershey, PA, Information Science Publishing, 162–83.

Ally, M. (2004c) Using Learning Theories to Design Instruction for Mobile Learning Devices, *Third International Conference on Mobile Learning 2004, Rome*.

Attewell, J. (2005) *Mobile Technologies and Learning: a technology update and mlearning project summary*, Learning and Skills Development Agency.

Baggaley, J. (2004) M-learning. How to M-teach, *Diverse Newsletter*, http://csalt.lancs.ac.uk/diverse/diversenl1104jb1.htm [accessed 4 June 2005].

BECTA (British Educational Communications Technology Agency) (2004) *What the Research Says About Portable ICT Devices in Teaching and Learning*, 2nd edn revised and updated, www.becta.org.uk/corporate/publications/documents/Research3_Portable%20Devices.pdf [accessed 28 June 2004].

Brown, T. (2004) The Role of M-learning in the Future of E-learning in Africa. In Murphy, D., Carr, R., Taylor, J. and Tat-meng, W. (eds), *Distance Education and Technology: issues and practice*, Hong Kong, University of Hong Kong, 197–216.

Bull, S., Cui, Y., Roebig, H. and Sharples, M. (2005) Adapting to Different Needs in Different Locations: handheld computers in university education, *Wireless and Mobile Technologies in Education (IEEE) Conference, 2005*, Tokushima, Japan, IEEE Computer Society.

Davis, M., Good, N. and Sarvas, R. (2004) *From Context to Content: leveraging context for mobile media metadata*, http://sigmobile.org/mobisys/2004/context_awareness/papers/davis.pdf [accessed 10 September 2005].

Esmahi, L. and Lin, F. (2004) A Multiagent Framework for an Adaptive E-learning System. In Lin, F. (ed.), *Designing Distributed Learning Environments with Intelligent Software Agents*, Hershey, PA, Idea Group Publishing, 218–41.

Friesen, N., Hesemeier, S. and Roberts, T. (2005) CanCore: guidelines for learning object metadata. In McGreal, R. (ed.), *Online Education Using Learning Objects*, Routledge/Falmer.

Holzinger, A., Nischelwitzer, A. and Meisenberger, M. (2005) Lifelong-learning Support by M-learning: example scenarios, *E-learn Magazine*, www.elearnmag.org/subpage.cfm?section=research&article=6-1 [accessed 1 December 2005].

Kawarasaki, M., Ooto, K., Nakanishi, T. and Suzuki, H. (2004) Metadata Driven Seamless Content Handover in Ubiquitous Environment, *International Symposium on Applications and the Internet (SAINT '04)*, http://csdl.computer.org/comp/proceedings/saint/2004/2068/00/20680287abs.htm [accessed 2 September 2004].

Keegan, D. (2002) *The Future of Learning: ZIFF papiere 119: from eLearning to mLearning*, www.fernuni-hagen.de/ZIFF/ZP_119.pdf.

Lin, F. (ed.) (2004) *Designing Distributed Learning Environments with Intelligent Software Agents*, Hershey, PA, Idea Group Publishing.

Lin, F. and Esmahi, L. (2004) Integrating Agent Technologies and Web Services into Distributed Learning Environments. In Lin, F. (ed.), *Designing Distributed Learning Environments with Intelligent Software Agents*, Hershey, PA, Idea Group Publishing.

Magusin, E., Johnson, K. and Tin, T. (2003) Library Services: designing the digital reading room to support online learning, *Proceedings of the19th Annual Conference on Distance Teaching and Learning*, www.uwex.edu/disted/conference/Resource_library/proceedings/03_65.pdf [accessed 31 March 2005].

McGreal, R., Anderson, T., Hubick, C., Lin, F., Sosteric, M., Tin, T. et al. (2005) Case Study: EduSource and the Athabasca University Digital Library Project, *E-Learning Network News*, 1 (1), www.astd.org/astd/Publications/Newsletters/elearn_news/jan05_mcgreal.htm [accessed 28 January 2005].

McGreal, R., Cheung, B., Tin, T. and Schafer, S. (2005) Implementing Mobile Environments Using Learning Objects: the Athabasca University Digital Reading Room, *IEEE International Workshop on Wireless and Mobile Technologies in Education Conference (WMTE) 2005*, Tokushima, Japan, IEEE.

McGreal, R., Tin, T., Cheung, B. and Schafer, S. (2005) The Athabasca University Digital Reading Room: library resources for mobile students, *Proceedings of the MLearn 2005 Conference*, Qawra, Malta, IADIS.

Moseley, D. and Higgins, S. (1999) *Ways Forward with ICT Effective Pedagogy Using Information and Communications Technology for Literacy and Numeracy in Primary Schools*, University of Newcastle.

O'Driscoll, J. (1988) *Basic English Grammar*, Penguin.

O'Driscoll, J. (1990) *English Grammar Exercises*, Penguin.

Perry, D. (2000) *Portable Computers in Primary Schools: literature review*, Lambeth Education Action Zone, Psion netBooks Project.

Savill-Smith, C. and Kent, P. (2003) *The Use of Palmtop Computers for Learning: a review of the literature*, www.m-learning.org/docs/the_use_of_palmtop_computers_for_learning_sept03.pdf [accessed 28 March 2004].

Song, Y. and Fox, R. (2005) Integrating M-technology into Web-based ESL Vocabulary Learning for Working Adult Learners. *Wireless and Mobile Technologies in Education (IEEE) Conference, 2005*, Tokushima, Japan, IEEE Computer Society.

Taylor, R. (2005) Kenya Pilots Handheld Education, *BBC News*, http://news.bbc.co.uk/2/hi/programmes/click_online/4727617.stm [accessed 4 August 2005].

Uther, M., Zipetria, I., Uther, J. and Singh, P. (2005) Mobile Adaptive CALL(MAC): a case study in developing a mobile learning application for speech/audio language training, *Wireless and Mobile Technologies in Education (IEEE) Conference, 2005,* Tokushima, Japan, IEEE Computer Society.

White, N. (2004) M-Learning with Disadvantaged Kids, *Full Circle Associates Community Blog* (2 November) [accessed 30 November 2004].

Yang, S. J. H., Shao, N. W. Y. and Sue, A. Y. S. (2005) Personalized Metadata Mechanism Applied to Adaptive Mobile Learning, *2nd IEEE International Workshop on Wireless and Mobile Technologies in Education (WMTE '04)*, http://csdl2.computer.org/persagen/DLAbsToc.jsp?resourcePath=/dl/proceedings/&toc=comp/proceedings/wmte/2004/1989/00/1989toc.xml&DOI=10.1109/WMTE.2004.1281377 [accessed 10 September 2005].

20

Digilab: a case study in encouraging mobile learning through library innovation

Keren Mills, Non Scantlebury and Rhodri Thomas

Introduction: creating an experimental space

The Digilab began life in 2005 as an Open University internal collaborative partnership project between four institutional units. These were Library, Learning and Teaching Solutions (LTS), the Institute of Educational Technology (IET) and the Knowledge Media Institute (KMi). Collectively these departments support the development of e-learning by contributing skills and expertise in pedagogy, research, information literacy and learning resource development. The project piloted the establishment of an innovative and technologically rich physical space to encourage collaborative working around e-learning. The project was funded by the Open University's Learning and Teaching Office and its key aims were to support the organization's priorities in creating market-responsive innovations to strengthen leadership in modern pedagogy for supported distance learning.

In terms of the Digilab project, our core users were defined as the staff responsible for developing, delivering and supporting Open University courses to students. Open University staff are able to drop in to the Digilab and engage in a range of hands-on exploratory activities using existing standard market technologies. Staff are encouraged to reflect on the potential use of these technologies to support and develop learning and a key strand of activity has centred on evaluating the potential of mobile technologies to deliver and support accessible learning wherever users choose.

Marketing mobile technologies to users

During its first phase, the Digilab pioneered a new type of loan service for users on campus. A range of mobile devices was already available for experimentation in the physical space. In order for staff to have more time to engage in hands-on experimentation with these technologies and sample course materials, a further set of devices was made available for loan via the Library's counter services. Loans were available to Open University staff and full-time postgraduate research students on campus. Initially two Edirol digital recorders, four iPod photos, ten iPod shuffles, two Game Boy Advanced, two Nintendo Game cubes and four PlayStation Portables were made available for loan. The iPods were loaded with an introductory MP3 message requesting feedback from users on the potential use of the technology to support learning development in the broadest sense, i.e. in the context of their own personal development needs as well as course development for students.

In parallel to the development of the physical space, a website was created which aimed to provide a range of additional web-accessible resources, guides and information on related themes. Information regarding the mobile loan service was made available via the main library website[1] which in turn was linked to the Digilab website.[2] Presentations were made to staff, promoting the mobile loan service. As a result of the proactive initiative taken by project staff in offering this new pilot service, the project manager suggested the setting-up of a university-wide mobile learning interest group.

A community of interest

The Mobile Technologies Knowledge Sharing Group was set up in May 2006 to facilitate knowledge-sharing and cross-departmental communication about mobile learning and mobile learner support. The 'M-Tech' group continues to meet quarterly for informal knowledge sharing discussions on a predetermined theme (e.g. Podcasting workshop; social networking; mobile web services; PlayStation Portables in education), and between meetings maintains contact via a wiki and a mailing list.

Participants include staff doing active research into mobile learning, those providing technical support and those engaged in horizon scanning. They are representative of academic and research, learner support and organizational business departments. Attendance at group meetings has helped to foster collaboration among the participants and has helped developers to avoid duplication of effort. For example, the group was able to identify a number of teams across the University experimenting with educational podcasting. This has resulted in a co-ordinated effort to standardize practice and identify opportunities for service users to access the relevant technology. The Digital Services Development Officer, who managed the Digilab through its project phase and who now has responsibility for operational management for the service, continues to maintain a del.icio.us account to manage relevant information and useful links available to the group.[3]

Showcasing research

The Digilab proved a particularly useful asset in enabling discussion and drawing colleagues in to consider approaches to mobile learning. As an example, at an early stage in 2005, the OU's Digital Education and Enhancement Project (DEEP) had already trained a number of teachers on how to use mobile technologies in teaching and learning (Leach et al., 2005). In the dissemination phase of DEEP, it was decided to provide example resources so that the wider OU community could see what had been created for the mobile devices (Power and Thomas, 2007), using demonstrations and independent exploration with guidance notes. The Digilab's physical space was used for informal discussions of project work, supplementing formal presentations and seminars held elsewhere in the Library.

Leading on from this dissemination work, it was decided that large-screen live presentation and tailored emulator-based content could both play a useful part in bringing the concepts behind provision of mobile learning and mobile content to a wider audience. Thus, for group discussions connection to a Personal Digital Assistant (PDA) device and real-time demonstrations could be enhanced by projecting a desktop PC running a PDA emulator. The set-up enabled participants to engage in subsequent investigation of the functionality and navigation of PDAs, even if they did not have access to the devices themselves.

The Mobile Learner Support Project

The Digilab project has run parallel to the University's Mobile Learner Support Project but the active networking facilitated by the M-Tech group means that the Business Project Leader, tasked with scoping and developing this 'mLearn' project, continues to capitalize on the potential of the Digilab facility and services to support the work.

A key recommendation to senior managers that has emerged from the Mobile Learner Support Project highlights the potential for building on current services to promote greater staff awareness and development of skills relevant to the use of mobile technologies.

> In taking forward this work within the OU, an essential focus will be to familiarize our staff with the particular affordances gained through mobile learning, which need to be achieved by a blend of up skilling, hands-on staff development and awareness-raising of models of good practice. Staff development sessions provided as part of the Educational and Professional Development programme, and those provided by the Library Digilab will need to be revisited and extended.
>
> (Internal mobile learning position paper)

Technical infrastructure and support

Examples of presentations and discussions held in the Digilab include:

- comparing the approaches and benefits of using e-book reader applications on mobile devices
- illustrating the differences of approach for creating Flash learning objects for mobile use
- evaluating scaled-down desktop and web applets to assess their suitability for stand-alone usage
- demonstrating the current possibilities available in mobile web browsing and the differing approaches taken by different browsers.

All these activities have proved useful in preparing future web-based services for learners.

Since the early work in presenting these aspects of mobile provision and support, the OU's specialist IT support team has also been able to customize, configure and distribute a PDA emulator for wider groups of staff to explore on their own desktop machines. This also is already set up and promoted within the Digilab.

From project into service

Surveying the market

The initial intention of the Digilab project was to facilitate a self-service approach to user engagement with the physical space and the technologies housed in it. In order to get a clearer picture of what types of staff development resources might be required and to ensure full take-up of services, an online questionnaire was used to gather data that would help to scope and inform requirements. It soon became obvious that there was a broad interest in using the Digilab for staff development beyond course-specific e-learning initiatives. Academic, academic-related and business support staff were therefore invited to participate in the questionnaire.

Table 20.1 reveals a need for much more work with academic staff to encourage greater experimentation and reflection on the potential use of mobile technologies in learning. See also Figure 20.1.

Table 20.1 Responses to question: To what extent do you agree with the statement 'I am looking forward to the challenge of keeping up with the new technologies over the next 5 years?'

Staff role	Academic			Academic related			Secretarial and clerical		
Total number of responses	94			207			96		
Time at OU	Less than 5 years	5 to 10 years	More than 10 years	Less than 5 years	5 to 10 years	More than 10 years	Less than 5 years	5 to 10 years	More than 10 years
Number of responses	39	24	31	81	55	71	49	28	19
Strongly agree	26%	33%	19%	38%	36%	32%	51%	50%	11%
Agree	49%	42%	42%	48%	40%	35%	41%	36%	42%
Neutral	15%	25%	23%	11%	24%	23%	6%	11%	37%
Disagree	8%	0%	16%	2%	0%	8%	2%	0%	0%
Strongly disagree	3%	0%	0%	0%	0%	1%	0%	4%	11%

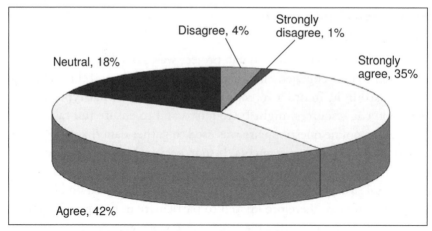

Figure 20.1 Looking forward to the challenge of new technologies (397 responses)

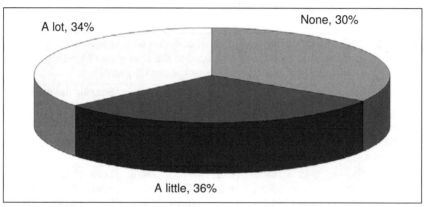

Figure 20.2 Staff experience in taking photos with a camera phone (398 responses)

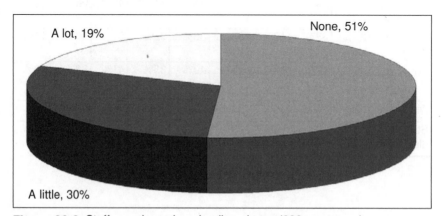

Figure 20.3 Staff experience in uploading photos (398 responses)

Table 20.2 reveals that although the majority of respondents have experience of using mobile phones to take pictures, a significant number have not followed through with uploading these to other services or transferring them between devices. See also Figures 20.2 and 20.3.

Table 20.2 Responses to question: How much experience have you had of the following?								
		Staff role			**Age of respondents**			
		Academic	Academic related	Secretarial and clerical	18–30	31–40	41–50	over 50
Total number of responses		95	207	96	44	129	116	109
Taking a photograph with your mobile phone	None	41%	29%	21%	7%	19%	34%	50%
	A little	39%	39%	26%	32%	33%	41%	35%
	A lot	20%	31%	52%	61%	48%	25%	14%
Loading photos into Flickr or a similar photo-sharing site	None	58%	48%	45%	36%	39%	58%	59%
	A little	24%	31%	29%	25%	32%	28%	28%
	A lot	16%	18%	23%	39%	27%	10%	10%
Creating a podcast	None	75%	84%	83%	80%	81%	84%	80%
	A little	16%	12%	6%	16%	13%	9%	10%
	A lot	3%	1%	3%	5%	2%	2%	2%
Transferring files to or from a PDA or smartphone	None	61%	57%	60%	48%	54%	64%	64%
	A little	15%	19%	17%	32%	18%	15%	14%
	A lot	20%	21%	16%	18%	25%	17%	17%
	A little	12%	16%	4%	18%	16%	10%	6%
	A lot	4%	1%	1%	5%	1%	2%	2%

Table 20.3 reveals that there is a general lack of in-depth knowledge regarding mobile learning and Web 2.0, although it is greater than knowledge regarding geocaching and ambient technologies. See also Figure 20.4 (page 237).

Table 20.3 Responses to question: How much do you know about the following?

		Age of respondents			
		18–30	31–40	41–50	over 50
Total number of responses		44	129	116	109
Web 2.0	Nothing	50%	32%	37%	39%
	Heard of it	16%	22%	28%	26%
	Know a little	9%	10%	16%	13%
	Could explain it	25%	31%	19%	20%
	Expert	0%	4%	0%	1%
Mobile learning	Nothing	41%	27%	28%	42%
	Heard of it	23%	24%	26%	18%
	Know a little	20%	25%	30%	22%
	Could explain it	16%	21%	14%	16%
	Expert	0%	2%	1%	1%
Geocaching	Nothing	73%	71%	79%	81%
	Heard of it	11%	11%	7%	10%
	Know a little	11%	7%	6%	6%
	Could explain it	5%	9%	8%	2%
	Expert	0%	1%	0%	1%
Ambient technology	Nothing	68%	59%	62%	60%
	Heard of it	16%	27%	24%	26%
	Know a little	11%	10%	10%	9%
	Could explain it	5%	2%	3%	5%
	Expert	0%	1%	0%	1%

Table 20.4 reveals some interesting results which appear to demonstrate that respondents who classed themselves as support staff engage more in using the functions available on their mobile devices than do academic staff. See also Figure 20.5 (page 238).

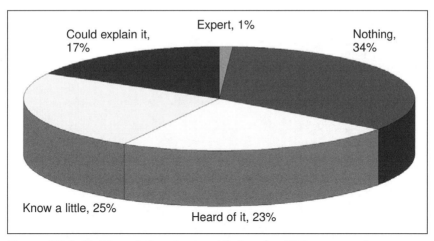

Figure 20.4 Staff knowledge about mobile learning (398 responses)

Table 20.4 Responses to question: Today, mobile devices can provide one function (e.g. a phone) or combine several functions (e.g. a phone that plays music). How do you use the mobile device/s you have? (Respondents were asked to tick all applicable categories.)

	Staff role			Age of respondents			
	Academic	Academic related	Secretarial and clerical	18–30	31–40	41–50	over 50
Total number of responses	95	207	96	44	129	116	109
Mobile phone calls	89%	98%	94%	95%	98%	92%	93%
Mobile text messaging	81%	89%	91%	98%	98%	85%	74%
Mobile internet	23%	31%	31%	52%	36%	24%	17%
Smartphone features such as e-mail, games, applications	16%	25%	28%	43%	29%	20%	14%
Mobile audio (inc. radio)	21%	30%	32%	43%	35%	24%	20%
Mobile video	9%	17%	24%	27%	22%	13%	11%
I don't own a mobile device	7%	2%	3%	0%	0%	6%	6%

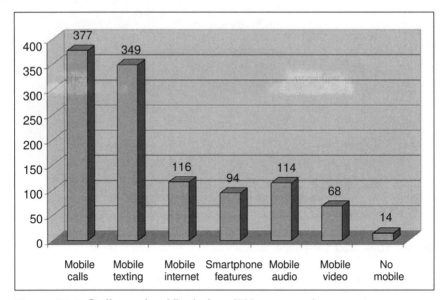

Figure 20.5 Staff use of mobile devices (398 responses)

Taking all these results into consideration, the project team decided to pilot a series of facilitated hands-on learning opportunities which could enable all staff to further their knowledge and increase their confidence in using mobile devices to support their work.

Service planning

After piloting the project for a period of 18 months, the team had gathered sufficient data to present a convincing case to senior managers to move the Digilab from the project phase to a standard service. The service plan outlined the Digilab service on a three-tiered model, showing different levels of service that could be offered depending on resource availability.

The service plan contained a full market appraisal of the various customer segments identified as potential users. The services available to these segments were mapped out in detail, highlighting take-up during the pilot phase. Detailed costing of the packages was undertaken and a full operational plan was developed for the first year of service.

Although the original project specification was for provision of a drop-in space, with staff support on request, it became apparent through discussion with users that some felt they would benefit from facilitated hands-on staff development activities. The higher levels of service proposed in the plan allowed for the provision of half-hour to one-hour activities dubbed 'DigiBytes' and half-day or full-day 'DigiQuests'.

In order to pilot the development of a 'Digibyte' a collaborative activity was developed with the Mobile Learner Support Project Leader for a Faculty of Education and Languages (FELS) staff development session.

Taking all these results into consideration, the project team decided to pilot a series of facilitated 'first hand' experiential learning opportunities which could enable all staff to further their knowledge and increase their confidence in using mobile devices to support their work. They were then asked to upload photos and videos to a web-based mediaBoard service[4] via text or multimedia messaging.

Evaluating success

The project team sought feedback from users on what they felt to be the real benefits of the facility to them as professional practitioners and researchers. We include here some of the comments, which reveal the extent to which users value the service currently on offer.

> If we want to start looking at newer technologies, then there are places in the university that have got hold of these, but it's quite difficult for most people in the university to get into those projects and find out about them and then also get a hands-on experience with those devices. So having something here, which could be booked out and can also be part of a hands-on activity, and giving a follow-up opportunity is one of the strengths of the Digilab and that's something that I hope that we can move forward with. Every time I do any presentations about Mobile Learning or Mobile Learner Support, I always mention that the Digilab is the space that's available if people want to try things for themselves, using the physical devices or talking through the concepts and using some of the emulation tools to get an idea of how the software works.
>
> (Mobile Learner Support Project Leader,
> OU Virtual Learning Environment Programme)

> Participants on the FELS Learning and Teaching Development day found using the Digilab a very enjoyable experience. It opened to them windows that no doubt will inspire the development of their courses and their teaching. In particular it helped

them reflect on how what they do now can be enhanced by the use of the Digilab tools explored. It is early days, but I have no doubt that as a result of the careful and thorough 'induction' facilitated by the Digilab team, colleagues in FELS will be keen to explore new ways of teaching and learning using these tools.

(Senior Lecturer, Department of Languages)

The room is very valuable – primarily because it is a relaxed place to meet with people and talk about interesting things. I have only really used it as a meeting room – when I want to encourage free-flowing creative discussion – or just want folk to relax. I know that folk on the Schome Park Project have used it to gain access to Second Life (due to the difficulties of gaining access elsewhere on campus).

I am sure that the design of the room encourages a different sort of discussion compared with formal meeting rooms. The availability of interesting kit and relaxed meeting facilities (and free hot chocolate) certainly encourages folk to congregate there – helping with the sharing of good practice and ideas.

(Senior Lecturer, Department of Education)

The Digilab rejuvenates thinking. Discussions there quickly identify superior approaches not appreciated in more formal settings. . . .To prosper in the modern world you must understand the tools available – the Digilab is a gateway to those tools. . . . The modern student does not work in isolated silence, but works surrounded by tools, technologies and distractions. Digilab helps understand how they work.

(Interactive Media Advisor, LTS)

I think we tend to get a bit isolated; the Digilab inspires and reminds us that real users will be interacting with our work.   (Media Developer, LTS)

Brilliant up to date technology, in a relaxing environment. (Media Assistant, LTS)

I like the drop-in nature of it so you can just pop in whenever you need to. . . . It really helps for a Media Developer to know what kind of technology is out there that isn't just PC-based. I tested several of my websites on a Playstation3, Nintendo Wii and PDA, something I would never had the opportunity to do inside LTS despite them being fairly common technology for home users.   (Media Developer, LTS)

The freedom to use the tools with contextual notes or commentaries is liberating.

(Media Developer, LTS)

Conclusions

The success of the Digilab is due to the Library's collaboration with stakeholders to ensure that services remain relevant and valuable within the scope of available resources. Calculating the full cost of providing staff development activities is crucial in order to forecast and balance appropriate resourcing.

Mobile devices are mainstream mass-market technologies which are available for libraries and others to capitalize on for e-learning and knowledge-management purposes. However, staff need to feel supported with regards to using these devices and to feel confident enough to support users of mobile library services. The Digilab has supported awareness raising, confidence building and professional development for library staff. For example, a member of Library staff used the PDA emulator in Digilab to test how well the Library's short course 'Beyond Google' worked on mobile devices. Through Digilab sessions Library staff have engaged with the provision of mobile library services at a strategic level, and this has resulted in work on content delivery and on skills development delivery via mobile devices.

Strategic support within the institution is critical for success in pioneering new types of library services such as the Digilab. Take-up of services during the project phase was largely due to a strong project team and individual champions. If the facility is to become established to support change management for e-learning, Digilab services will need to be integrated into workforce development planning. Staff need time and support if they are to participate in skills development and reflective practice. As an organization, the Open University needs to fully understand this commitment and invest accordingly so as to reap the full benefits and become more effective.

References

Leach, J. et al. (2005) *DEEP IMPACT: an investigation of the use of information and communication technologies for teacher education in the global south*, Department for International Development (DfID), Researching the Issues, 58, www.open.ac.uk/deep/Public/web/publications/pdfs/ReportFeb2006.pdf.

Power, T. and Thomas, R. (2007) The Classroom in your Pocket? *The Curriculum Journal*, 18, (3), 373–88.

URLs

1   http://library.open.ac.uk/services/digilab/index.cfm
2   www.open.ac.uk/digilab
3   http://del.icio.us/OU_MTech
4   www.portal.m-learning.org/mboard.php

Part 4

Practice perspectives

21

From shelf to PDA: how to transform mobile devices into a library information tool

Àngels Carles, Ana Castellano and Fernando Guerrero

Introduction

The UABMS (Universitat Autònoma de Barcelona Medical School) has set up a new project: to create a platform to help final-year students on clinical placements. Because these sessions involve dealing with real patients in university hospitals, it is essential for students to be able to respond quickly in cases where they may be unable to find answers to their doubts and queries. We consider the PDA (Personal Digital Assistant) to be a good solution, as it could enable easy access to library documentation, such as catalogues, databases, digital journals, e-books, etc. in the field. The ultimate objective is to make mobile devices a normal tool for consultation.

The main objective of the Learning Resources Centre, Informatics Services and Medical Library is to contribute content and make access to and consultation of the Library's documentary resources easier and more practical. Meanwhile, we also seek to collaborate with students and professors to develop educational materials.

Background

The aim of the project is to create a platform to help final-year medical students on clinical placements to access just-in-time information. These students work in hospitals, visiting real patients with assistance from a professor. Response time is a determining factor, and it is essential for students to answer patients' questions quickly. Patients trust physicians and physicians in training, but if they feel students are unsure about their illness or seem insecure in their behaviour, this could have a negative effect on their recovery. Patients must trust their physicians, and physicians must generate a sense of security. It can sometimes be difficult for medical students to achieve such a relationship, because without the possibility of consulting medical literature or clinical guides to answer patients' questions, they may not make the right diagnosis.

Medical students need to improve their clinical skills and also integrate fully into the doctor–patient relationship. To do so, they must improve their self-confidence and gain a better understanding of the practices being carried out. Current manuals do not solve their real needs, and are not available to them when they are visiting patients in hospital. Our students found that one solution was to write their own pocket handbooks as an aid to their clinical work. They wrote a short report and presented it at the Educational Innovation Workshop held at the UABMS in April 2006. The idea received an enthusiastic response and the students asked for help in developing the handbook. Under the leadership of the Medical School, the initial project developed into an authentic Educational Innovation Project in collaboration with the Medical Educational Unit. The UABMS presented the draft to the annual MQD (Teaching Quality Improvement) in association with the Catalan government and obtained a grant to develop the project with the involvement of several of the UABMS services.

The PDA was first designed as an electronic agenda, but people are now discovering many more uses for these portable devices. They are indeed a good solution for libraries. Our project is an educational innovation that we believe could prove helpful to final-year students. We are making a pocket handbook, an e-book consultable by PDA and containing the essential requirements for work in clinical placements. These are designed for students, but also present a good opportunity to libraries as they could provide a new user service whereby library users would be able to access resources without needing to go to the library in person.

By implementing mobile devices, we are seeking to introduce new technologies and promote their use as everyday tools for solving any user's questions. Our aim is to make an easy, practical, schematic, visual and complete tool for accessing medical resources in digital format. This will be our contribution to the further education of medical students who are fully immersed in the learning process. We calculate that it will involve around 15 clinical specialists, with 20 clinical cases each. This way students will be able to put questions to reference librarians, and access the library catalogue and the library's other documentation in order to solve problems, check the validity of information and perform basic queries.

Description

Transforming the students' initial idea into a real tool of educational innovation requires the collaboration of the all elements of the Medical School, including students, faculty and other service staff. The students' participation is of utmost importance because the project is designed as a free-choice credit (or option). All of the students are volunteers and should also receive academic credits for their contributions, as for any other optional subject offered by the UAB (Autonomous University of Barcelona).

The students' work involves filling in forms preformatted by their teachers. There is one form per clinical speciality. The form contains several sections: a brief description of the illness, aetiology, clinical features and treatment. Teaching units are the equivalents of a clinical speciality, such as cardiology, neurology, dermatology, etc. Every teaching unit is made up of 15 to 20 clinical cases, and may be illustrated with photos to help students make their diagnosis. After the students have filled in the forms, teachers and hospital residents check the work and validate it. A teacher co-ordinator then arranges for the material to be revised and approved for publication in an e-book. The Informatics Services and Learning Resources Centre transforms all the documentation into iSilo format, a PDA reader. We did this conversion using a *handicraft* search method. This led to a minor problem: finding an 'end to end' publishing system for efficient publication of the materials in PDA format – but we believe this issue will be resolved very soon. The Informatics Services' current priority is to find a good 'end to end' publishing system.

Findings

The project is currently in the initial phase. Further user training will be provided to make the system easier to use and handle. At present, we only have one teaching unit available: Dermatology. This unit contains 23 clinical cases and several photographs to help students. We carried out a pilot project with 15 students for three weeks. The feedback from the students and teachers involved has been very good. The results were excellent, and the attitudes of students to using PDAs in their clinical practices are positive. The students now feel more secure when dealing with patients and their diagnoses are better. The next stage will involve collaborating with students and professors to create educational material to enable use of PDAs to access library information and digital medical resources.

Conclusions

Students are involved in the writing of educational material and, at the same time, learn much more. Some materials provided by commercial publishers are on the market, but there are none quite like the materials developed for this project, which has involved the joint participation of students and faculty.

Mobile devices provide flexibility in terms of time and location, i.e. information and knowledge can be accessed anywhere and at any time, and this is a significant opportunity for libraries. We are in a position to exploit mobile technology to provide new services and improve old ones.

Acknowledgement

We wish to acknowledge the Catalan government for the grant it provided to develop this project, and the computing company Acer for facilitating a pilot trial with 15 PDA devices.

22

Working towards the ubiquitous library: an exploratory case study of cell phone informatics for new student library orientation

Jim Hahn

Introduction

The University of Illinois at Urbana–Champaign, a research university situated in east central Illinois, 140 miles south of Chicago, has 30,695 undergraduate students of whom 6949 are first-year students enrolled in Fall 2007. The departmental library structure of the University of Illinois mirrors the development of the modern American research university, which evolved along the path of departmental specialization (Geiger, 2004). There are around 40 departmental libraries, each serving unique needs of the University. A number of these libraries are housed in the departmental buildings, while others are in the main library building. The collections of the library comprise nearly 11 million volumes – making it the largest publicly funded research library in the United States. While departmental specialization may indeed be advantageous for researchers and scholars, it does make it difficult for first-year students to locate items and rooms within the library complex. A dedicated Undergraduate Library helps to alleviate 'library anxiety' for first-year students.

The Undergraduate Library is one of the larger departmental libraries and is oriented toward serving first- and second-year students. The services provided include in-person reference service at a single-point service desk, virtual reference service (instant messaging and chat), and online web help guides and instructional material, as well as an instructional programme which provides introductory information literacy workshops to first-year students and services specifically targeted to support University 101, the campus version of a national first-year student success movement. The collections of the Undergraduate Library reflect the needs of this population as well, supporting the general research needs of students and also providing them with checkout for media such as DVDs, books on CD, and gaming resources. In this way, the Undergraduate Library does somewhat resemble the services and collections one might expect to find in the standard American public library.

A particular challenge in reaching undergraduate students is the nature of their highly scheduled lives. An as-yet unanswered question for librarians is how to situate the library into the existence of the modern student. The goal for the librarian is to connect students to the library, with the aim of helping them in their studies and supporting their higher education. The fact that massive amounts of information are available without the intervention of a librarian as mediator presents a serious challenge to this goal. The library can remain relevant as an informational–educational space by inventing or seeking out innovative integrative strategies. Though no two students are alike, they are generally somewhat nomadic and quite bound up in technology, to the point that (although they may not realize it) they carry in their pockets the processing power of the desktop computers of a decade ago – on a cell phone. This device is a possible channel between the students and the library. The aim of cell phone research in the Undergraduate Library is to invent new ways of connecting students to the library.

Orientation to the library has attributes of instruction and of a tour. Orientation as conceptualized by this librarian involves complementary instruction and preparation for the information literacy workshops in which students may participate. Library orientation also seeks to lay the foundations for education at university level. The orientation programming takes a two-pronged approach, being intellectually rigorous in its instructional objectives yet speaking to the students in a manner conducive to learning. The scholarship which informs library orientation programming and partnership efforts stems from nationwide research on first-year initiative and transition (Upcraft et al., 2005; Tobolowsky and Cox, 2007).

Pilot project goal and objectives

Because of the nature of the decentralized library system – somewhat akin to a large new city for some students – a way-finder video on a librarian's cell phone was constructed to better guide students through the physical library space. The way-finder is a 'proof of concept' for a librarian using a video-enabled cell phone to instruct students on how to locate rooms that are frequently asked for in the library and which are not easy for first-time library users to find. It was perceived that navigation would be easier using a three-dimensional model rather than the typical two-dimensional model given to students on paper.

The informatics involved in placing a video on a cellular device include constructing the animation on a personal computer, reformatting the video file for use on a cellular device, and then transferring the content from the PC to the device. The animation is then accessed and played via the cell phone user interface that is packaged with the cell phone.

This proof-of-concept project uses the following software and hardware: Google SketchUp 6 for map construction and animation, Media Convert (http://media-convert.com) for file conversion and a SanDisk MicroSD disk with MiniSD adapter for file movement from PC to cell phone. The cell phone used in this project is an LG VX8300, which comes with a microSD Expansion Slot as standard, and the standard packaged Verizon VCAST-enabled operating system. A more detailed explanation of the technical specification of this phone is reviewed by Nass (2007).

Map construction

Google SketchUp 6 is an easy-to-use software application for modelling three-dimensional objects. Any user can download and freely use SketchUp for eight hours before they must purchase the software. Though the software is easy to use for a beginner, it does require the user to be somewhat skilled in 3-D modelling for the representative model to resemble an actual building. The work entailed creating a directional map using segments to represent the path a student would take to navigate between one departmental library, the undergraduate library, and a lecture hall in a different library building (this being an often-requested room in the main library, reflecting a library-wide need for a service solution).

There is an animation feature in Google SketchUp, though this is not the main purpose of the program. One very easy way to go about making an animation is to take a variety of views, which the application calls 'Scenes', of the model and then record them in the order that the user will experience during playback. Once the series is constructed the next step is to export the animation. For this project, the animation is output in the .AVI file format.

The .AVI file format is not playable on the LG VX8300 but the blog (http://vx8300.blogspot.com) was helpful in finding the proper file format. Identifying free web services for file conversion uncovered the Media Convert webpage (http://media-convert.com). Reformatting consists of uploading the .AVI file and then using the conversion tools of the web page to convert the file format to the file specification for cellular devices, .3GPP. The new file is then saved to the desktop PC.

The blog reference material is extremely helpful also for learning how to move content from the desktop PC to the cellular device.[1] The actual technique varied slightly in this project, but the reference material was nonetheless useful. This project did not include a USB adapter but instead relied on an all-SanDisk (SD) solution of MicroSD to MiniSD converter, a subtle and insubstantial difference.

The next step in moving the file is to copy the .3GPP file to the MiniSD adapter, which has the MicroSD drive inside it. Once the file has been copied over to the adapter, the drive is removed from the PC. Removing the MicroSD from inside of the MiniSD and placing the MicroSD inside the cellular phone then makes the file accessible to the cellular device's user interface. The interface is fairly intuitive and greatly helps this project because the phone has been built to handle this type of video playback. It may be the case that only early adopters will be interested in these features of the phone. Librarians as early adopters may realize considerable instructional benefits for their innovative use of cell phone technology in the library.

Usability and delivery

At present, this proof of concept shows a route of line segments. Further refinement of the concept would make use of picture data ported into Google SketchUp, which would be used to better model the actual environment that the student needs to navigate. Once a more accurate model was developed human intervention would not be needed for assistance in using route information; with picture data, the route could better represent itself. The map could be placed on a server from which the user could access a digital library of animations to help in navigation of the library. Conceptual maps of the research process are another possible resource for development. A student in the throes of information-seeking frustration could consult a 'research process' map which would help the student to determine a route to a completed project. The maps could be accessed by Bluetooth, a data transmission protocol. Other access solutions would depend on the physical library being equipped with data cables for cellular devices.

One possible scenario would be to equip battery charging stations with data provision. One can envisage a student charging a mobile device and then realizing that, while the phone is being charged, it can be loaded with library tutorials such as short instructional videos, e-books, navigating maps, citations that the student has browsed, weather updates, and possibly flight or bus schedules. The applicability of loading content to the cellular device would depend on students' individual needs.

The LG VX8300 phone is also capable of playing MP3s. Using the functionality of Verizon's VCAST interface it was also possible to move the library MP3 tour from a personal computer to the cellular phone. The front of the phone has accessible player features, so if this is the only MP3 loaded onto the phone, simply pressing 'play' will enable the user to listen to the MP3 tour of the library. Future development of in-library cell phone informatics may rely on other capabilities of the cellular device paired with context-aware sensors.

An independent server formatted with digital library software could, in theory, be configured to supply content formatted for cellular or mobile devices. Further, wireless informatics initiatives may investigate using an intermediate transmitter to deliver content via Bluetooth. Consider, that a file normally delivered from a hard drive and sent to the user interface by way of an integrated motherboard can be extrapolated to include a cellular phone as another data conduit for arrival at its destination.

Conclusion

A wireless mobile digital library can be regarded as an additional step toward ubiquitous library computing. Viewing the cellular device as an additional component in students' everyday computing may well lead to innovations in delivery of library content; extension of the library to the student's computing accessories may well be a means to realizing integrating the library and assistance with information seeking for new students.

Acknowledgements

The author gratefully acknowledges the help of Lisa Hinchliffe, who commented on a draft of this chapter.

References

Geiger, R. (2004) *To Advance Knowledge: the growth of American research universities, 1900–1940,* Transaction Publishers.

Nass, R. (2007) LG Handset Gets it Right, *Electronic Engineering Times*, 1460, (29 January), 50.

Tobolowsky, B. F. and Cox, B. E. (2007) *Shedding Light on Sophomores: an exploration of the second college year*, University of South Carolina.

Upcraft, M. L., Gardner, J. N. and Barefoot, B. O. (2005) *Challenging and Supporting the First-year Student: a handbook for improving the first year of college*, Jossey-Bass.

URL

1   http://vx8300.blogspot.com/2006/08/microsd-memory-card-for-cell-phone. html

23

A basic plan for mobile service connectivity for the library system of the Open University of Sri Lanka

Wathmanel Seneviratne

Introduction

Information technology is constantly evolving, posing a challenge for those of us who are using it to provide information. The situation is the same with mobile telephony.

As Malhan (2003) indicates, the electronic information environment is more effective for exchanging information, and results in better user satisfaction, than the physical library, even though the user is miles away. The versatile nature of modern ICTs has influenced information systems constructively, and learning systems also. According to Yi Jia, use of modern ICTs improves the knowledge level of weaker students and provides less-skilled students with more opportunities for learning (Yi, 2005).

The Open University of Sri Lanka (OUSL) library system currently operates as a network of libraries, consisting of the main library in Colombo, five regional centre libraries and 17 study/teaching centre libraries. Out of these, the regional centre libraries operate both as libraries and as information centres; the other libraries are merely essential collections.

The main library has a collection of books, journals and multimedia resources. There are approximately 92,000 books and bound journals spanning a variety of subject areas and over 2000 AV resources and multimedia titles. There are around 35 staff in the library system as a whole. The student population registered for different courses as at April 2007 was 24,400 and most of the student population is in employment. The student population is scattered widely across the island.

The learning system in the university is based on the open and distance learning (ODL) method, using both face-to-face and electronic classrooms, supported by printed study materials. The new project undertaken by the university is the Moodle-based e-learning strategy supported by the Asian Development Bank's Distance Education Modernization Project. At present the OUSL library is planning to link into the virtual learning environment being developed by the University. The OUSL library embarked on developing collaborative learning support materials in consultation with the faculty. According to studies (Fang et al., 2007; Suresh Kumar, 1996; Radar, 1998; Adikata, 2006) conducted in some overseas universities, this collaborative work can help to reduce unnecessary student workload.

Situation analysis

At present the library services at OUSL are confined to the main campus library in Colombo. There are two regional centre libraries which are established to fulfil the needs of users scattered island-wide, but they are considerably inferior to the main library in terms of resource base, staff strength, access mechanisms and other modern facilities. Another regional library will be established in the very near future towards the north side of the island. It is expected that this library will develop in line with the other regional centre libraries.

Thus, catering equally for the users' varying information needs and library service needs is not an easy task, as the ODL clients are scattered around the island. It was observed that the students attached to the OUSL system find it difficult to travel long distances to OUSL regional libraries and to access study centre collections, sometimes to obtain a small piece of information that doesn't really justify the cost of travelling such a distance. In some cases, when students have travelled a long distance to the study centres, some of the information they need is not available at the point of access, and they still have to contact the main library to obtain it.

Even though some have internet access, many remote learners are unable to access the OUSL library website (which provides a lot of information for distance learners), because some remote areas either do not have electricity or connectivity to the national grid or do not provide a consistent supply.

It is reported that, in 2007, there were many National Access Centres established in remote regions, providing access to all types of distance learners scattered around the country via the Asian Development Bank's Distance Education Participatory Programme (DEPP). However, these centres have not had much impact on distance learners' ability to access electronic resources to support their learning.

An alternative approach is therefore needed to provide remote learners with access to the OUSL's learning and information resources and services. Possible options for the OUSL to pursue include television networks or broadcasting services, but these do not support a user-driven, personalized approach to information delivery. However, a significant interest has emerged within the library and information sector in the concept of mobile learning using mobile telephony. Experiments are being carried out to deliver information to remote library users via mobile phones.

The strategy

The strategy proposed is to reach the remote learner/user through mobile telephony. According to the statistics there has been a rapid increase in mobile phone use, especially among youth and the working population. Recent reports have mentioned that there were three million mobile phone users in Sri Lanka and that 80% of the land area is covered by the mobile networks. This trend provides an opportunity to implement mobile technology-based library services for distance learners as an outreach strategy.

According to the m-learning systems explored, mobile technology is unlikely to be able to supply the necessary service on its own, but needs to be integrated with digital technology. The following prerequisites were identified:

- digitized information base
- information products designed for an e-platform
- electronic information service delivery
- design of electronic access systems.

The OUSL library portal

When considering the OUSL library background, the following conditions can be identified as favourable to embarking on a mobile technology-based library service:

- fully automated catalogue with web-based OPAC
- automated circulation system
- automated Selective Dissemination of Information (SDI) service
- system-generated new acquisition lists
- web-based OUSL library portal.

The OUSL library portal embraces most of the automated and e-services, hence it is considered significant in planning mobile-based services for library clients. It is intended to reach remote learners as a course-oriented learning support, a lifelong learning support and an information delivery portal. The website has facilities to search the catalogue, databases, access to e-journals and printed holdings, circulation-related searching and reservations, question paper search, query handling service and access to information products such as CAS (Central Authentication Service) and services such as SDI (Figure 23.1).

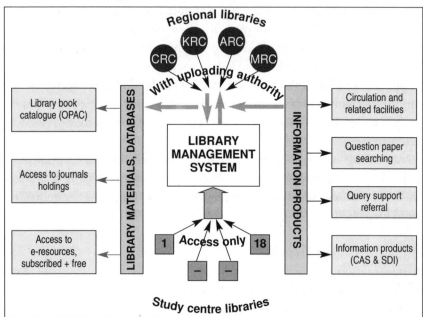

Figure 23.1 The interactive library web portal

It is hoped that when the mobile network is configured as an information delivery mechanism, some special web-based services will be earmarked for delivery to users' mobiles. The library services that can be connected from the start are shown in Figure 23.2. The service functions already in operation are indicated in shaded boxes under 'e-environment'. The services that can be connected through the mobile telephones are shown on the left-hand side.

It is important that the information we provide is presented in such a way as to match the limited display capability of the mobile phone. The following services are selected for the first phase of mobile connectivity:

■ Library OPAC (can be given shortened titles and location/class numbers)
■ SMS-based responses for subject queries
■ question papers (online searchable by course codes or years)
■ indexed or annotated recommended literature as learning support
■ course materials listings by levels and course codes
■ My OUSL service On-Mobile connected to library services
■ Ask-the-librarian online query service.

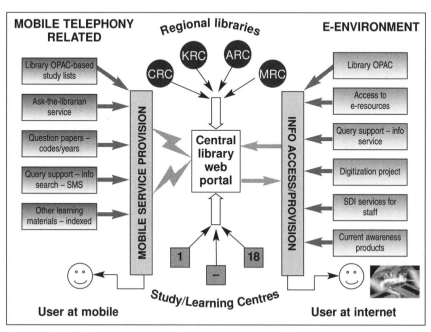

Figure 23.2 E-library- and mobile telephony-related library architecture

Some indexing or abstracting of materials is needed at the documentation stage and it may seem like extra work for the information processing staff. Nevertheless, the effort is fully justified by the benefits to be attained and will provide ample return on the investment in terms of the service being delivered to the remote users.

The 'mobile service strategy' could be arranged under four functional areas:

1 *Awareness*: This function is important for the users to locate the information they need or to make arrangements to obtain that information, wherever the user is located.
2 *Catalogue/information search*: Beyond the Awareness function, remote users will need to be able to search for references on information that they need and to identify the location of that material or information.
3 *Information delivery*: Information will be delivered on the mobile, although that information may be in the form of references and abstracts.
4 *Ask-the-Librarian*: This is an enquiry service operated from 8.30 am to 5.00 pm as an online helpdesk service.

Conclusion

The Open University of Sri Lanka's library users are scattered around the island and have not had access to an effective online library system through regular networked technology. Therefore, it is very important to use an alternative strategy to bring remote users into a library and learning support system. Mobile technology is a convenient and inexpensive method for the open and distance information services to adopt to reach remote students, as more than 90% of the students have adopted this technology for their personal use.

With growing enthusiasm for using new technology among young learners, the level of adoption of mobile technology in library services is high. According to the experience of other countries, the learning benefits a remote learner can achieve through mobile-operated library services are much higher and more cost effective than those obtained from on-site library services.

References

Ali Adikata, A. (2006) Students' Library Use: a study on faculty perception in a Malaysian university, *Library Review*, 55 (2),106–19.

Fang, M., Jinghai Rao, Xiomeng Su, Tieyang Li (2007) *A Web Based Collaborative Learning System*, www.cs.cmu.edu/~jinghai/papers/WCLS.pdf.

Malhan, I. V. (2003) Challenges for Information Users in the Turbulent Times, Technological Transitions and Changing Work Environment, *Proceedings. First International Convention on 'Mapping Technologies on Libraries and People'*, organized by INFLIBNET and Nirma Education and Research Foundation, Ahmedabad, 501–12.

Radar, H. B. (1998) *Faculty–Librarian Collaboration in Building the Curriculum for the Millennium – the US experience*, www.ifla.org/iv/ifla64/040-112e.htm.

Suresh Kumar, V. (1996) *Why Collaborative Learning?* www.cs.usask.ca/grads /vsk719/ academic/890/project2/node2.html.

Yi Jia (2005) Building a Web Based Collaborative Learning Environment, *IEEE ITHET 6th Annual International Conference, Juan Dolio, Dominican Republic, 7–9 July 2005*, http://fie.engrng.pitt.edu/ithet2005/papers/.

24

Information literacy: sharing ideas for delivery on the move

Peter Godwin, Anne Hewling and Jo Parker

Introduction

Librarians involved in the delivery of information literacy (IL) are always looking for new ways to engage learners. We have concluded that students not only come in different age groups and study modes but also have different learning styles, requiring us to consider different methods of delivery. In particular, it is leading to investigation of the potential of Web 2.0 tools. However, armed with the knowledge that there are 3 billion mobiles worldwide, we should also consider the benefits of using this technology. It would be unlikely to replace the core instruction or learning delivered in other ways, but the advantages for getting snippets of information to remote users, or for reinforcing existing messages, should not be overlooked. With this in mind a group of interested librarians took part in a workshop to discuss how the potential of mobile technologies might be harnessed to assist students with their information literacy.

Defining information literacy

Worldwide, there are many definitions and models of IL which practitioners use as frameworks to support the development of their information literacy interventions. These include models from Australia and New Zealand (Bundy, 2004), the USA (Association of College and Research Libraries, 2000) and the UK's CILIP (Chartered Institute of Library and Information Professionals) definition (Armstrong et al., 2005) and the SCONUL Seven Pillars model (SCONUL, 1999). But while practitioners use the models, there are additional factors that influence the success of information literacy interventions. So what constitutes 'good' information literacy development – and how might mobile delivery help to support it? There are a number of recognized critical success factors which work alongside the various definitions and models and enable practitioners to deliver effective information literacy sessions and services. These include:

■ the need for harmony with academic programmes, in that any attempts to influence students have to be delivered at the point of need and to appear relevant to their current study and later life
■ good quality materials, delivered by professionally competent staff
■ incorporating and encouraging critical thinking
■ measurable outcomes.

What follows is an exploration of some of the issues raised in the workshop.

Mobile IL: challenges, issues, solutions?

One of the real challenges that the group was sure must be faced by all developers of mobile learning materials is the huge range of mobile devices available, from basic mobile phones to fully enabled web browsers, e.g. the new iPhone. This creates challenges in terms of designing flexible and suitable materials. We reached no conclusion as to whether a resource is genuinely 'mobile' if the material is already on the web generally, and just accessed via one of these devices, though we did acknowledge that larger-screened devices would lend themselves better to displaying material not specifically designed for mobile devices.

Typically in higher education (in the UK, at least), information literacy sessions led by library staff feature induction tours, or lectures at the start of the year, with big groups of students. Most practitioners would agree that these methods of delivery are far from ideal for getting across some of the more complex aspects of information literacy. Mobile technology may not be any more appropriate. Where practitioners do negotiate classroom time with students, based on the support of lecturers, any group or collaborative activities would need to be rethought if mobiles were to be introduced. Mobiles tend to be used for 'private' interactions, rather than for fostering a sense of group interaction. They are certainly not suitable for delivering lots of text. We would need to think again, and render information differently, in small chunks, which could be very popular with many users, representing the way they prefer to pick up information. The huge expansion in available information has led to the need to acquire a deeper understanding of what our users require or will be interested in using (Morville, 2005). In what Morville calls 'a world of ambient findability', where we can find anyone or anything from anywhere at any time, librarians should consider using mobiles to deliver their instruction and content. For example, learning could be delivered as small 'bolt-ons', supplementing existing web-based materials.

One example of this approach is Mobile Safari, produced by the Open University Library in collaboration with Athabasca University. Content is inspired by the existing Safari programme (the Open University, 2007b), which has recently been completely updated. It reprises the main lessons from that programme and adds worked examples. Thanks to software from Athabasca, this is delivered formatted for use on mobile devices – smartphones, PDAs etc. The development of Mobile Safari was motivated both by the wish to make important information literacy materials as widely available as possible, and in response to an awareness that mobile technology potentially offers access to an even wider population than presenting a programme like Safari via a 'traditional' web format. Since the Library's web pages are themselves available as a mobile version, it made sense not to reproduce the same materials, but to develop complementary and extension materials when creating the mobile-only content. The individual learning objects that this produces can also be inserted directly into course materials. For example, a course which requires students to use the Safari PROMPT tool (the Open University Library, 2007a) to evaluate material for an assignment might embed the Mobile Safari object for PROMPT right into the materials (via their Moodle VLE site) at the point in the course when students should be preparing their assignments. This would then offer not only a quick revision tool but also one that could be used 'on the move'. Mobile Safari also has potential for use in areas and locations where students cannot easily get PC and/or wired internet access but do have access to mobile telephony, e.g. rural areas – both in the UK and internationally. At the time of writing, the PROMPT learning object was being informally evaluated on different mobile devices, but it was expected that learning objects to complement the sections of Safari would be finalized by 2008. Negotiation is under way to decide exactly how, other than from the main Safari page on Open Library, students will access these objects. The objects will also join the collection of resources available for all course developers to use.

Further suggestions for use of mobiles

The strength of mobile devices clearly lies in widening access to material rather than in reading great screeds of text – using the mobile as a 'pulling down' device rather than 'pushing up'. Participants at the workshop suggested that they might be used for:

- getting hints and tips for an assignment
- showing students how to get to an electronic journal article (rather than for delivering it in its entirety)
- communication, e.g. about workshop schedules
- providing one-to-one support as follow up to face-to-face sessions (this would raise questions about SMS support and staffing)
- accessing traditional lectures delivered via podcasts, which would help to free up any available face-to-face time for more in-depth learning opportunities
- podcast versions of guides to the library and tours (the example of Arizona University was cited here as a work in progress).

The increasing potential for audio and video learning, harnessing the power of the next generation of mobile devices, was also acknowledged. A colleague from Napier University (UK) gave some examples of current work: the Napier information literacy website is available via Wireless Application Protocol (WAP), and podcasts are provided. Audio clips of students talking about best practice (and bad practice) for the benefit of other students have also been produced.

Conclusion

These ideas indicate that mobiles present information literacy practitioners with a real opportunity to take advantage of the anytime/anyplace/anywhere delivery that they afford. They represent opportunities for delivery on what is likely to become the ideal device of the future. Mobile tools for information literacy could be embedded into course work like any other virtual learning device. Information literacy practitioners must come up with solutions to meet the future needs of students, and there is no doubt that, armed with appropriate staff development, creativity and enthusiasm, they can deliver it effectively.

Acknowledgements

The authors would like to thank colleagues who attended the workshop for their active participation.

References

Armstrong, C. et al. (2005) CILIP Defines Information Literacy for the UK, *Library and information update*, 4 (1), 22–5, www.cilip.org.uk/publications/updatemagazine/archive/archive2005/janfeb/armstrong.htm.

Association of College and Research Libraries (2000) *Information Literacy Competency Standards for Higher Education*, American Library Association, www.ala.org/ala/acrl/acrlstandards/informationliteracycompetency.htm.

Bundy, A. (ed.) (2004) *Australian and New Zealand Information Literacy Framework: Principles, Standards and Practice*, 2nd edn, Australian and New Zealand Institute for Information Literacy, www.anziil.org/resources/Safari.

Morville, P. (2005) *Ambient Findability*, O'Reilly.

Open University Library (2007a) *PROMPT: evaluating information, Safari section 5*, www.open.ac.uk/safari.

Open University Library (2007b) *Safari: skills in accessing, finding and reviewing information*, www.open.ac.uk/safari.

SCONUL (1999) *Information Skills in Higher Education: a SCONUL position paper*, www.sconul.ac.uk/groups/information_literacy/papers/Seven_pillars2.pdf.

Conclusion: thoughts on the future of m-libraries

Gill Needham

Introduction

This volume has brought together a diverse and stimulating array of theory and practice in the relatively new world of m-libraries. There appears to be a clear consensus among the authors that there is a great deal still to come. So what of the future? Will the increasing sophistication of mobile technologies offer exciting opportunities for libraries which will help to secure their future in this changing landscape? Or will it perhaps sound their death knell as users take up more tempting offers from competing information providers so that, as suggested by Naughton in Chapter 1, their fate mirrors that of travel agents?

We asked some well-known commentators on both digital libraries and m-learning to give us their predictions about the future of libraries and mobile technologies. Their comments and suggestions form the basis of this concluding chapter.

The technology

The use of mobile technology has increased exponentially in recent years. At the same time, the technology is becoming smaller, more portable and more powerful. Mobile devices are now part of daily lives in the affluent world and are also playing an increasingly significant role in the developing nations.

All our commentators seem to agree on the future pervasiveness of mobile technology. Brophy (2008) suggests that the term 'mobile' will indeed become obsolete:

> I think we have to assume that the term 'mobile' will sound fairly quaint before very long, since internet access will be largely ubiquitous and services like GPS will be better integrated into mainstream devices. That suggests that personal devices, whatever they turn out to be, will be dominant.

What of the devices themselves and their functionality? How will they develop? The iPhone is regarded by many as the way forward in terms of mobile design.

> iPhone style phones will dominate more quickly than predicted. The fact that app[lication]s on the phone are appearing on Apple phones fifty times more than [on] regular phones tells us something.   (Abram, 2008)

> I'm sure for example that something like an iPhone with a foldable decent sized screen/keyboard (or other input device) will be commonplace.   (Brophy, 2008)

Abram (2008) also predicts a shift from the emphasis on voice to other forms of communication:

> Voice will not be the dominant form of communication in the future. It will stay static as new forms – even beyond texting and SMS – take over. Jetson style videophones are already here. . . . Mobiles will have a large component of asynchronous voice messaging including threaded discussions using v-mail technologies.

There appeared to be some scepticism about the ability of mobile devices to support effective reading of scholarly articles but some optimism about the future development of the e-book reader.

> . . . but will it become the tool of choice for reading the PDF of a scholarly article? I'm not so sure about that, at least until devices such as the Philips prototype with the expanding e-ink screen reach maturity.   (Miller, 2008)

> E-ink combined with flexible screens should soon make e-books more of a reality than at present.   (Sharples, 2008)

Convergence and lifestyle

As these devices become increasingly sophisticated, how many will we wish to carry around with us? I currently carry a mobile phone, a digital camera, an iPod and a PDA. My phone, recently upgraded, actually duplicates most of the functions of the other devices.

The role of mobile technology in the individual's lifestyle is discussed by all our commentators. Abram (2008) envisages each of us with one device to organize our working life:

> Mobile devices will be individuals' primary electronic device including for their calendar, voice and e-mail, search, GIS, etc.

to engage in e-commerce:

> The ability for a phone to read barcodes or RFIDs and search for a better price will rock the retail industry as price comparison sites go wild . . .

> Mobile and auction are a perfect fit (think what Skype and eBay could do if they thought it through!) . . .

> eCommerce on the phone through OpenID and your provider's billing system will be common within five years. Micropayments may finally have a business case. The early beneficiaries of ecommerce on digital mobiles will be products that do not require delivery – like advice, music, movies, ringtones, ebooks, storyhours, audiobooks, podcasts, radio, alerts, financial transactions like stocks/insurance, and more

to participate in e-government:

> The transition from surveys based on home to individual will be complete. If anything has been learned by the pollsters in the current US election it is that they were really off on the role of mobiles in the new generation and that their polls of landlines in homes were off by a major factor;

to undertake our social and leisure activities:

> Your called and calling numbers as well as your nicknames and directory will start to support social networking applications.

Gaming on the mobile is just the tip of the iceberg. As ringtones taught folks how to download, games are the killer commercial app[lication];

and for formal and informal learning:

Learning app[lication]s will follow with e-learning on mobiles being popular.

And Kukulska-Hulme (2008) poses an interesting suggestion about changing relationships with advertising:

Yet another development that looks set to increase is the close relationship between information access, learning and advertising. The resistance to advertising will fade away as adverts become more ingenious, rewarding and tailored to one's personality and preferences. Advertising may even become integrated with semantic linking so that delving deeper into an advert will be the beginning of an interesting journey, with several paths depending on which way a person chooses to go. The alignment with mobile devices is partly through the playfulness of the experience and also the congruence with interruptions and short attention spans.

Content

What kinds of content are appropriate for delivery to mobile devices? Currently the development of content designed for mobiles is at a relatively early stage, but this is an important area for libraries.

There will be new types of content presented in more flexible ways:

E-ink combined with flexible screens should soon make e-books more of a reality than at present. Although they will initially mimic paper books, the opportunity is to provide new forms of content, including customised content (such as personalised newspaper, magazines, and even fiction) and content that seamlessly incorporates dynamic media. (Sharples, 2008)

I predict a more visual future, as heralded by the popularity of something like the Visual Bookshelf on Facebook, and facilities to search and navigate the illustrations contained in books, rather than just the text. What we know as book covers may well become entry points to virtual worlds, simulations, games and other visual experiences. This lines up well with mobile devices – their affinity with sound and vision, which are more convenient than text on the move. (Kukulska-Hulme, 2008)

And an increasing emphasis on user-generated content and content sharing:

> And I'm just back from a holiday in China where most of the people on the trip have a digital camera. I've suggested that we agree on a tag and upload photos to a photographic sharing site such as Flickr. This is another example of how digital devices and networked and social applications will have impact on the wider society and not just higher education. (Kelly, 2008)

> Social networking applications will be huge on the mobile but not for a few years. (Abram, 2008)

Personalization

The phenomenal success of Amazon, eBay and iGoogle has created an expectation of personalized services. The ability to access personalized services from mobile devices and customize them to order will be even more desirable. This is closely linked to the theme of developing context- and location-specific services:

> But a significant trend is that of mobile and location-based content creation, so that people are creating media content in situ or linked to a location (moblogging, linking Wikipedia to Google maps etc). That will offer opportunities and pose challenges to catalogue, manage rights to, and provide access to heterogeneous location-based content).
>
> . . .
>
> Another trend that combines the two above is just-in-time access to dynamic content – including context-specific multimedia tourist guides, repair manuals, etc., which may combine professionally created and user-created content. (Sharples, 2008)

Kukulska-Hulme (2008) is similarly interested in this idea of location-specific information and the opportunities offered by semantic linking of information:

> Another area I think will become very important is the ability to access semantically related information, for example everything about an author or everything that relates to a particular publication. In as much as some information is related to location, it will be possible to declare one's interests or current pursuits and get notifications when

entering a zone that relates to the plot of a novel, an author's childhood, an area associated with the birth of certain academic ideas . . . and this will be a two-way
process as more location-based information is uncovered.

And Abram (2008) picks up the location theme:

GIS features will be key to the growth of mobile applications. 3D maps of your local
area, context sensitive ads and coupons, smart mobs, political rallies, etc. will all come
to popular consciousness.

The future role of libraries

There is no clear consensus from our commentators on the role of libraries
in this new and evolving landscape. They make some interesting suggestions about the use of mobiles to enhance the use of traditional library space
and traditional library services:

On a mundane level, I guess we'll see more thoughtful catering to the mobile
devices that people bring into the library; power, open wifi, an evolution of the 'no
cellphones' poster. . . . More fundamentally, we need to rethink the library 'experience'; most OPACs look pretty grim on a tiny screen. Redesigning the interface is
one step, but there's actually a more important process to understand first in terms
of the tasks that the mobile user wishes to engage with the library for. They may be
quite different from the tasks they're involved in at a desktop or laptop computer,
so simply reskinning the OPAC for a smaller screen is unhelpful.   (Miller, 2008)

OPACs will develop GIS sensitivity and be able to communicate with users through
their mobiles for holds, fines, lates, etc.   (Abram, 2008)

I think there must also be plenty of scope for inventions around the physical library
space such as gadgets that you could borrow to learn more about collections of books
or journals as you explore a library. This would require some kind of change of attitudes and perceptions of what the library space is all about, changing existing
habits and inviting people to spend some time in an engaging experience of discovery.
                                                          (Kukulska-Hulme, 2008)

While the relationship between e-book publishing and libraries is yet to
be understood:

Digital Rights Management will be a huge issue, of course, with competing hard-ware-based eBook readers appearing all over the place at the moment. The publishers might wish to drive content toward those devices . . . but the library would presumably have to buy and maintain them . . . and ask users to borrow them in order to read, instead of loading content onto their own device. That hardly seems ideal for anyone except the publisher.   (Miller, 2008)

Brophy (2008) expresses some reservations about the ability of libraries to adapt to changing roles and relationships with users:

I've also argued that libraries need to move away from an information delivery model to become enablers of information/knowledge sharing. By this I mean that they need to provide facilities to enable users to publish and share their data/creativity as well as to look at what others are producing. Increasingly this will involve ongoing dialogues. We can see this in various Web 2.0 services but libraries are slow to adapt to these ideas.

Returning to our original question, how will libraries fare in this new future? How active a role will they assume?

There would appear to be no doubt that the 'future is mobile'. Mobile technology is part of everyday life and the functions it offers are multiplying day by day. In the developing world, mobile phones are of paramount importance in bridging the digital divide:

Phones will leap laptops and PCs in the developing world as the main form. Charging will be by solar.   (Abram, 2008)

Traxler (2008) reminds us of how fundamental a challenge is being faced by libraries:

As mobile devices and technologies become universal and increasingly powerful, pervasive and ubiquitous in our societies, we will see the nature of knowledge, learning, work, resources, disadvantage and community transformed, challenging the roles of libraries and universities and specifically challenging them to exploit these devices and technologies in order to take their work beyond the fixed times and places they often currently occupy and into a more and more mobile world.

Is this a signal, then, of make-or-break time for libraries? For several years now the library community has been committed to developing 'user-centred' services and has bemoaned the fact that so many of us choose Google as our primary information service and prefer to spend time in Facebook and Flickr rather than in the library website. Does mobile technology offer a new opportunity to work creatively and collaboratively to develop services with and for users in their chosen spaces?

> That suggests to me that the future of libraries and mobile services is indistinguishable from the future of library services per se. (I leave aside here the enduring concept of the library as place.) So it boils down to how to secure a presence in a kind of ubiquitous virtual space–time information continuum!! I have been suggesting in a number of recent papers that the key to this is to embed the library in the workflow/leisureflow/lifeflow, and that the key to success there is clear alignment with the 'language' of the individual user community. For example, to deliver meaningful services to research astronomers we need to understand, at a deep level, their discourse so as to be able to participate in it. A public library equivalent would be to localise services to the specifics of the locality and the community interest.
>
> (Brophy, 2008)

In this volume, there are numerous examples of librarians, researchers and developers responding to this challenge. This is, of course, just the beginning, and we look forward to future m-libraries conferences to explore the use of technology in the library of the future.

References

Abram, S. (2008) E-mail communication 18 February 2008.

Brophy, P. (2008) E-mail communication 1 February 2008.

Kelly, B. (2008) E-mail communication 4 February 2008.

Kukulska-Hulme, A. (2008) E-mail communication 28 January 2008.

Miller, P. (2008) E-mail communication 30 January 2008.

Sharples, M. (2008) E-mail communication 29 January 2008.

Traxler, J. M. (2008) E-mail communication 27 January 2008.

Acknowledgements

I would like to thank the following colleagues for so generously sharing their thoughts:

Stephen Abram

Stephen Abram has over 25 years of expertise in libraries as a practising librarian and in the information industry. He is Vice President of Innovation for Sirsi Corporation. His most recent role was as Vice President of Corporate Development for Micromedia ProQuest.

Abram's other roles include publisher for Thomson and Carswell and director of Information Resources for the Hay Group. He is a frequent keynote speaker on issues that affect libraries, their communities and librarians. Abram was named by *Library Journal* in 2002 as one of the key people who are influencing the future of libraries and librarianship.

He is the incoming president of the Canadian Library Association and was President of the Ontario Library Association in 2002. He has also served on the International Board of Directors of the Special Libraries Association.

Abram is a Fellow of SLA; and in June 2003 he was awarded SLA's highest honour, the John Cotton Dana Award.

In 2001, Abram was presented with the University of Toronto Faculty of Information Studies, Alumni of the Year award.

Peter Brophy

Peter Brophy is Director of the Centre for Research in Library & Information Management (CERLIM) at Manchester Metropolitan University, UK and holds the Chair in Information Management at that university. He is the author of *The Library in the Twenty-First Century* (Facet, 2nd edn, 2007) and *The Academic Library* (Facet, 2nd edn, 2005). Before moving to MMU in 1998, he was Head of Library and Learning Resource Services and of the Learning Technologies Centre at the University of Central Lancashire. His earlier career included posts at the Universities of Lancaster and Strathclyde and at the then Teesside and Bristol polytechnics. He is a Fellow and Honorary Fellow of CILIP, and was President of the Institute of Information Scientists in 1998–9.

Brian Kelly

Brian Kelly's job title is 'UK Web Focus'. Based at the University of Bath, his remit is to support the higher and further education and cultural heritage communities in making effective use of web technologies. His post is funded by JISC (the Joint Information Systems Committee) and the MLA (Museums, Libraries and Archives Council).

Brian is an experienced web developer, having set up his first website in January 1993. Brian has been employed at UKOLN, a national centre of expertise in digital information management, since 1996.

Brian's interests include standards for web development and web accessibility. A particular current area of interest is in strategies for exploiting Web 2.0 technologies and ways of addressing institutional inertia. He blogs on these issues on the UK Web Focus blog at ukwebfocus.wordpress.com.

Agnes Kukulska-Hulme

Agnes Kukulska-Hulme is Deputy Director and Senior Lecturer in Educational Technology in the Open University's Institute of Educational Technology, where she convenes the Telelearning Research Group and chaired the production of the postgraduate course, Innovations in eLearning. She is the co-editor of *Mobile Learning: a handbook for educators and trainers*, published by Routledge in 2005.

Agnes led two JISC-funded projects: Case Studies of Wireless and Mobile Learning in the Post-16 Sector, and the Landscape Study reports on the use of mobile and wireless technologies for learning and teaching.[1]

She also led the literature review for a Becta-funded project on the use of tablet PCs in schools. Agnes's background is in foreign language learning and from this perspective she has a long-standing research interest in user interface and communication requirements, with particular reference to non-technical users. Her 1999 book on user interface design explored the language elements of user interfaces, and this work has been taken forward through collaborative projects on the usability of educational websites and the usability of mobile devices in the context of learning.

Her most recent projects include investigations of spontaneous innovation with mobile devices among postgraduate learners, and a staff development project using smartphones.

Paul Miller

Paul joined Talis in September 2005 from the Common Information Environment (CIE), where as Director he was instrumental in scoping policy and attracting new members such as the BBC, National Library of Scotland and English Heritage to this group of UK public sector organizations. Previously, Paul was at UKOLN where he was active in a range of cross-domain standardization and advocacy activities, and prior to that he was Collections Manager at the Archaeology Data Service. At Talis, Paul is exploring new models of collaboration and identifying further areas in which our technology or knowledge would be of value. Paul has a doctorate in Archaeology from the University of York.

Mike Sharples

Mike Sharples is Professor of Learning Sciences and Director of the Learning Sciences Research Institute at the University of Nottingham. The focus of the LSRI is to explore theories and practices of learning and to design and evaluate novel learning technologies and environments. Mike's research interests include human-centred design of new technologies for learning, mobile and contextual learning, and the application of studies of human cognition and social interaction to the design of novel interactive systems. He is Deputy Scientific Manager of the Kaleidoscope European Network of Excellence in Technology Enabled Learning.

John M. Traxler

John is a Director of the Applied Innovative Digital Technologies Research Group at the University of Wolverhampton. He also works with the University's HEFCE-funded Centre of Excellence (CETL), looking at ways of using sustainable innovative technologies to support diverse communities of students and with the University's Centre for International Development and Training, exploring ways of using appropriate innovative technologies to deliver education in sub-Saharan Africa.

John has recently co-written a guide to mobile learning in developing countries for the Commonwealth of Learning and is co-editor of a book on mobile learning which includes 12 international case study chapters (Kukulska-Hulme, A. and Traxler, J. (eds) (2005) *Mobile Learning: a handbook for educators and trainers*, Routledge). During

2004–5 he worked on the JISC-funded Landscape Study on the use of mobile and wireless technologies in the post-16 sector and on implementing support for Kenyan teachers' in-service training using mobile technologies.

His recent research and publication interests include the ethics and techniques of evaluating innovative technology-supported learning; mobile learning and social inclusion; factors affecting the nature and extent of lecturer take-up of VLEs; the use of 'contrived' techniques in evaluation; and the diffusion of learning technology innovations within educational organizations.

URL

1   www.jisc.ac.uk/eli_outcomes.html.

Index

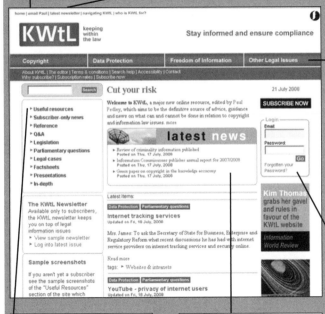

CILIP: taking you where you want to be

Is job satisfaction important to you? Would you like greater recognition within your organisation? Are you hoping to progress up the career ladder?

If your answer is yes to one or more of these questions CILIP can help.

We believe that job satisfaction comes from doing a job to the best of your ability and from getting recognition from your manager, your colleagues and your customers.

By investing in CILIP membership you can benefit from a range of services, including new online content, which will help you do your job better and enhance your career prospects.

For your free membership pack, email findoutmore@cilip.org.uk today.

Chartered Institute of
Library and Information
Professionals

www.cilip.org.uk/member
Now even more reasons to belong